Eros Mama

Embracing Your Sensual Feminine Power Through Pregnancy, Birth, and Postpartum

Eros Mama

Embracing Your Sensual Feminine Power Through Pregnancy, Birth, and Postpartum

Megan D. Lambert

Copyright © 2025 by Megan D. Lambert

All rights reserved. No part of this publication may be reproduced, distributed, or transmitted in any form or by any means, including photocopying, recording, or other electronic or mechanical methods, without prior written permission from the author, except in the case of brief quotations embodied in critical reviews and certain other noncommercial uses permitted by copyright law.

This is a work of nonfiction. To protect the privacy of individuals, names and identifying details have been changed or omitted. The author assumes no responsibility for errors, omissions, or any consequences arising from the use of the information contained in this book.

The author disclaims any liability in connection with the use of the information presented in this book. Readers are encouraged to seek professional guidance where appropriate.

Published by Megan D. Lambert

Cover design by Debbie O'Byrne
Book Interior Design and E-book formatting by
Amit Dey (amitdey2528@gmail.com)

First Ebook Edition: 2025

First Paperback Edition: 2025

ISBN: 979-8-9986064-1-0 (Paperback)
ISBN: 979-8-9986064-2-7 (Hardcover)
ISBN: 979-8-9986064-0-3 (E-book)

Printed in the United States of America

Visit www.megandlambert.com for the latest updates and additional resources.

Other titles by Megan D. Lambert
Eros: A Journey Home

*To the women who mothered before - thank you.
Your wisdom, grit, and love ripple through the generations.
May us new mamas stand on your shoulders
and cherish all you've given.*

PRAYER FOR THE BOOK

May this book hold your hand into becoming a mama,
May you feel held and supported by a millennia of mothers before you,
Whispering to you, *"You can trust yourself, my love. You know the way."*

May this journey into motherhood empower and humble you,
Destroy and remake you through the fire of devotion,
Into a woman fiercer, stronger, softer, wiser than before,
And most of all,
Guided by your ever-expanding heart.

May this book herald a mama revolution,
Of waking up, of remembering, of reclaiming your feminine power.
You, stepping into matriarchal leadership.

The matriarchs of this world, together,
Tending to our families and communities,
Knitting back together what has unraveled,
Finding togetherness amidst division,
And common humanity in our uniqueness.

The matriarchs of this world,
Trusting our hearts and intuition above any expert or authority,
Making bold decisions for our families and communities,
Following the red thread vision of a world that is more vibrant, connected, and compassionate.

We are the change we've been waiting for.
The women who will create a new earth,
One child at a time, one family at a time, one community at a time.

So that our children feel wild and free, truly themselves, and woven into the web of life,
Inheriting a beautiful, thriving earth for generations and millennia to come.

And so it is. Amen.

TABLE OF CONTENTS

Prayer for the Book ix
Welcome xix
A Quick Note Before We Begin. xxvii
Where We're Going xxxi

Chapter 1: Hearing the Call to Be a Mama 1

    Are We Ever Truly Ready? 3
    What Are You Afraid Of? 5
    Hearing the Call 6

  Body 7
    Go Do: Hearing the Call Meditation 8
    Reflect: Hearing the Call 10

  Sensuality 11
    My "Slut Era". 14
    Go Do: Desire Exploration 15
    Love Dates. 18
    Go Do: Set Up a Love Date 20
    Love Date FAQs. 23

  Relationship 29

Conception Conversations. 29
　　Open: Seven Conception Conversations 30
　　How Men vs. Women Prepare to Conceive 33
　Ecosystem 36
　　How Mamas Got So Isolated 38
　　Reflect: Dream into Your Ecosystem 42
　Chapter Summary. 45

Chapter 2: Calling in Your Baby (Conception) 47
　　Conceiving Lila 49
　　A Note on the Timing of Conception 52
　　Conceiving Latham 53
　Body 57
　　Physical Preparation 57
　　Emotional and Spiritual Preparation 58
　　Go Do: Thanking Your Womb Ritual 59
　　The Egg and Sperm Story 62
　　Reflect: Conception Beliefs 65
　Sensuality 66
　　Go Do: Sensual Movement Class 69
　　Go Do: Opening the Gates Ritual 70
　Relationship 72
　　When It's Faster Than You Wanted 72
　　When It's Slower Than You Want 73
　　When You Conceive 75
　　Celebrate Conception 76

Open: Our Conception Journey 77
Ecosystem 78
    Social Support. 79
    Environment. 79
    Home. 80
Chapter 2 Summary 81

Chapter 3: Your Body as a Home for Two (Pregnancy) 83
    Will I Regret This?. 85
Body 86
    You are a Goddess 86
    Remembering the Wonder Through Ritual 87
    Go Do: Create a Pregnancy Ritual 89
    Who's Body is This?! 90
    Nausea as My Great Embodiment Teacher 94
    Reflect: What's My Body Telling Me? 99
Sensuality 100
    Bringing All of You Into the Erotic 102
    First Trimester 103
    Open: The Adjustment Sandwich 108
    Open: Active Surrender 110
    Second Trimester 111
    Go Do: Breast Massage 111
    Sexy Troubleshooting 114
    Third Trimester 120
    Go Do: Intuitive Movement 121

    Third Trimester Lovemaking 123

Relationship 124
    Open: See into My World *128*

Ecosystem 130
    Home. 130
    Nature 132
    Community 134

Chapter 3 Summary 136

Chapter 4: The Underworld Journey (Birth) **139**

Body 141
    My Unlearning 144
    Mining Your Beliefs 146
    Reflect: Your Birth Beliefs *147*
    Unraveling Your Beliefs 148
    Reflect: Unraveling Your Beliefs *152*

Sensuality 155
    Sex as Birth Prep 157
    Moment-to-Moment Impulse 158
    Breath 159
    Limbic Connection 161
    Sounds. 162
    Pain vs. Pleasure 163
    Go Do: Lovemaking as Birth Prep *166*

Relationship 167
    He Surrenders to Her Power 170

  Open: Prepare for Birth Together *171*

 Ecosystem 173

  Where Will You Birth? 175

  Who Will Be At Your Birth?. 179

  What Other Support Do You Need? 183

  Reflect: My Birth Ecosystem. *184*

 My Story 185

  Lila's Birth 185

  Conscious Pause 188

  Latham's Birth. 189

  Check-In 193

 Chapter 4 Summary 194

Chapter 5: Being Reborn (The Fourth Trimester) 197

 Body 199

  Go Slow, Go Gentle. 200

  Let Yourself Be Tended To. 201

  Go Do: Ask for Help *207*

  Welcoming the Duality 208

  The Identity Death of Postpartum 210

  Integrating Your Birth 212

  Reflect: Birth Wisdom *214*

  Caring for Your Body 216

 Sensuality 219

  Rediscovering your sensuality 219

  Coming Home to Myself 221

Intimacy Post-Birth 224
Relationship 231
  A New Way to Love 232
  Open: New Ways to Love Each Other. *235*
  "Maleness" vs. "Femaleness" in Postpartum 236
  The Resentment Wall 239
  Go Do: Take Down the Resentment Wall *245*
  Daily GADs practice. 246
Ecosystem 249
  Finding Your Nature Haven 249
  Go Do: Earthly Delights Walking Meditation. *250*
  Tending to the Earth and Your Baby 251
Chapter 5 Summary 255

Chapter 6: Babyhood & Beyond (Your New Life). 259
  Moving Beyond the Baby Bubble 261
Body 262
  Coming Home to Your Body 264
  Your Changing Emotions. 266
  Mom Guilt 267
  Meeting Your "Mother" Self 274
  Go Do: Meet Your Mother Self *274*
Sensuality 276
  Schedule Love Dates 278
  Nourish Your Sensuality 278
  Show Up Goalless. 279

Explore Desire. 280
  Open: The Desire Game *281*
Relationship 283
  The 1:1:1 Rule for New Parents 286
  Weekly Planning Ritual 287
  Getting Support. 289
  Lastly, Don't Forget Fun 290
  Reflect: Relationship Tune-Up *291*
Ecosystem 293
  Parenting Philosophies. 295
  The Earth Your Kids Inherit 297
Chapter 6 Summary 300

Conclusion 303
  Your Insights 306

Share Your Experience 313

Go Deeper 315

Acknowledgements 317

About the Author 319

WELCOME

To be a woman means to know change deep in your bones.

Have you heard of the feminine *holy trinity*—the Maiden, the Mother, and the Crone?

This is a way of looking at womanhood through the lifecycle.

The Maiden embodies youthful innocence and self-discovery. The Mother holds the power of creation and nurturance. The Crone carries the wisdom of a life fully lived.

And yet, our culture distorts these phases:

We *fetishize* the Maiden.
We *use* the Mother.
We *ignore* the Crone.

What a shame.

But what if, instead of following this distortion, we honored the **true** journey of a woman's evolution?

- **In the Maiden phase** (*the focus of my first book*), we grow by rejecting external expectations and self-objectification, turning inward, and **claiming our own desires and truths.**
- **In the Mother phase** (*the focus of this book*), we grow by refusing to be used as a martyr, refusing to become invisible in our sacred service. Instead, we become the matriarch,

the leaders of our homes, **nourishing our families—and ourselves**.
- **In the Crone phase**, rather than fading into the background, we grow by taking up space, by sharing our hard-earned wisdom with the world and **fiercely protecting our communities**.

With each phase of womanhood, our attention and capacity expands outwards—first to hold ourselves, then to hold our families, and finally, to hold our communities and the earth.

"Fetishize the maiden, use the mother, ignore the crone" becomes:

Empower the Maiden. Enliven the Mother. Honor the Crone.

Powerful, huh?

Now for the sake of this book, let's focus on the Mother phase and what it means to you.

Does Radiant Motherhood Exist?

After witnessing many of my clients and friends become mothers, I found myself asking:

"Does a woman lose her radiance when she becomes a mother? And if so, why?"

I watched women—once full of life and passion—slowly dull under the weight of motherhood. They gave and gave, until there was nothing left of themselves.

Why does this happen?

Here's what I see:

- A woman overwhelmed, stressed, and stuck in survival mode.
- A woman who has put everyone's needs ahead of her own.

- A woman who stops caring for her body and her pleasure.
- A woman who has lost touch with Eros—her sensual life force.

Growing up, I rarely saw mothers who were *passionately alive, thriving,* and *proud* of their life-giving role. Instead, I saw women who were exhausted, depleted, and quietly resentful. It seemed like they had lost a part of themselves in the process of raising their little ones.

What about you? What examples of motherhood did you see growing up?

Of course, this type of motherhood is a **natural result of our culture**. How could it be any other way in a culture that devalues the service of mothers and expects one woman to do the job of an entire village?

I wanted to understand how we got here, so I asked ChatGPT, "If you were the devil and wanted to take away a woman's power through motherhood, what would you do?" Here is the response:

If I were the devil and wanted to strip a woman of her power through motherhood, I wouldn't do it by force—I'd do it by illusion. I'd make her believe she was losing herself so she didn't know the truth: that she was becoming more powerful than ever.

Here's how I'd do it:

1. **Convince Her That Self-Sacrifice Is the Ultimate Virtue**
   I'd whisper that a "good mother" puts herself last—her desires, dreams, body, and time belong to her children. I'd make her feel guilty for wanting anything just for herself. No pleasure, no ambition, no identity beyond being "Mom."

2. **Isolate Her from Other Women**
   I'd ensure she feels alone, cut off from the deep well of feminine wisdom that has guided mothers for centuries.

Instead of sitting in a supportive circle of women who remind her of her strength, she'd be left scrolling social media and comparing herself to curated highlight reels.

3. **Make Her Doubt Her Intuition**

   I'd flood her mind with expert opinions, parenting books, and conflicting advice until she no longer trusts her own instincts. I'd have her second-guess every decision, convincing her that she needs someone else to tell her what's best for her child.

4. **Redefine Her Body as 'Used Up'**

   I'd have her believe that pregnancy, birth, and breastfeeding have "ruined" her body rather than transformed it into something more powerful, sensual, and wise. I'd make her chase pre-baby weight, cover stretch marks, and feel disconnected from her own pleasure.

5. **Shift Her Focus from Power to Perfection**

   I'd set impossible standards—demanding she be the perfect mom, wife, career woman, and remain perfectly fit and patient. I'd ensure she constantly feels like she's failing, so she never notices the true power she wields.

6. **Make Her Forget She's a Creator**

   More than anything, I'd distract her from the truth—that she hasn't just given birth to a child, but to a new, powerful version of herself: wilder, deeper, stronger. I'd keep her so busy, exhausted, and self-doubting that she never fully steps into this new power especially meant for her.

But of course, the devil only wins when a woman believes these lies. However, if she remembers who she is, meaning her body, her pleasure, her intuition, her sisterhood, and her fire, then she is unstoppable! She becomes an Eros Mama.

A New Way Forward

So, if the "devil" thrives on you forgetting who you are, **here is how we fight back**:

1. We remember that devotion applies to our families—and ourselves.
2. We connect with other women and build strong ecosystems of support.
3. We trust our intuition above all else.
4. We recognize the miracle and beauty of our bodies.
5. We let go of perfection and unrealistic ideals to focus on our true power.
6. We remember that we are the creators of life and we embrace our wholeness.

When we do these 6 things—**we become revolutionaries.**

The Revolution of Motherhood

There is a movement happening—can you feel it?

A revolution is rising, and you, Eros Mama, are a part of it.

You are not alone.

We, women, are being called to create a new future—not just for ourselves, but for generations to come.

We are being drawn to live in harmony—with ourselves, with others, with nature.

This revolution is guided by our Eros, our deep life force. It is a call to reclaim our bodies, our desires, and our intuition. Together, we can resist unnecessary struggle, outdated paradigms, and the myth of doing it *alone*.

We are being called to simplify. To collaborate. To connect.

To return to our innate nature.

To remember that nature is not *outside* of us—it *is* us. We are woven into its web, and are a part of its rhythm.

And it is us, *mothers*, who will lead this movement.

Matriarchal Leadership
Why will mothers lead this movement?

Because a mother feels with her heart first.

Sometimes it swells so full of love, it feels it might burst.

Sometimes it aches so deeply, it feels it might break.

But that is the key–a mother is never far from her heart.

It beats, achingly alive, pulling her toward a more heart-led way of living. For herself. For her children. For the generations that follow.

She senses how linked we all are. She *knows* the actions she takes today ripple through time.

Do you feel it, too?

Do you sense what I'm pointing to?

If so, take a deep breath.

We are in this together.

My Personal Journey
When I became pregnant four years ago, I knew in my bones that everything would change.

And it did.

My priorities. My identity. My relationships. My career.

But the one constant—the *true north* guiding me through it all—was my body. My sensuality. The deep wisdom of my desires. My sense of interconnectedness with life.

This book is my love letter to that wisdom. To the path of motherhood that is *sensual, profound, and alive*. To the tools that helped me return to myself in the hardest moments of this transformation.

It's not an accident that my pregnancy was one of the sexiest times of my life. Or that my husband and I now have a thriving intimate relationship, even with a baby and a toddler. That, despite the stretch marks and sleepless nights, I feel more powerful and beautiful than ever. Or that I am held by a thriving community of friends and family.

No, that is the result of integrating the **feminine art of desire** with the **path of motherhood**.

Over the past decade, I have taught thousands of women about the power of the feminine through coaching, group programs, and retreats. I've seen my clients' lives transform with more love, hotter intimacy, and deeper self-trust, again and again. **It's 100% possible for you too.**

And now, I want to show you how.

Your Invitation to Begin

There are very few role models for this.

This is *radical* soul work.

It's not easy. But it is *beautiful*.

Know that you are not alone.

We are doing this *together*.

Feel the other women walking this path beside you.

Know that you are held.

Are you ready? Let's go.

A QUICK NOTE BEFORE WE BEGIN

Before we dive in, I want to take a moment to clarify a few things.

This book is deeply personal. It is shaped by my own experiences, my work, and my perspective as a white, able-bodied, cisgender, heterosexual woman from the United States of America. I fully acknowledge that my vantage point is just that—*one* vantage point. Motherhood is vast. It is as unique as the women who walk this path. While I aim to write in an inclusive way, I know my words will not always reflect your experience. If anything in this book feels distant from your reality, I invite you to take what resonates and leave the rest.

This book also explores sensuality, sexuality, and feminine embodiment. We are diving into taboo, edgy territory here, so please know---you are welcome to skim past any sections you feel uncomfortable with. I use certain words that may feel unfamiliar or provocative so let me take a moment to define them for you.

God

Let's start with the big one—the G-word. No, not G-spot. *God.*

Depending on your background, this word may carry different meanings.

When I use *God*, I'm referring to a universal life force—pure love, deep wisdom, the divine intelligence that flows through all things.

I sometimes use *he* and *she* interchangeably, or even the word *Goddess*, to remind myself that the divine is not patriarchal.

But more importantly—what does *God* mean to you?

If the word God doesn't resonate, feel free to replace it with something that does: *Spirit, Source, Universe, Life Force, Prana, Chi, Divine Mother*. Or, if you don't believe in a *Higher Power*, feel free to skip those parts.

Sensuality vs. Sexuality

Sensuality and sexuality are not the same, though they are deeply intertwined.

Sensuality is about being **in your body**—feeling, tasting, touching, listening, savoring. It's about living in a way that is intimate with life itself.

Sexuality, on the other hand, is a more specific expression of sensuality—one that includes arousal, erotic energy, and the power of our reproductive center.

Throughout this book, we will explore both.

Pussy

Ah, the most provocative word of them all.

According to Merriam Webster, pussy is listed as vulgar, and in many circles, it is still used in a vulgar and violent way. The word "pussy" has been weaponized against women—either as an insult (*"Don't be a pussy"*) or as a way to objectify us sexually.

But here, we redefine the word pussy. Throughout the book, I use the word pussy to describe female genitals. Why? Well part of reclaiming our power requires removing the sting of the words used against us.

By using the word pussy, we are part of a movement to **restore reverence** to this part of our body. To remind us that our pussy is not something to be ashamed of or objectified, but something to be honored—a source of pleasure, wisdom, and creation itself. To go deeper into this work, I highly recommend the book *Pussy: A Reclamation* by Regena Thomashauser.

I'll use the word pussy even and especially when describing birth and postpartum. Why? Because, here more than anywhere, women's erotic selves are divorced from their maternal selves. By using the word pussy, I invite a unification of these seemingly opposite parts of us.

If pussy feels uncomfortable for you, of course feel free to replace it with whatever word feels right. This book is about your experience. Your body. Your language.

Eros

Eros is our life force energy—the primal pulse of our aliveness. While it encompasses our sexuality, it is far more than that.

Eros is our innate creative impulse: the drive to generate life, spark innovation, and form meaningful connections. It is the heartbeat of our deepest yearnings.

By embracing Eros, we celebrate life. We allow stagnant energy to flow freely through our bodies, fueling our pleasure and creativity. In doing so, we open ourselves to deeper connection with others and inspire our creative endeavors toward a more vibrant life for ourselves, our families, and our world.

Eros is the feminine voice of the soul, a reminder of the transformative power within each of us.

Feminine power

Each of us, regardless of gender, have both masculine and feminine energy.

At the highest level, masculine energy is witness, consciousness, the observer of all that is, while feminine energy is life itself. In Tantra, this is called Shiva (masculine) and Shakti (feminine).

We have both, and to be whole, we must have access to both.

As I describe in my first book, *Eros: The Journey Home*:

> Masculine energy is linear, directed, goal oriented, logical, and factual. In contrast, feminine energy is intuitive, emotional, creative, sensitive, receptive, and connected.
>
> Put more poetically:
>
>> She is the river. He is the bank that holds her.
>>
>> She is raw electric power. He is the direction in which power flows.
>>
>> She is deep, intuitive knowing. He is the logical explanation.
>>
>> She feels the desire. He is the structure that brings it to life.
>>
>> She is radiance and beauty. He is the one who witnesses and honors beauty.

So, what is feminine power? It's deliberately embracing our feminine energy—and discovering how powerful this energy truly is.

We live in a patriarchal world that has devalued the feminine in all its forms. Yet becoming a mother is the most feminine journey there is. So, this rite of passage is an invitation to discover more deeply your feminine essence, reclaim its inherent power, and become the matriarch you were born to be.

WHERE WE'RE GOING

This book is a journey—one that takes you from the dreams of motherhood to conception, pregnancy, through birth, and into the early years of raising a child.

At every stage, we'll focus on four key areas that are essential to your experience as an Eros Mama:

1. Your Body & Emotions
- How does your physical body change through each phase?
- What emotions and sensations may arise?
- How can you stay connected to your body and your inner world?

2. Your Sensuality & Sex
- How do you return to your sensuality as a place of nourishment and rejuvenation?
- What does sex feel like in each stage of motherhood?
- How can you nurture your sensuality and stay connected to your erotic self?

3. Your Relationship with Your Partner (If applicable)
- How might your relationship shift as you become parents?
- How can you stay intimately connected while navigating the changes?

- What tools are essential to strengthening your relationship through the "baby bomb"?

(If you don't have a partner, you're welcome to skip these sections—or read them as preparation for any future relationship you may have.)

4. Your Ecosystem of Support
- What is the context in which you are becoming a mother?
- How do you build the "village" that will support you and your growing family?
- What role does nature and the earth play in your mama journey?

Throughout this book, I'll share my own stories—the struggles, the triumphs, the messy, and the beautiful in-between. I'll also share my client stories (with their permission and with names removed). My hope is that these stories help you feel a part of this movement, that you feel seen and understood. May these stories give you guidance and trust to lead yourself forward.

There are plenty of guides out there that cover the logistics of motherhood—health, finances, parenting strategies. While I may mention some of my favorites, this book is different.

This book is about **you**.

It is about keeping **your** fire lit.

Your body alive.

Your soul connected to the sensual, intuitive woman you are—not just before motherhood, but through it.

How to Read This Book

There is no "right" way to move through this book. You can read it front to back, following the full arc of transformation, or you can skip ahead to the sections that resonate most with where you are now.

(This book makes an excellent bedside table companion—something you can return to again and again, depending on what phase of the journey you're in.)

More than just reading, I encourage you to interact with the book.

- Highlight or underline the passages that move you.
- Take notes or write in the margins—your thoughts, your reactions, your own wisdom.
- Make it yours.

This book is not just here to be read. It's here to be *experienced*.

To help you do this, I have provided practices for you to do along with the reading. In each chapter there are suggested ways for you to engage in the learning. Here are the four types:

- **Go Do:** An exercise, meditation, or ritual to deepen your experience.
- **Reflect:** Journaling prompts to help you integrate your insights.
- **Open:** Questions or activities to do with your partner to strengthen your partnership.
- **Widen:** Recommended books and resources to continue learning.

These are active Invitations for you to not just learn but GROW through the experience of this book. I know you're busy, so each practice will take twenty minutes or less. I encourage you to pause the reading and do the practice right away, if possible, so you don't forget.

You Know You Best

While this book is full of insights, tools, and stories, I do not pretend to have all the answers. *How could I?*

Your journey is uniquely yours.

Your circumstances, your desires, your challenges—they all belong to you, and no book, no expert, no single philosophy can claim to know exactly what you need.

So rather than seeing this book as a prescription, I invite you to see it as a conversation between sisters, sharing our stories, discovering our own truths as we walk this path together, and trusting each other to know what's best for ourselves.

Engage, Share, Connect

This book is meant to be read in community.

Maybe you want to share a passage with a friend who needs it. Maybe you want to discuss an insight with your partner. Maybe you feel called to post a favorite line on Instagram to inspire others.

If something moves you, let it ripple outward.

I love when you share your favorite parts of the book on Instagram! Use the hashtag **#ErosMama** and tag me **@megandlambert** so I can see what resonates with you. It truly makes my day to hear what you're loving.

If you want to share more personally, I'd love to hear from you. Feel free to send me a direct message on Instagram to share your insights.

It's Time

Take a breath.

Trust that you are exactly where you need to be.

Know that you are held in this work.

The journey starts now. Let's begin.

Chapter 1

HEARING THE CALL TO BE A MAMA

Baby.
Thinking of it brings tears to my eyes
Goosebumps

Now? Are we ready?
How would I know?

I slip my hand in yours,
And dream of our family,
So sweet it hurts,
Could it really be?

Are We Ever Truly Ready?

"Honey, wait! I need to heal my intergenerational trauma!" I exclaim anxiously to my new husband.

We're on the way home from a family trip, sitting at the airport, while I read a book about preparing for motherhood. I'm not pregnant yet, but I can feel such a deep yearning to conceive soon.

The book informs me that, while pregnant, my unborn child is absorbing all of my unhealed traumas, neurosis, and intergenerational karma. Just as casually as you'd read a grocery list, the author recommends healing these before getting pregnant.

Healing *all* my intergenerational karma?

Yikes.

I definitely haven't done that yet.

I've been working on my personal growth and spiritual journey for almost a decade by this point, but have I healed it all? Most definitely not. I still have lots of broken and crazy parts. (Don't we all?)

I remember feeling so anxious and daunted by this book. Of course I want to give my child-to-be the best start to life I can. Of course I don't want him or her to absorb all my unhealed traumas. And suddenly I felt so unprepared and full of doubts about my desire to get pregnant.

Am I actually ready?

How will I know when I'm ready?

> Becoming a mother is an invitation to heal ourselves on deeper levels than we ever could prior to having children.

Looking back on that moment, I laugh now, because the audacity to assume I could heal all my intergenerational trauma before motherhood is absurd. It's impossible.

In fact, I now believe that becoming a mother is an invitation to heal ourselves on deeper levels than we ever could prior to having children.

So we move forward and trust.

Trust that when we conceive, it is exactly the right time. Trust that, if I feel the call to be a mama, I am ready. Trust that my baby is getting the unique dose of trauma that he or she needs to develop the character they will become. (I know! Radical, right?) Trust that there is a bigger plan to all this than I can understand or control.

None of us are perfect, and we will never be perfectly ready for motherhood.

We will discuss ways to prepare your body, sensuality, relationship, and ecosystem together through this chapter. And still, nothing will make you feel completely ready.

There is nothing you can do that will fully prepare you for the biggest initiation possible—bringing new life to earth. Becoming a mother invites you to surrender, leap into the unknown, and open to uncertainty and mystery.

On this journey you will often feel unprepared and unequipped. This feeling is part of the portal of motherhood. When we feel the call to conceive, we don't know how this story ends. Will we conceive? How will pregnancy go? The birth? Raising babies?

> What clouds our deepest knowing the most is fear.

So many unknowns. What clouds our deepest knowing the most is *fear*. Fear can make our minds loud, so loud that it drowns out the quiet voice of our soul. So first, let's look at some of the common fears you may have.

What Are You Afraid Of?

The idea of having a child can bring up many fears. Here is how one of my clients described it:

> "Since I met my partner, we have always been clear that we both want kids. It's been his dream since he was a child to become a father—he could always see them and feel them and love them long before they're even born. For me, I wasn't always sure if I wanted kids.
>
> The deepest underlying truth is, the desire **was** always there. But that desire was a treasure buried beneath layers and layers of fear and doubt that for the longest time made me question if I **did** want to become a mother!
>
> Fears like—
>
> - Am I healed enough? (*I don't want to pass my trauma down to my kids!*)
> - Do I know enough? (*What if something horribly wrong happens to my baby and I can't or don't know how to fix it?*)
> - Am I enough? (*Do I have what it takes mentally, emotionally, practically, spiritually to bring a baby into this world?*)
> - Do I want to have a child for the right reasons? (*Do I want to have a baby from an overflow of love and goodness in my life and my relationship, or am I trying to fill some selfish void within me by having a child—which isn't fair to them!*)

Yikes—the inner chatter and inner debate has been immense in this preconception journey! Yet, every day, I lean more and more into self-trust. I put more and more trust in my relationship. I trust the divine timing and will of this spirit baby to arrive when the time is right. I trust that an entire humanity of mothers have been through this before and figured it out. And I remember **that the mother is born *through* the experiences of motherhood, not before it.**"

She shares such beautiful self-awareness of her fears—and also trust that this is an on-going journey between herself, her future baby, her partner, and God. She realized that she doesn't need to have all the answers yet.

Hearing the Call
October of 2020

"The father in me sees the father in you," our friend told my partner, James, as we sat in a circle at our commitment ceremony.

As he spoke those words, my eyes filled with tears and I felt shivers.

Yes. 100 percent yes.

James and I were vowing to be together for life, witnessed by twenty of our closest friends. Sadly, our family couldn't make it, as COVID lockdowns were strictly in place.

During the ceremony, we asked for a blessing from each person. As our friend said those mic-dropping words, it felt like the room stilled.

There was gravity in those words. Truth.

I wasn't pregnant yet, and we hadn't started "trying," but I could feel the call to become a mama deep in my bones. Every time I thought about having a baby, it felt like my heart exploded. Tears filled my eyes, and a chill ran down my arms. The yearning was undeniable.

———————

Have you felt that way? Perhaps while you're reading this book you're feeling the yearning deep within you to bring new life to earth. Or perhaps you're not feeling the call yet, but you're curious enough to want to learn. This book will walk you through your own journey of discovery, helping you find your path toward motherhood—or toward something more resonant for you.

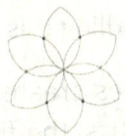

BODY

The call to have a baby is both a mind and a bodily decision.

Our minds need to wrap themselves around this decision, to feel like we have our "ducks in a row," and we are ready to call a baby in. If you tend to be a logical person, this part of you may be especially loud. You may wonder:

- Am I prepared?
- Is this the right time to bring a baby into the world (financially, emotionally, career-wise, etc.)?
- Is my relationship solid and steady enough? Is this the right father of my children?
- Why do I want a baby?
- Am I taking a prenatal vitamin?
    Note: Folate or methylfolate (rather than folic acid, which many people can't metabolize) is especially important to have before conceiving.

These are important questions to consider, from the biggest and deepest practical questions to the most straight-forward. Having a baby is a major, life-altering decision that requires deep thought.

Yet, ultimately, hearing the call to conceive is a body-based, gut knowing. It can be felt as a yearning, an ache, a tug from your heart.

Perhaps when you imagine having a baby, you feel physical sensations like I did—tears in your eyes, goosebumps, tingles down your arms and legs.

Or perhaps you feel the call in your heart—a swelling and lifting sensation as you imagine cradling this new baby.

Having a baby can sometimes create a lot of mental noise. You may be thinking about logistics, the financial aspects, the impact on your work and career, and on your body. All of this can make thinking about having a baby challenging. Ironically, here we need the quiet voice of Soul more than the loud voice of Mind.

Go Do: Hearing the Call Meditation

Below is a meditation to help you check in with your body around sensations, emotions, and thoughts related to becoming a mother. Read through the meditation. Then find a quiet space where you can be alone for ten minutes to talk yourself through each of the steps.

> **Bonus:** To get the most from this meditation, I strongly recommend listening to the audio version of this meditation, which you can find on my website: www.megandlambert.com/emresources.
>
>

Instructions:

1. Take a few deep breaths. Relax your belly, your chest, your throat, and your face.

2. As your body settles, place your hands on your womb and imagine a baby growing inside you. Imagine the cells of sperm and egg uniting, the cells forming, and the baby growing.

    a. Notice first what thoughts come to mind: "Am I ready?" "Do I really want this?" etc.

    b. Then drop a layer deeper, into your heart, and notice what feelings arise: Excited? Nervous? Calm? Anxious?

    c. Last, falling behind the thoughts and the feelings, notice what sensations you feel in your body. Pay particular attention to your belly and womb area.

3. Next, imagine giving birth. The waves of contractions, the opening of your hips, and the emerging of your baby.

    a. Again, walk through your thoughts, feelings, and sensations, step by step.

    b. What thoughts arise as you imagine birth?

    c. What emotions do you sense? Excited, trusting, terror, love? Welcome it all.

    d. What sensations do you feel?

4. Last, imagine caring for a new baby. Changing diapers, feeding the baby, holding them, rocking them. Imagine the sweet moments and also the challenging ones.

    a. Again, notice thoughts first, then emotions, then sensation.

5. Bring the meditation to a close and thank your body for this wisdom.

Then continue on to the next activity.

Reflect: Hearing the Call

Journal what you thought, felt, and sensed during this meditation.

Consider these questions:

- What sensations did I notice in my body when I visualized becoming a mother? Did I notice tightness? Warmth or softness? Discomfort? Pay particular attention to your heart, solar plexus, womb, and pussy.
- Did I feel a pull, a yearning? What did it feel like?
- What are the major thoughts and feelings that arise around becoming a mama?
- Are there any fears about becoming a mother that you want to share and process with someone (e.g., a therapist, a supportive friend, or your partner)?
- Are there any unhelpful thoughts (e.g., "Birth is terrifying" or "I'm never going to sleep with a newborn") that you'd like to journal on, and perhaps get more information about (e.g., talk to someone who had an empowering birth, learn about infant sleep, etc.)

This meditation is designed to help you come face-to-face with your inner world around this massive step toward motherhood. Whatever arose—joy, excitement, fear, anxiety—can you welcome it all? Can you make space for the duality of this moment?

Often when taking a big step like this, you'll be feeling both "high" emotions like excitement, joy, and gratitude, as well as "low" emotions like fear, disbelief, and grief. In my experience, motherhood invites us to expand our amplitude of feeling, welcoming both "higher highs" and "lower lows."

That starts right here, in this meditation. All your thoughts, feelings, and sensations try to whisper wisdom to you. They try to help you prepare for this big step that is motherhood.

That doesn't mean you need to let each feeling guide the decision – especially fear! It isn't a good driver – but can you welcome each feeling with love?

Lastly – and this is a big step – I invite you to continually reach out for support from other wise mamas who have walked this path and been at this spot. It will strengthen you and give you courage to take the next step, as well as help you align yourself with what you *do* want.

Now that we've covered your thoughts, feelings, and sensations, let's turn toward your erotic self.

SENSUALITY

Have you had your slut era yet? If not, go do it, baby!

I say this tongue-in-cheek, but seriously, this is a great time to check in with your desires, especially any "wild and crazy" ones that may be lurking in the corners of your subconscious.

> *The point is not to compare your "slut era" to anyone else's - it is to give yourself permission to explore your own edges and desires.*

For every woman, being free in your sensual self will look different. For some, freedom looks like exploring a new room of the house with your husband, or simply turning the lights on during lovemaking. For other women, it may include edgier activities like power dynamics or group interactions (more ideas below). The point is not to compare your "slut era" to anyone else's - it is to give yourself permission to explore your *own* edges and desires.

As one of my clients put it, "Fulfilling my slut era helped me get *very* clear around the type of relationship, father of my child, and sexual dynamic I wanted to inhabit before starting a family. It gave me peace of mind and a sense of 'Okay, now I am ready.' I also firmly believe it helped me anchor in my self-love to endure the changes of pregnancy."

People often say to get everything wild done before the baby comes, with the unspoken message that once the baby is here, your life is over. Now, this is definitely *not* true—you can still fulfill wild and crazy desires after having a baby—but it *is* true that you're in a precious window before having a child.

For a short while longer, your body is fully and completely your own. You have full sovereignty right now, and you can try or do anything that delights you. Once you conceive, your body will be shared by another little human for at least nine months, and then if you breastfeed, possibly months or years longer.

All this to say, now is the time to explore your erotic edges and discover your own desires. Ask yourself, if I weren't constrained or limited, what might I want to try erotically? What have I been curious about but haven't explored?

Ideas to consider. Would you like to try . . .

- A sex toy? A vibrator? A new position?
- Being restrained (handcuffs, tied-up wrists, etc.)?
- Involving other people (play party, threesome, group experience, etc.)?
- Going to a temple or sacred sexuality party?
- Exploring BDSM and power dynamics?
- Learning tantra or conscious intimacy practices?
- Making love somewhere novel (a hotel, your kitchen, the parking lot, etc.)?
- Role-play ("Hey, Doctor!")?
- Psychedelics? (Hopefully with good guidance, if you're new to these.)

As you read that list, listen to your body. Do any of these light you up? Might you be willing to explore them?

It's also possible that right now, in a non-aroused state, perhaps none of these sound appealing. You may even feel afraid, judgmental, or uncomfortable reading this list. That is okay! We women have been taught to tamp down and judge our desires for millennia. It may take more inner safety for your tender desires to emerge. Let's look at a "go do" activity that will help you create safety and privacy for these desires.

My "Slut Era"

Hey, my parents, if you're reading this, skip ahead! It's gonna get juicy.

Before becoming a mama, I went on a wild, sensual journey that began with a deep dive into a mindful erotic community that taught Orgasmic Meditation.

What's that, you ask? Basically, Orgasmic Meditation (OM) is a fifteen-minute partnered practice where one person touches a woman's clitoris with no goal except to feel and be present to what arises. I discovered this practice when I was twenty-two, and it radically changed my life.

From there, I spent five years learning about OM and how it reflected the intersection of mindfulness, feminism, and sexuality—and I also did some crazy exploration in the process. (My book, **Eros: The Journey Home**, has more of the story).

This journey took me down many different erotic rabbit holes, learning about power, seduction, magnetism, erotic play, and more. I won't tell you all the juicy details here, (perhaps we can share stories in my private coaching!) but I will say it was 100 percent worth it.

My "Slut" Era was an incredible journey that taught me from the inside out how to turn myself on by listening deeply to what my body is asking for. Rather than waiting for "Prince Charming" to turn me on (as many of us are subconsciously taught), I discovered my own pleasure - and how to guide another person there. It taught me to connect with others around desires and boundaries, rather than by conditioned fears or expectations.

Best of all, this time of my life gave me a spirit of empowerment, exploration, and adventure in my sensuality that I will never forget—even now that I'm a mama of two, often covered in milk, with my mom bun tight.

Because of this time, I can now say confidently that it's never too late to discover your desires or sense of erotic adventure. That part of you may feel dormant (or it may be totally alive!), but she is always here, right now, just waiting for an invitation to emerge. And best of all, she holds the key to your most alive, sensual, and powerful self.

You don't have to run off and join a sex cult to access her. You can start right now, right here, in your own home.

The way to start? By creating a safe container to explore your own desires.

Go Do: Desire Exploration

This short meditation will help you connect with your body and make space for desire to arise. It is a potent way to access your erotic, exploratory self—in a safe and gentle way.

Bonus: I have this meditation as an audio you can follow along for free on my website: www.megandlambert.com/emresources.

Instructions:

1. Create a cozy and private cocoon for yourself, where you will be uninterrupted. Perhaps you find a soft blanket and comfy chair, or maybe you lie down in bed.

2. As you lie down, close your eyes softly and make yourself comfortable.

3. Bring your awareness into your pussy. Imagine your inhales can breathe life into your pussy, while your exhales melt away any tension. Inhale, exhale.

4. Continue for a few minutes, softening your body and breathing deeply into your belly and your pussy. Let your body relax, feeling cozy and safe, in this little cocoon you've created.

5. Now begin your physical exploration by asking your body: What part of my body wants to be touched right now? In what way?

    a. For example, maybe your feet are craving a massage, or your head scratched, or your breasts cupped, or your pussy stroked.

    b. Listen in, try out a few different types of touch, noticing where you can find pleasure.

    c. Avoid doing routine movements or aiming for a goal (say, of climax); instead, become aware of the subtle moment-to-moment yearnings of your body.

6. After a few minutes of physical exploration, it's time for psychological exploration. Allow your mind to wander to different movie or book scenes you've seen that felt exciting or arousing to you. Was there a sexy movie scene you saw recently? Maybe an intriguing book passage? What type of erotic scenes appeal to you right now?

a. If you haven't read or seen anything exciting in a while, what could you imagine?
   b. Remember, this is safe, private exploration in your own mind. None of this ever needs to come to life, nor ever needs to be shared with others.
   c. Continue touching your body as you bring these scenes or images to mind
7. Explore different fantasies and ideas, with different touches, for as long as you'd like.
8. When you're complete, open your journal and jot down responses to these questions:
   a. What type of touch was my body wanting today? Was I surprised by any desires I felt?
   b. What type of scenes or images did I find arousing? What about them was so intriguing to me?
   c. Did I learn something new about my erotic self, or discover any erotic desires I have?
   d. Is there anything from today's exploration that I want to bring into an erotic moment with a partner(s)?

The power of this practice is creating a short, safe cocoon to allow your body and mind to explore new terrain.

Now that you've explored a solo practice, perhaps you'd like to share this juiciness with a partner?

If you're ready to explore with a partner, let me introduce you to a life-changing practice— my husband and I call these containers "Love Dates." You can do this with an intimate partner, your spouse, or anyone you'd like to explore deeper intimacy with.

A love date is a sensual practice where you can explore all kinds of new ideas and experiences, in a safe container. It is an agreed-upon time where you and your partner(s) meet to explore a particular sensual experience. It has a set start and end time, plus an agreement on what you'll be doing. This clarity creates safety, which is foundational if you explore new terrain.

Love Dates

Love dates are a life-changing practice that will become increasingly important on your motherhood journey.

Why?

If you're in a partnership, it's likely that, at the beginning of your relationship when it was just the two of you, you probably made love spontaneously, when you both were ready and had desire. Perhaps after a nice dinner out, or maybe a passionate reunion after one of you took a trip.

The spontaneity can be so exciting and thrilling, particularly if you feel your partner's desire for you. Who doesn't want to feel wanted, right?

Yet, over time, spontaneity decreases as the initial hormone high of your union fades and settles into an established partnership. This is true for 100 percent of the couples James and I have worked with (which is hundreds over the last five years).

This shift doesn't mean you want each other any less or that your sex is doomed—quite the contrary. Less spontaneous sex simply signals a change of season, and with this change, a need for a new arrangement together. It is a maturation of your partnership that invites new tools and practices.

My advice? Set aside a dedicated time to be intimate, and treat that time as sacred. (Because it is!) Yes, I mean literally open your calendars and schedule "Love Dates" into them.

> *Less spontaneous sex simply signals a change of season, and with this change, a need for a new arrangement together. It is a maturation of your partnership that invites new tools and practices.*

By carving out this time, you do four things:

1. **You make a declaration that your intimacy matters**. It matters enough to create time for that experience, and to protect it.

2. **You eliminate the need for someone to initiate intimacy**, which is often fraught with past hurts and obligations.

    One typical scenario: Person A initiates intimacy, then Person B doesn't want to. Person A feels hurt and rejected, while Person B feels burdened by their partner's desire and either feels guilty about saying no or says yes and has sex out of obligation. Can you relate?

    This is not true for all couples, but it's common enough to be worth stating.

3. **You actually make love!** As you get busier and life gets more complex with children, if you don't schedule intimacy, most couples simply stop being intimate. They go weeks or months without sex.

4. **You create a safe container for erotic exploration.** The set Start and End time helps your vigilance center relax, so you can try out new things without as much fear or anxiety.

Sounds pretty good, right?

It is! Let's talk about how to get started.

Go Do: Set Up a Love Date

Love Dates are a potent way to keep the spark alive and fire-hot, especially as life gets busier when you two become parents.

Instructions:

So, you're convinced enough to give it a try? Great! Here's what I recommend:

1. Invite your partner to schedule intimacy with you by sharing how important it is for you to stay connected (you can even share this section of the book with them).
   - If they are skeptical, suggest you do a two-week experiment of regular love dates and see how the love dates feel to you both.
   - If your partner is still not on board, perhaps reach out to a coach who can help you untangle any painful feelings that may be bubbling up around your sex life.
2. Once you're both on board, decide how often you'd like to schedule intimacy.
   - I recommend you each privately choose a number of times you'd ideally like to have scheduled intimacy each week (you can have spontaneous intimacy as well, but this question is just for scheduled). This can range from once per week to seven per week (every day). Don't share it with each other yet!
   - Then each close your eyes and hold up your fingers with the number of times you'd like.
   - Now you can peek! Notice your partner's number and your own.

- If there is a big difference (say you want 6x/week and he wants 1x/week), have a chat about why that is, and what sex means to each of you.
- Find a number you can both agree on. It may be the number you both said, or a number in the middle.

3. Open your calendars and schedule your time!
    - I recommend an hour block for your love dates, but you're welcome to do as short or as long as you'd like. Some couples I know do twenty-minute dates, while others do two-hour dates on Sunday afternoons. Your call!

4. Choose a "leader" and a "follower" for this love date.
    - The leader sets the tone for the love date. They consider the scene: Where will this love date take place? The bedroom? The living room? They also decide how to enhance the scene: candles, music, etc.
    - The leader considers what erotic desires may bubble up either in themselves or in their partner. What could be fun to try and explore? If it's a particularly edgy idea (for example, handcuffs), check in with the follower well before the Love Date to see if they are a "yes," or to ask about any boundaries the couple should be aware of.
    - The follower arrives, ready and willing to connect! (PS, It's just as much work to be a follower as it is to be a leader, and leaders are only made by great followers! More on that later.)
    - I recommend taking turns being the leader, so you each have a chance to design the love date, as well as receive each other's leadership.

5. Once the time is scheduled, protect it like it's sacred. (Because it is!) That means not scheduling meetings, or anything else, on top of it.
    - If something urgent comes up and you *must* reschedule, the person who has to reschedule takes responsibility for finding a new time that works for both of you.
6. At your love date . . .
    - Set a timer, and stick to it. This creates safety in the container.
    - Remind each other what you're exploring during your love date—any desires or boundaries.
    - Enjoy the erotic play.

This practice sounds relatively simple, but it's surprisingly deep and life-changing. Here is a short story from one of our couple clients:

> "My partner and I first learned about love dates at Megan and James's couples retreat a couple of years ago. Hearing about it, I was stoked! (Virgo girl, that structure and scheduling like this turns me on, and the anticipation of having sex excited me!) My partner, on the other hand, was skeptical. To him, the thought of scheduling sex sounded so mundane and a massive buzzkill. But through staying open and committing to the practice for one month after the retreat, we both came to love it. **Having a dedicated and consistent love date is a practice that keeps our spark alive even when life gets busy.**"

Another couple described love dates this way:

> "The power of love dates for us has been in the time boxing. Creating the time boundary feels like a **real honoring of us both**."

That is enough to get started, but you may still have some questions about this rather radical idea of erotic containers. So, let's dive into a few of the most common "Love Date FAQs" we receive.

Love Date FAQs

Q: What if it's time for our love date, but I don't feel sexy or turned-on?

You can show up to the love date *exactly as you are* – you don't need to be in any particular state. However, taking a few minutes to transition from the hecticness of daily life into a lover mode is well-worth the time. I recommend preparing for a love date just like you might get ready for a dinner date. Perhaps you want to shower, get dressed up, dance around a bit . . . anything that helps you feel more in your body and more open for love.

Then, once the date starts, it's absolutely okay to not feel sexy right away. In the life-changing erotic education book, *Come as You Are*, author Emily Nagowski explains that there are two types of desire: spontaneous and responsive.

Spontaneous desire arises in anticipation of pleasure (a.k.a. you get turned-on before the love date, just by thinking about how fun it will be). Only 15 percent of women have a purely spontaneous desire, according to Nagowski's book. Responsive desire, by contrast, is only activated once you're already experiencing pleasure.

Here's an example of responsive desire: Imagine you start slowly kissing your partner. You're not turned-on or aroused yet, but as their soft lips meet yours, you think, "Mmm, I like that," and you feel open to trying a bit more. Then they kiss your neck, and you melt a little. You think, "Okay, that's nice," so you keep going. After a few minutes, you may start to feel your own arousal.

(And if not, you can totally stop the love date and say no. Your body's sovereignty is valid and primary, always.)

Most women have either purely responsive desire (30 percent, according to Nagowski's book) or a mix of spontaneous and responsive (55 percent). That means, for many of you, you often *won't* feel sexy or turned-on until something pleasurable is already occurring.

All this to say, if you're not turned-on right away, there is nothing wrong with you. Try a few minutes of erotic play and notice how your body feels. Are you open to more? Keep going.

Not into it? Offer something that would feel good to you. Perhaps a massage, a slower kiss, or cuddling. What type of touch could you genuinely say yes to?

By taking off the pressure to be turned-on right away and, instead, listening to your body moment-to-moment, you create a safe space for pleasure to arise naturally.

Q: Won't scheduled intimacy take the fun and spontaneity out of our sex life?

This is such a common belief because we live in a culture that idolizes the myth of spontaneity. As if the only passion that matters is the one that happens "by chance." (*But is it ever really "by chance?" At least one person is usually planning to get lucky.*)

In my experience while coaching hundreds of couples, scheduling intimacy and regularly making love helps them feel more desire for each other. They are stoking the fire, keeping it hot, through scheduled time to be intimate. They may start flirting more in their everyday life with small, sensual touches or sending playful, erotic texts. Then spontaneous sex is far more likely than if the couple had only relied on spontaneity.

Also, when you schedule love dates, it can be so helpful to take turns "leading" the date and crafting a particularly sexy experience for your partner. What have you never tried? What could be fun? Can you bring that element in?

By taking turns leading, you keep an element of surprise, fun, and spontaneity in your sex life. Even though you know you'll be intimate at that time (say, Wednesday at 3:00 p.m.), you never know what will happen!

Q: What if my partner keeps canceling or scheduling over our love date?

Ouch! This can be such a tender spot, because going back to benefit #1 of love dates, carving out and protecting this time is a way that you two can communicate to each other how important your intimacy is.

So, naturally, if your partner is canceling or overscheduling, you may start to wonder, "Is our intimacy as important to you as it is to me?"

If this is your situation, I'd recommend sharing your feelings with your partner as vulnerably and blame-free as you can while inviting them to help create a solution.

I worked with a woman where this continually happened in her relationship. Her partner was working a lot and under big pressure in his career as an executive. Meanwhile, she craved more quality time with him.

I suggested the idea of love dates, and they jumped on it eagerly, putting time in their calendar. But when the time came to connect, he canceled the love date because he was on a big work deadline. She was devastated.

She started our next call with, "He's always canceling on me! He doesn't even care. I knew this idea was stupid and wouldn't work." I listened, really hearing her hurt and frustration, creating space for her to vent it out. (Sometimes that's all we really need, am I right?)

After a bit, I asked if she was open to solutions (she was). I suggested that she share her feelings with him as vulnerably as she can, and invite him back into intimacy with her.

For example, she could say: "I feel so sad when you cancel our love dates because I worry that our intimacy doesn't matter to you. Can you reassure me that it does? And can you help us find a solution that works? I really want to be intimately connected to you."

She had to let go of her (justified) self-righteous anger to be this vulnerable, but she was willing to give it a shot. And guess what? It worked like a charm. He apologized for canceling, reassured her that she matters to him, and they put a new date on the calendar for after his deadline ended.

She later told me, "That was a big lesson for me. A part of me wanted to hold on to my anger and blame because it felt safe and righteous. But I realized our intimacy can only be found through vulnerability, and when I express my feelings gently, he comes closer to me."

> *Our intimacy can only be found through vulnerability, and when I express my feelings gently, he comes closer to me."*

Well said!

Q: What do we do if one of us has more desire for intimacy than the other?

I can't tell you how often I hear this question, and what a tender spot it is for many couples. Are you in this situation? If so, I'm sending you so much love, as it can be challenging for both sides.

For the partner who feels that they have higher levels of desire, you may feel frustrated and hurt by your partner's seemingly lack of desire to connect erotically. You might feel rejected or ashamed of your own desire.

For the partner who feels like they have lower desire, you may feel burdened, obligated, guilty, or resentful about your partner's sexual desire. You may say "yes" when you're not into it, or feel bad about saying "no" yet again.

If you want to dive deeper into this, I highly recommend the book *Come Together* by Emily Nagowski, where she outlines exactly what couples can do in this situation (as well as shares her own story of being the "lower desire" partner!)

In the meantime, here are three ideas you can try to prioritize intimacy with different levels of desire:

1. **Find a Yes:** If your partner initiates intimacy, practice finding one thing you can say yes to. Maybe you can't say yes to sexual intercourse, but can you say yes to kissing? Maybe you're a no to cock-sucking but a yes to a breast massage? What could you say yes to (and thereby validate your partner's desire) while respecting your body?

   Remember, if you have a responsive desire, you may not feel "into it" until the action gets started, so practice saying yes to some type of touch before you necessarily feel like it (while listening to your body every step of the way).

Important caveat: Please don't bypass your body and do anything out of obligation or that feels like a genuine "no."

2. **Reverse Roles**: Over time, couples often polarize into roles of "the initiator" (who wants more intimacy) and "the rejector" (who doesn't). So, do a one-month experiment where you consciously switch roles, and the "rejector" is fully responsible for initiating all the intimacy (agree ahead how many times they will initiate intimacy each week, and refer to the guide to love dates for help).

3. **Each Initiate Once a Week:** Later, I'll introduce the 1:1:1 rule of sustaining a long-term relationship, but for now, I'll tell you that one of the tenets is that you and your partner are each responsible for initiating intimacy once a week. That way, the "burden" (and vulnerability) of initiating falls on both of you.

Which one of these three ideas appeal to you? What would you add?

This is such a tender spot, and there can often be resentment and hurt feelings. If this is true for you, I also invite you to seek out support from a relationship and intimacy coach or therapist.

Now that we've looked at keeping your sensuality alive through conscious exploration, let's look at your overall relationship and the important conversations to have before calling in your baby.

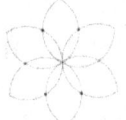

RELATIONSHIP

Remember that moment in our commitment ceremony where I felt the undeniable truth of wanting a baby with James?

My heart was saying "yes."

But we still needed to have some important conversations before I was fully ready. First, we needed to prepare our relationship for the massive bomb that a baby is.

Here is how we prepared ourselves . . .

_____

Conception Conversations

Before opening up to conceiving life together, I recommend having a number of deep, honest heart-to-hearts with your partner. These conversations will help you two connect over this life-changing decision and feel more prepared for taking the leap together.

Know that the decision to conceive a baby is a *big* one and will likely bring up many fears for both of you. It may trigger reflection about your own childhoods and the way you both were parented. It may invite you two to get more real and honest about the life you envision together. All of this is wonderful preparation for a baby.

I've also heard many stories of couples who struggled to conceive for months, and then after having these honest, heartfelt discussions about a baby, they immediately conceived, almost as if the spirit baby was waiting for the channels to be clear and connected to come through.

Open: Seven Conception Conversations

This will help you two connect over your visions and desires, as well as create space to talk about any fears that arise.

> **Bonus:** I have this list as a downloadable PDF guide on my website at www.megandlambert.com/emresources.

Instructions:

Here are the conversations I recommend having with your partner before conceiving.

I recommend splitting this list into **seven unique dates**, choosing one topic per date. That way you can really take your time with each question, letting the questions percolate deeper inside you. Perhaps you spread the questions out over seven weeks, bringing them up on your weekly date night. In numerology, the number seven is associated with wisdom, intuition, and mystery—powerful factors as you two dream into your next possible season together as co-parents.

Note: Know that if you conceive without talking about these questions, that's okay too! It's never too late for you and your partner to get even more intentional about being parents.

- Date #1: Readiness for Children
    - How will we each know when we're ready to have a baby? Make a list!
    - Why do we want a baby?

- What do we imagine our daily life will be like with a baby, from waking up to going to bed? What parts sound exciting? What parts sound challenging?
- What can we do to strengthen our relationship before this next phase of having children? Do we need any external support (coaching, a retreat, etc.)?
- Date #2: Lifestyle
    - Where do we want to raise our family? In this home? A new home? This town or another one?
    - What kind of childhood do we want to give our children? What memories will we make as a family?
    - What are our long-term dreams? How do we imagine a child fitting into those dreams?
    - What's important to us when it comes to parenting? What three values will guide us in raising our children?
- Date #3: Childcare
    - How do we envision sharing childcare duties?
    - Make a list of responsibilities for children. (E.g. feeding, diapering, night wake ups, healthcare, etc.)
    - What roles will you take, and what do you expect me to do?
    - What did we see modeled by our own parents in terms of sharing childcare? For example, did Mom do most of the childcare and Dad "helped"? Was it 50/50? Did Dad stay home while Mom worked?
- Date #4: Work
    - Who will earn the income for our family? How will they earn money?
    - How much time away from the family will this work require? Who will care for the kids while the parent(s) is at work?

- What do we need to have done professionally in the next decade to feel successful or fulfilled, with or without children?
- Date #5: Finances
    - How much money do we need to earn monthly to feel prepared to support a child?
    - How much savings do we need to feel safe enough to have a baby?
    - How much do we imagine a baby would cost anyway? (There are great resources online to help you calculate this!)
- Date #6: Sex & Intimacy
    - How do we imagine having a baby will impact our sex life?
    - What do we want our sex life to be like while pregnant, and later, with a baby?
    - How will we nourish our intimacy through this next chapter? Are there any rituals we can design or create to keep us connected?
- Date #7: In-Laws
    - How often do we want our in-laws to visit the children? Are there any boundaries we can anticipate needing to hold here?
    - What relationship do we hope our children have with our families of origin? How will we foster this relationship (or not)?

This is not an exhaustive list but this can give you two a great starting point to dream into, and prepare for, a baby bomb.

How Men vs. Women Prepare to Conceive

This is a gendered generalization, but I've seen it time and again, so I'm going to say it:

Men and women prepare very differently for having a baby.

Women often feel the call to have a baby, like a soul yearning. It's deep, primal, and emotional. There isn't often a strong, logical reason to have a baby – more like an embodied desire.

For me, I knew when I was being called to have a baby because I got tears in my eyes every time I thought about it. I felt chills across my body. It felt like my heart was opening and expanding as I imagined our little baby. It felt *right* in a way that I couldn't explain.

Now, as a general rule, men prepare for having a baby in a more practical, logistical way. He thinks about: Do we have enough money to support a child? Am I at a stable enough place in my career? Do we have a suitable home for children? Does a child fit into my life plan? And so on.

When I told James I was ready to have a baby, it was this sweet desire to hold our little one. When he said he was ready, it was a calculated move based on all the factors involved.

Does that make this any less romantic?

Nope. It's just a practical difference between men and women, because the feminine moves from desire, and the masculine tends to move from his plan.

All this to say, if your partner seems a bit less emotional about the prospect of your baby, and a bit more practical, it doesn't necessarily mean that he is less excited than you are. It might just be that he's speaking a different language.

If you relate to this, ask him, "What comes to mind when we think of conceiving a baby? What worries, fears, or excitement? What do you need to figure out before you feel ready to conceive?" Then listen. Really listen. Notice that he may come to conception from a completely different vantage point than you, but it does not mean he's any less willing or happy about the decision.

What if you and your partner don't agree on the timing of having a baby?

Is one of you ready, and the other one not yet?

If that's your situation, I recommend asking each other these questions:

1. What do you need to do before you feel ready to have children?
    - (e.g., Earn a certain amount of funds, travel the world, get this promotion, find a house, etc.)
2. What do those items from the list above represent to you?
    - (e.g., If it's "find a house," that might represent security or safety; if it's "travel the world," that might represent freedom, etc.)
    - This will help you get to the values underlying your partner's needs.
3. Why is that value important to you?
    - This helps you "get into their world" and really understand your partner's perspective on this desire.
4. How can we both get our needs met here?
    - (e.g., If you want a baby within the year because you're worried about fertility while your partner wants to wait until they're financially secure . . . perhaps you can start saving together now each month while also being open to conceiving.

I hope these questions help you both express your needs and desires in a way that each of you can understand and hear each other. I believe that, most times, there is a way to align around a timeline by deeply understanding each other's perspectives.

There is one situation where it may not be possible to get aligned.

What if your partner doesn't want children, period?

Sorry, love, this might be harsh, but this is a deal-breaker spot for couples, no matter how much you love each other.

If one of you sincerely wants to become a parent, and the other adamantly doesn't . . . that is a cause to end the relationship. You need to be on the same page about the choice to have children.

Trying to convince a partner to want kids when they don't want them disrespects both of you. It disrespects your partner's "no," and dishonors your desire by staying in a situation that doesn't align with your life vision.

However, if you want children and your partner is skeptical but open to considering it, that may warrant a number of conversations to learn more about each other's life vision.

When I met James, he wasn't sure whether or not he wanted to be a father. He was open to it, but he could also see his life without children. Meanwhile, I was passionate about becoming a mother—it was nonnegotiable for me, and I said so on our second date.

Over time, he came around to the idea and realized he would love to become a parent with me. Today, he is so grateful for our children and couldn't imagine his life any other way.

So, if your partner is open to having children but not yet certain, it's worth more conversations and exploration. If they are a hard no, that is a deal-breaker.

Now that you two are (hopefully) on the same page about getting ready to conceive, let's broaden our lens and look at the whole ecosystem needed to support you two.

ECOSYSTEM

The journey to become a parent does not happen in isolation. It's not just a "you" moment, nor a "you + your partner" moment. No. Becoming a mother happens in the context of your ecosystem—your home and neighborhood, your community, your natural surroundings, and, dare I say it, your spirituality.

For a plant to bloom flowers, it needs a healthy ecosystem—nutrient-rich soil, the right amount of rain, the exact sun-to-shade ratio for the specific plant, and the right insects and animals around it.

If the plant is not producing flowers, or not thriving, you don't yell at the plant to "Try harder!" No.

You look at the ecosystem around the plant and wonder, "What might this plant need to thrive? Does it need more sun or less? Is it getting enough nutrients? Are there any pests or weeds to remove?"

You are the same way. To thrive in your motherhood journey, you need to be embedded in a healthy ecosystem of support and nature. Do you have enough community? A cozy and comfortable home? Peaceful nature to rejuvenate you? Your ecosystem matters immensely.

The focus on ecosystem may be unusual for those of us who grew up in the Global North. As a general rule, Global North cultures (e.g., European, American) have a stronger focus on independence and personal autonomy. In those cultural contexts, people tend to see themselves as self-reliant and personally responsible. With that lens, becoming a mama is an individual experience happening between a mother and baby, plus a partner or close family members. This reductionist lens misses the context and ecosystem of motherhood.

For example, when treating postpartum depression in the United States, we focus on prescribing drugs and potentially psychotherapy to the mama (which may be helpful and needed!), which emphasizes that the problem and the solution are inside the individual, rather than looking at her context.

By contrast, if you take an ecosystem lens to postpartum depression, you'd notice that more and more mamas are suffering because the ecosystem around motherhood is dysfunctional. Paid parental leave is minimal, the mythical "village" is nonexistent for many families, many new mamas live far from their extended families, and the role of the mother is not honored. So, to treat postpartum depression from an ecosystem lens, you'd start by looking at the context that surrounds the mother, rather than simply assume that the problem lies within her.

It's natural that you wouldn't thrive in a context that isn't conducive to life. It's normal to need support, to need nature, to need a healthy ecosystem to belong to.

At a physiological level, our bodies know that we are meant to belong to a tribe, to have a land we know intimately, to feel supported by a wider

> *Our bodies know that we are meant to belong to a tribe, to have a land we know intimately, to feel supported by a wider community. When this is not true for a new mama—if, for example, she lacks friends, a connection to nature, or elders to guide her—her biological alarm bells will go off.*

community. When this is not true for a new mama—if, for example, she lacks friends, a connection to nature, or elders to guide her—her biological alarm bells will go off. Her body knows something isn't right.

In the ecosystem section, we're looking at the context that surrounds you. How do we create a setting where you can thrive as you become a mother, flowering into the mama you were meant to be? That's what this section is all about.

How Mamas Got So Isolated

Motherhood wasn't always so lonely. Not long ago, raising children was something women did together. In many cultures, it still is. Here in Bali, it's not uncommon to see grandmothers, aunties, and neighbors stepping in to help raise children, much like they've done for centuries.

But in many Global North societies, this communal support has largely disappeared. The result? A kind of quiet isolation many mothers feel today.

How did we get here?

Before the Industrial Revolution (late 1800s, early 1900s), many families lived in close-knit communities with multiple generations and shared child rearing more collectively. However, with the Industrial revolution, many families moved to the cities in search of work, which broke up traditional extended-family structures.

As people moved to the city, the nuclear family (father, mother, children) became the dominant unit with women often confined to homes to raise children while men worked outside the home. This meant that women were now solely responsible for the children, without the network of support she once had.

As the twentieth century continued, the rise of suburban living and cultural norms focused on self-sufficiency and privacy, with families living in single-family homes far from extended family. At the same time, there was a rise in "intensive mothering," which is a cultural shift to place heightened expectations on mothers to single-handedly meet all of their children's emotional and development needs. At the same time, many community structures like churches and town gatherings began to unravel.

All of these factors—unraveled community structures, higher expectations for mothers, and isolated nuclear-family living—have created an experience for mothers that is often lonely, stressful, and overwhelming.

Here is the truth: We are not meant to do this alone. Mothering is *not* a one-woman job, nor is it a nuclear-family job. It takes a village to raise a child—it's a cliché, but it's true.

Your Village

Motherhood is the biggest call to interdependence that I know. I felt more vulnerable, more needy, and more reliant on others while becoming a mother than at any other point in my life.

Now I believe that's by design—having children is not a one-woman job. It's a community activity that invites us to gather closer, to share and learn from each other. We're meant to do this together.

It takes a village to raise a child, *and* it also takes a village to raise a *mother*. You will become the mother you were meant to be by surrounding yourself with mentors, friends, and loved ones—as well as enriching your connection with earth and spirit.

If you felt sad reading this, or notice you have a lack of community, you are far from alone. In fact, you are in the norm.

As one client shared:

> "I wasn't in a position of having family close by, I didn't speak the language of the country I lived in, and I hadn't made friends there yet. This was the context where I became a mother—and it was lonely."

> *With care and intention, you can rebel against the cultural norm of an isolated mother and create your village.*

Many women crave this village, but it isn't their experience (yet). However, with care and intention, you can rebel against the cultural norm of an isolated mother and create your village.

Doing this is countercultural and radical, yet so much more nourishing for you and your children. So, what can you do if you don't currently have a strong community network? There are many ideas.

The first step is awareness, to take stock of your connections currently and to make a "wish list" of the types of connections you'd like to have.

For example, maybe you're dreaming of:

- Neighbors that you know by name and feel safe watching your kids play in their yard.
- Friends that send over extras of their home-cooked meal for you and your family.
- Other families you get together with at the park, where your kids can play together.
- A yoga buddy you get coffee with after class each week to share about your motherhood journey one-on-one.

What kinds of connections would you love to have? What is your desired community? This can feel vulnerable and bring up feelings of isolation or loneliness. That is okay! Everybody gets lonely from time to time, and wanting more connection doesn't mean there is anything wrong with you.

Then the next step is to move through your day with an openness to meeting new people. Say hi when you pass people on the street. Strike up a conversation with the person in your yoga class. Smile at another parent at the park. This creates openings for new connections to flow.

Making new friends is tender. In a way, it's like dating—you can set out your intentions and be open to connection, and then you let go and trust that life will bring you the perfect people for this stage of life.

Building your village is an important topic that I will continue to expand on in every chapter. For now, if you just get clear on your desired village and communal support, that is enough, and together, we will help you get a stronger, more vibrant ecosystem.

A key aspect of your ecosystem is a deep sense of trust. Let's expand on that here . . .

Your Faith

How easily do you trust life? The Universe? How easily can you let go and surrender to what is?

I believe with all my heart that we need a sense of faith to thrive in motherhood. That faith can be in a higher power, in God, in Allah, in universal love. Whatever name or face you attribute to spirit, I believe a connection with that entity or energy is vital, because without that connection, it is too challenging to surrender. Surrender into what? Without connection to something greater than yourself, it is easy to fall into patterns of trying to control everything, which rarely works in motherhood.

Maybe you already have a deep relationship with your higher power. Maybe this is a budding spot for you, a relationship you'd like to cultivate deeper. Or maybe you're ready to chuck this book out just because I brought the G-word in. Either way, I invite you to stay here and to stay curious about what your unique relationship to Higher Power might be like during this journey into motherhood (or not! As with everything, take what you like and leave the rest).

I'll share more ways to connect with your higher power throughout this book, because motherhood requires surrender. Surrender requires trust and faith. Of course, you can always skip these sections if faith gives you the heebie-jeebies.

Your Land

Finally, the physical land you choose to create life on has a big impact on your family. Our original mother is Mother Nature.

For me, the journey into motherhood brought a renewed interest and passion for nature as I felt how nourishing it was to be near life while growing life. Maybe you already have a deep connection to nature with lots of wild land nearby, or maybe you're reading this in a big city where your only nature is a little potted plant you're barely keeping alive. Either way, it's great! It's less about trying to find some perfect place and more about finding ways to connect with, tend to, and be nourished by the land you're on.

Reflect: Dream into Your Ecosystem

By journaling on the questions below, you'll have a clear idea of your current ecosystem and where you want to devote extra attention to as you become a mother. Building a strong, supportive ecosystem is one of the best ways to prepare for having a baby.

Instructions:

Take time to journal on each of the below questions. This can be done in multiple sittings, perhaps taking one section at a time, so you can fully digest each of them.

Community

- Overall, how supported by your community do you feel?
- Do you have family nearby? Is that important to you?
- Do you have other women friends who are mamas who you can turn to for advice?
- How deep and lasting are your friendships? How nourished do you feel by spending time with them?
- These people will be uncles and aunties (by choice or by blood) to your children. Consider thoughtfully who you want influencing your little ones.

Spirituality

- What do you call your higher power?
- What attributes does your higher power have?
- How can you connect with your higher power each day?
- What burdens or fears are you currently carrying that you could ask a higher power to support you with? What can you give up to your high power?
- What are you thankful for in your life that you can attribute to your higher power?

Land

- On what land do you want to have children?
- Consider the feeling of the environment around you.

- Is there nature? Do you crave more nature? How could you access more nature? (Parks? A mini-garden on your balcony? A weekend hike?)
- What is the history of the land you're on right now? (Consider its indigenous roots and cultural background.)
- Know that the land you are on is steeped in tradition and has a particular vibration to it that will affect your family. How does this land feel to you? How might it shape your family?

Home

- What type of home would you like to raise your babies in? Is it your current home, or are you interested in moving? If you want to move, where would you like to go?
- Consider basics like how babyproof (or not) your home is, as well as the overall "feel" of the home.
- Is there anything you could do to make your home more welcoming to new life?
- What can you do to make your home as natural, clean, and toxin-free as possible to support a future pregnancy? The book *Really Very Crunchy* by Emily Morrow is a great resource on creating a healthy, low-tox home.

Please use this simply as an invitation for inquiry, rather than a checklist. It's unlikely that all aspects of your ecosystem feel perfect already, and they don't need to be to feel ready to have a baby.

However, this list might inspire you to make a few little changes, perhaps aiming to improve your ecosystem by just 10 percent.

Or maybe this list touches on a niggling feeling you've had that it's time for a big change in your ecosystem. Either way, I'm sending you so much love as you find the right ecosystem for your budding family to thrive.

Putting these elements together—your village, your faith, and your land—creates a vibrant ecosystem to support you and your budding family.

CHAPTER SUMMARY

We may never feel fully "ready" to have a baby, nor do we need to be fully healed from all our intergenerational trauma to become a "good enough" mother.

Having a baby is both a mind and a body decision. It's worth getting to know your fears and considering the logistic aspects of having a child. Yet, ultimately, you can trust your gut intuition here. Your body knows.

Before conceiving, this is a great time to explore your own erotic or wild desires—do you want a Slut Era? Go for it! It's also a great time to deepen your intimacy with your current partner, if applicable, through a life-changing practice called Love Dates.

You and your partner can prepare for conception by having a series of powerful Conception Conversations that I shared in this book.

I also walked through common disagreements between couples when it comes to conceiving, and how to resolve them.

Last, we explore how motherhood became such an isolated journey for many women, and how you can start building your community and connection to nature now, so that your motherhood experience is more supported, lush, and nourishing.

Ways to GROW

In this chapter, I shared the following invitations for you:

- **Go Do: Hearing the Call Meditation**—This meditation will help you imagine what it might be like to have a baby and become aware of any hidden fears or desires that are under the surface so you can feel more prepared to conceive.
- **Reflect: Hearing the Call**—an invitation to journal on your insights from the meditation and integrate the lessons.
- **Go Do: Plan a Love Date**—Love Dates are a life-changing practice for couples to intentionally plan time for the erotic, and to bring more exploration and fun into their sexual lives.
- **Open: Seven Conception Conversations**—I shared a list of powerful questions for you and your partner to discuss so that you feel on the same page about the decision to conceive a baby.
- **Reflect: Dreaming into Your Ecosystem**—Building your network of support now will help you feel more supported, nourished, and held as you embark on the journey to becoming a mother.
- **Widen:** If you'd like to read another book on this topic, you might enjoy *The Baby Decision: How to Make the Most Important Choice of Your Life* by Merle Bombardieri.

Chapter 2

CALLING IN YOUR BABY (CONCEPTION)

Moving, swirling, opening,
Love building,
Yes.

We nod, we know.
A bold decision.

The earth quakes and shakes.
Timelines leap.
Nothing will ever be the same again.

Conceiving Lila

> **Note:** We're about to share a juicy story that involves sex (of course, it's conception). Skip if you don't want to read it (looking at you, mom and dad ☺).

"Go conceive your baby!" My friends said, laughing, while sitting on the couch after my thirtieth birthday celebration.

"Ahhh!" was all I could manage to respond with. I felt shy and prudish, but also excited.

We had just finished an amazing surprise birthday party, planned by James, with forty of my friends. There were surprises like a drumming lesson, group painting, massages, and a photo booth. It was such a fun birthday, and I left in awe of the community we had created around us.

It was no secret that James and I were considering conceiving a baby soon, but we weren't sure we were quite ready yet. Our commitment ceremony was only three months ago, and by God, I still hadn't healed all my intergenerational trauma. Joking!

We went upstairs and kissed passionately, moving into deeply connected lovemaking. Stay with me here, because this is where my experience turns from pleasurable to full-on mystical.

At the pinnacle moment, I felt a white orb floating up to my right side. It clearly felt like our spirit baby, knocking on the metaphorical door, asking if we were ready.

I looked at James, and I believe he felt it too. All I said was "Yes." Then we both let go into this beautiful, simultaneous orgasm of creation.

Afterward, I shared what I saw, and he confirmed he had seen and felt the same thing. It felt like our spirit baby was here. We decided that this was the moment when we officially opened the gates to conceive a baby.

I know this sounds woo-woo and a little crazy. Despite living in Bali and surrounding myself with tons of self-described hippies, I'm not normally this "out there." Generally speaking, I prefer to stay more grounded and practical. But this was one of the most inexplicable and transcendental moments of my life.

Two weeks later, I took a pregnancy test. I was devastated to see that it was negative. I had felt the spirit baby! What happened? My heart fell.

James took me out to dinner to try to cheer me up, but I was so disappointed. For the past two weeks, I was so sure that I was pregnant, and I had let myself get so excited. Now I felt like a fool.

(Have you ever felt that way? So hopeful, and then disappointed?)

The next day, I went away for a girls' weekend with five of my close friends. We stayed in this charming bamboo hut where we planned to dance, sunbathe, share deep heart-to-hearts, and indulge in some memorable experiences that allowed us to relax and reflect.

During the weekend, my friend laid her head on my womb and said matter-of-factly, "Oh, you're pregnant." You could hear a pin drop.

I replied, "Really? No, I took a test. It was negative."

She shook her head, "No, I still think you're pregnant."

have to do this alone. I'll share more thoughts on support in the ecosystem section of this chapter.

Conceiving Latham

When my first baby (Lila) was twenty months old, I started feeling the spirit of our second baby quite strongly. I'd imagine being pregnant again, holding a new baby, and watching Lila become a big sister. Each time I imagined this image, I got chills and tears in my eyes, just as I had when I first felt the call to conceive Lila. The desire was growing stronger.

In May 2023, James left for two weeks to go on a men's retreat, and while he was away, my mind continuously went to this new possible baby. Every time I was driving, or waiting in line, or in the shower, I just kept wondering if it was time to have another baby.

I believe this kind of persistent curiosity or daydreaming is a way that the spirit baby knocks on our door, getting us ready to welcome him or her in.

The day James was due to come home, I remember driving my scooter back home, thinking, "We're going to conceive our baby today."

My menstrual app confirmed that I was ovulating that day. My mind raced ahead as I imagined being pregnant and giving birth. I realized I wanted the same midwife I had with my firstborn.

I looked up the expected due date. February 12, 2024—if we did conceive that day. Then I messaged our midwife: "Are you free around February next year to attend our birth?"

"Are you pregnant?" she asked.

"Not yet! But I think I will be pregnant soon," I replied.

She laughed and confirmed she could be our midwife with those dates. I felt relieved and excited. She was a true Earth angel that helped us so much with our first birth (See the full story in chapter 4).

Are you thinking I'm a bit crazy to line up a midwife before I even got pregnant? I might be! But I love a good plan, even in places where it's impossible to plan, like having a baby. It's probably just a coping mechanism against uncertainty. ;)

Meanwhile, James was on the plane flying back from the US, unaware of my master plan (hehe).

When James returned home, there was so much erotic energy between us after two weeks away. While we got Lila ready for bed, I showed him a note on my phone that said, "Let's conceive our baby tonight!" He looked stunned, then smiled broadly.

Later, he said he felt a lot of love, joy, and turn-on in that moment.

After Lila was asleep, we made love. This lovemaking was so electric and intense, but also held a deep love and tenderness, with grief mingled in. I remember crying during a particularly deep moment, feeling the enormity of what we were saying yes to.

The first time we conceived, I was so excited about a baby that I didn't necessarily realize what a massive life change, sacrifice, and responsibility it is to bring life into the world. I couldn't, because I hadn't had that embodied experience yet.

But now my body knew what this "yes" meant, so this moment brought so many mixed emotions. We made love while moving through moments of arousal and passion, as well as grief and sadness. Tears and joy, all mingled into one.

When we went over together, I felt like my heart broke open and shattered as our family expanded. Tears streaked down my cheeks, a confusing mix of love, joy, and grief.

The wave of grief that happened at conception surprised me. I imagined it would be a 100 percent happy moment.

I believe that my confusing mix of feelings is the result of my heart expanding. Letting go of our tight-knit little family of three to expand into a family of four. Letting go of my body sovereignty to welcome in a little soul. Letting go of Lila being my one and only baby love, to loving two babies.

While I was surprised by the grief, I know now how normal this is. The more I talk to other mamas, the more I learn that welcoming the second baby (or third or fourth) often comes with both joy and grief—a welcoming and a letting go. Both.

Again and again, motherhood invites me to welcome the duality of the experience—the high highs, and the low lows—knowing they are two sides of the same coin. Tears of joy and grief commingled on my cheeks in that sacred moment of welcoming a new soul.

Then began the two-week waiting game again to discover if I was, in fact, pregnant. This time, I felt clear that I was pregnant. Each time I put my hands on my womb, I felt an aliveness and an energy of something happening inside my body.

During that waiting period, we had our big wedding! We had the commitment ceremony three years prior, but we had yet to have the big wedding I had dreamed of since being a little girl.

During the wedding, I secretly hoped that I was pregnant so I could later tell my two kids that they had both been at the wedding. I went through the ceremony with such joy, feeling that we had our little girl with us in the ceremony, and that we may have our next little baby in my womb.

The day after the wedding, James, Lila, and I went to our bedroom, where I took the pregnancy test. All three of us, sitting, excitedly watching for the answer of the test (Well, I'm not sure Lila really understood what was happening, as she was only twenty months old).

Finally, we saw it—two blue lines! We rejoiced and celebrated, cuddling, and telling Lila she was going to be a big sister!

As I write both conception stories, similar themes weave through for me:

- **Listening in to the spirit baby's timing.** Ask the baby when they are ready vs. when I think pregnancy should happen. Sensing into the baby's timing.
- **Lovemaking right on ovulation.** I timed each lovemaking to be on the day of ovulation to give us the best chances of conception. (I'll share more on that shortly).
- **Surrendering to the unknown.** While I had a plan of when I'd like to conceive, I held that plan loosely, knowing that Higher Power has the best plan for me.

I wonder which themes stand out to you in my story? How do you feel reading these?

I love sharing and hearing women's conception stories, because again, they are as unique as each woman's fingerprint. Your story will likely be completely different from mine, and beautiful in its twists, turns, and timing. I trust your body's timing and your higher power's plan for your budding family. Now, let's move on to your story!

BODY

You're ready to conceive! Congratulations, this is such a big step.

In this chapter, we will explore how to prepare for a baby—physically, emotionally, and spiritually. Let's start with the basics of your body.

Physical Preparation

If you're trying to conceive, an obvious but important point is to know when you're ovulating, so you can time lovemaking well for maximum chances of conception.

There are several ways to know that you're ovulating such as:

- **Menstrual app:** This is a simple way to track your cycle and predict ovulation, by simply entering in the last dates of your period. Note that it's not always accurate, so if conception is challenging, I'd explore a few other methods.
- **Cervical fluid:** When you're ovulating, your vaginal discharge becomes clear and stretchy, like an egg white. This is a good sign that you're fertile right now.
- **Body temperature:** Your body temperature increases slightly (0.5–0.9F) immediately after ovulation occurs, so by tracking body temperature for a few months, you'll get a clearer idea of when your ovulation occurs.
- **Ovulation testing strips:** These are simple strips you can buy at the drugstore that you pee on each morning, and it will tell you when you're ovulating.

These methods will help you know when you're ovulating, and help you cultivate bodily autonomy by understanding your cycle better. Then I'd recommend timing lovemaking for when you're ovulating, by making love either every day or every other day during your fertile window.

Did you know that you can only get pregnant in a <u>maximum six-day window around ovulation</u>? It's true! You can only conceive if you have sex up to five days before ovulation, and one day after. The rest of the month, conception isn't possible, as there is no egg accessible.

Honestly, I was in my late twenties before I knew that, as my school's sexual education made it sound like pregnancy was inevitable all month long (very fear-based). This is empowering information that I wish all women learned early on so we could feel more empowered around our fertility.

If you've been tracking your ovulation windows for a while and haven't conceived yet, I recommend reaching out to a naturopathic doctor or integrated health practitioner for support. There are many other ways to support the physicality of conception that doctors can help with. Your partner should visit the expert with you as well, because his sperm count and quality have an enormous impact on chances of conception.

Now let's turn to the emotional and spiritual aspects of preparing your body for conception.

Emotional and Spiritual Preparation

Opening the gates to conceive is opening your body to the great mystery of creation. The moment when the spirit baby comes in and you become pregnant is up to divine timing. There is no way to control that mystery, no matter how many scientific interventions you use.

Conception invites us to connect back to an older, more primal aspect of ourselves: faith and surrender. This is no small thing, especially if you're used to using your intellect and frontal cortex to navigate life (as many of us are in the modern world).

Over the years, I've watched many intelligent, high-achieving women struggle in their conception journeys, because they are deeply uncomfortable with the inability to control the process. The uncertainty can bring up intense feelings of tenderness and vulnerability.

Being with your own vulnerability during this time, without trying to fix or control it, is excellent practice for becoming a mother. Being a mother is the most vulnerable work I've ever done. There is so much love, so much tenderness, and so much uncertainty. That starts with conception.

Below, I'll share a ritual with you that mimics the experience of being a baby in the womb. This ritual invites you to imagine your spirit baby's journey and to open your body to receive new life.

Go Do: Thanking Your Womb Ritual

This ritual is a beautiful way to prepare your body to receive life, and to honor your womb for all it has already done to prepare your fertility for this moment.

Babies live for ten moons in the salty, sweet water of your amniotic fluid. In a similar vein, this ritual will invite you to take a salt bath to embrace the feeling of being in the womb.

> **Bonus:** I have this meditation as an audio you can follow along for free on my website: www.megandlambert.com/emresources.

Instructions:

1. The first thing to do is to prepare your space. Fill a bath with warm water and add Epsom salt, which can be found at most health food shops or pharmacies. If you have essential oils, add those to the bath as well (rose is especially nice for this). Feel free to light a candle or incense and dim the lights.

2. Slowly lower yourself into the bath, feeling how the tub wraps around you like a womb, and how the water warms your skin like amniotic fluid. Breathe for a moment. Then place your hands on your womb and make a humming sound. Humming vibrates your vagus nerve, which can help you access a parasympathetic state of your nervous system (rather than a sympathetic or fight-or-flight state).

3. Once you feel fully relaxed, take a moment to thank your womb for all it has done. All the monthly cycles you've had, all the times you've bled, all the ovulations . . . your womb has been working hard your whole post-pubescent life, preparing for this moment.

4. If you've had previous pregnancies, miscarriages, surgeries, or abortions, take an extra moment to acknowledge your womb for its fertility journey so far. Your womb has stories to tell you about these experiences. Notice any emotions or sensations that arise. Imagine holding yourself and any tenderness that comes up with deep compassion and welcoming.

5. Next, ask your womb if she is ready to welcome new life in. Listen for a response. I know this sounds woo-woo, but it can be so profound! A "response" may come as an intuitive idea, a gut feeling, an image, a sound, or a

sudden insight. Trust what comes to mind or body after you ask the question.

6. Then ask your womb if there is anything your body or spirit needs to become ready, any final ways of preparing. What can you do to get ready to welcome a new life?

7. Finally, imagine the eggs inside your ovaries. Send a golden warm light to your ovaries, as if you can wrap them in health and well-being. Each egg has been with you since before you were born. In fact, you developed these eggs while still inside your mama's womb. These eggs have been with you for your whole life, waiting for this moment.

   Imagine one egg, the perfect one, dropping down your fallopian tubes, preparing to meet the sperm that will be half of your baby. Visualize the sperm and egg meeting, the spark of life entering, and the cells dividing to form an embryo. It's quite miraculous, isn't it?

   As you imagine this conception, continue feeling any sensations in your womb, the future home of your baby.

8. To close the ritual, send a little prayer of love and gratitude to your womb and ovaries, thanking them for everything they've done.

9. After you get out of the bath, take a few minutes to journal on what you felt, noticed, and perhaps any messages you got from your body.

The Egg and Sperm Story

The Fairytale We've Been Taught

The conception narrative we tell ourselves has enormous implications for how we view life, as well as our role as women and men.

Traditionally, the conception narrative is that the egg is hanging out, passively waiting for a sperm to fertilize her. Meanwhile, the sperm are in a cut-throat, fight-to-the-death match to see which one is the biggest, fastest, strongest to make it to the egg. The "winner" breaks down the egg's protective barrier and enters her, creating fertilization.

Is that roughly the same conception story you learned in biology too?

Hmm . . . Can you see elements of patriarchy and capitalism in that story?

> Passive female, doing "nothing."
>
> Male competition and domination.
>
> The strongest wins.
>
> Breaking down her walls without any input from her.

Interesting once you pull the story apart, right?

The passive princess egg waiting for her knight-in-shining-armor sperm, that defeats all competition, to bring her to full fruition? It's just like the Disney fairytales I grew up with!

Yet, here is the weird thing about science: it's not objective truth. We can only see "science" through our own cultural lens. And the narratives we tell ourselves in "science" reflect our cultural conditioning.

What if science actually has a completely different story to tell us?[1]

So, how does conception actually happen?

> The narratives we tell ourselves in "science" reflect our cultural conditioning.

This is going to blow your mind. Are you ready?

(Well, maybe it just blew my mind because I'm a total biology nerd. You might not find this quite as cool, but bear with me, okay?)

According to "Is The Sperm Race A Fairy Tale?" shared on NPR's Short Wave podcast, Emily Kwong share what really happens.[2]

First of all, after ejaculation, the sperm aren't swimming on their own to the egg. No way. The reproduction tract inside the woman is contracting, moving the sperm toward the egg. (Notice an already more active female role than the traditional narrative?)

Then the reproductive tract secretes fluids that give the sperm more energy so they become better "swimmers," like bathing in coffee. It also strips off an extra layer from the sperm so they are more ready to bind to the egg. In essence, her body is ushering the sperm along, energizing them, and preparing them to meet the egg.

The egg guides the sperm to her by releasing super-attractive chemicals that draw the right sperm her way. Meanwhile, the woman's reproductive tract sends out immune cells that eat

---

[1] Emily Martin, "The Egg and the Sperm: How Science Has Constructed a Romance Based on Stereotypical Male Female Roles," *Signs* 16, no. 3 (Spring 1991): 485-501, https://web.stanford.edu/~eckert/PDF/Martin1991.pdf.
[2] Emily Kwong, "Is The Sperm Race A Fairy Tale?" March 5, 2021, in *Short Wave*, produced by NPR, podcast, MP3 audio, 12:53, https://www.npr.org/transcripts/971914242.

the dysfunctional sperm. In other words, the reproductive tract immune system is selecting only the healthiest sperm to continue.

Once the sperm reaches the egg, the sperm doesn't just bury itself inside. No, no, no. The egg is surrounded by special cells that attract and trap the healthiest sperm. Yes, the egg is a sperm catcher. (Are you hearing the song "Maneater" in your head right now too?)

The one specially chosen sperm is allowed to enter the egg. Once the sperm enters the egg, conception begins. First comes love, then comes marriage, then comes a baby in a baby carriage . . . or so the nursery rhyme goes. ☺

So, the narrative of the passive egg waiting for the big, strong sperm is scientifically false. It turns out that conception is a cooperative process, with significant effort on the part of the woman's reproductive tract and egg. Some people even say that the egg "chooses" the sperm.

Why Does This Matter?

Well, the narrative we tell ourselves about conception reflects and reveals the narratives we tell ourselves about what it means to be a man and a woman.

If you believe your role as a woman is to passively wait for a man to "save" you (or impregnate you) . . . well, that can be quite disempowering.

Instead, I invite you to see your body as a magical gateway of creation, actively welcoming the healthiest sperm toward you, choosing the sperm that will become half of your baby.

> *I invite you to see your body as a magical gateway of creation, actively welcoming the healthiest sperm toward you, choosing the sperm that will become half of your baby.*

This moment of conception is a symbiotic, cooperative effort between you and your chosen partner, with both of you showing up as active participants in welcoming new life.

Much more empowering, eh?

Now Disney, can you put that kind of storyline into a movie?

Reflect: Conception Beliefs

The beliefs you have about conception reveal so much about your relationship to men, to the masculine, and your role in this reproductive journey. By taking a minute to reflect on the above story and your beliefs, you create an empowering viewpoint in preparation for conception.

Instructions:

1. Set aside at least ten minutes where you can deeply reflect and journal.
2. Open your journal and write down reflections on these questions:
    a. What was I taught about conception growing up? What role did men or the sperm play? What role (if any) did God or the divine play?
    b. Now, as I stand on the precipice of conception, what do I want to believe about conceiving? What empowering or helpful beliefs do I want to adopt? You might consider writing down five or so affirmations such as: "My body was designed to do this," or "I will

> conceive in perfect timing," or "I am a powerful, fertile creatrix."
>
> c. How do I feel getting ready to conceive? Nervous, excited, anxious, fearful? Write it down, letting your pen reveal and alchemize any hidden feelings.
>
> 3. Once complete, close your journal and take a moment to thank yourself for your courage to look within and to boldly choose your beliefs for this chapter.

SENSUALITY

It's funny to write a section specifically on sensuality in the conception chapter, because obviously, babies are made through sex. So, in this phase of your motherhood journey, you're probably having a lot of sex! While this phase is clearly centered on sex, for many couples, sex can also be quite problematic in this phase.

Why?

Primarily because, in this phase, sex can become a mechanical chore to conceive your baby rather than an emotional, beautiful, and spiritual experience. It can become a point of tension and tightness in the relationship, rather than a relaxed and intimate journey.

Sometimes when a couple is trying to conceive, the sex takes on a mystical, magical quality as they welcome in new life. This is especially true at the beginning of the journey. Other times, especially if their conception journey has gone on a long time, sex becomes a problematic spot for the couple, a "have-to" to get the job done.

I'll tell you about a couple my husband James and I worked with who were struggling with sex and intimacy while trying to conceive.

This couple had been trying to conceive their baby for over two years and were extremely frustrated. They only made love while she was ovulating and described the sex as a frustrated "come inside me and be done with it" kind of affair. Neither of them enjoyed the experience of sex since trying to conceive. It had become heavy, tense, and obligatory.

They came to James and I for couples' coaching because by having purely obligatory sex, they no longer felt their core erotic spark. They were having sex yet had forgotten how to be intimate with each other.

Right away, we noticed the lack of sex unless she was ovulating. So, James and I recommended they delete their menstrual cycle app as a first step. For many couples, tracking ovulation and making love during the fertile window can be a special, bonding experience. But for this couple, it had become just another way to try to control the journey (and get frustrated when they couldn't). So, the app had to go.

(By the way, this is one of the many times I will give advice that counters earlier advice I've given. Why? Every couple is unique, and not every piece of advice is for everyone.)

Next, we helped the couple share and release stuck emotions from the past two years of trying to conceive. There was a lot of built-up hurt and frustration on both sides that needed to be witnessed and healed. I often find that when the spark of aliveness is gone, it's

> *When the spark of aliveness is gone, it's because the partnership has gotten bogged down with resentment, unsaid truths, and hurts. As we cleared these areas, their natural attraction emerged.*

because the partnership has gotten bogged down with resentment, unsaid truths, and hurts. As we cleared these areas, their natural attraction emerged.

Then we gave them practical advice on lovemaking. We encouraged them to make love every few days, all month long, focusing on their pleasure and desires. We asked them: What do you really want? How do you want to be kissed? How do you want to be touched? What kind of tempo and pace?

At first, they didn't really know what they wanted. (Have you ever felt that way?)

We recommended that they slow down the lovemaking and listen to their bodies, for the moment-to-moment impulse. Do they want a kiss now? A different touch? Rather than focusing on a mental plan, (in this case, of conception) we invited them to slow down enough to hear the subtle whispers of their bodies. This is good sex advice in any phase, but it's especially good sex advice when there is a hoped-for outcome – conception.

They become curious about each other's turn-ons—and their own.

Over the six weeks of working together, this couple transformed sex from a point of frustration and tension in their relationship into a place of pleasure and exploration. It was so beautiful! Then, a few months after we finished our work together, they told us that they had conceived their baby, and nine months later, they celebrated a beautiful, healthy baby girl.

Moral of the story: Even though sex in this phase has a purpose (conception), it can't *only* be a means to an end, or it will create disconnection. Instead, focus on creating pleasure, desire, and emotional intimacy through the journey.

Let's start with ways to activate your own sensual energy through movement, and then I'll share a partnered practice you two can do together.

This solo practice is a powerful way to awaken your sensuality and explore your body's wisdom. Best of all, it can be done in under an hour, in the privacy of your own home. Let's dive in.

> **Moral of the story:**
> *Even though sex in this phase has a purpose (conception), it can't only be a means to an end, or it will create disconnection. Instead, focus on creating pleasure, desire, and emotional intimacy through the journey.*

Go Do: Sensual Movement Class

This practice has helped me come home to my body, again and again, as a place of sensual pleasures, and helped me see myself as beautifully erotic, which is such an empowering way to feel while you're trying to conceive. Are you ready to try it?

This practice is inspired by S Factor from Sheila Kelley. I've modified it and made it my own. If you enjoy the practice, though, check out Sheila Kelley's work to go deeper.

Bonus: I've recorded this as a video on my website: www.megandlambert.com/emresources.

Instructions:

1. Create a cozy, dim space where you can move freely—perhaps laying a yoga mat and soft blanket on the floor, locking the door, and closing the curtains.

2. Open your digital device, and follow the video on my website on how to move your body. This will take around forty-five minutes.

3. After you move, take a moment to lay down, close your eyes, and notice how your body feels now. Do you feel 10 percent more soft or sensual? A bit more flowy or fluid? Celebrate yourself and your journey!

Now that you've done a solo practice to awaken your own eroticism, let's look at how to have the mystical, magical sex that some couples experience in this phase. We will start with a ritual.

Go Do: Opening the Gates Ritual

Purpose: The moment when you and your partner are ready to welcome in new life is such a special, profound moment. This is an amazing time to pause and consecrate this moment, to bring the sacred in, and to remind yourselves that something bigger than you is holding this journey (if that belief resonates with you).

Instructions:

Come together with your partner to cocreate a ritual that appeals to both of you. It can be as elaborate or as simple as you'd like.

If you remember from my story, our ritual was simple. Just eye-gazing and saying "yes" to each other at the moment of conception. But your ritual may be different!

Here are a few ideas:

- Say a prayer together or read religious texts you both love.
- Make a little altar in your bedroom for your spirit baby.
- Choose some crystals or pull out some tarot cards to ask the Universe for guidance.
- Write a letter to your spirit baby together, letting them know you're ready to welcome them into your body and into the family.
- Meditate together, envisioning your baby coming into your body.
- Go away for a romantic weekend together where you consciously are open to conception.
- Sing a song together to welcome your baby.

I wonder how you would like to honor and celebrate this important moment in your relationship? Is there any type of ritual to "open the gates" that would feel special and meaningful to you?

However you choose to "open the gates," remember the potent combination of intention *and* surrender. Set the intention lovingly, with your partner, and then give it up to God, the Universe, Spirit, or Source.

You might close the ritual by saying something like "We're ready and trust your timing, little one," or "We release control and open to the magic," or "All in good time." These words will help you remember you can consciously open the gates, but that the exact timing when the soul is ready for conception is beyond anyone's control.

RELATIONSHIP

So, you two have opened the gates to receive new life. Now what?

This is an exciting and tender time that likely comes with many emotions, while you wait to see when conception will occur. Let's look at two possibilities.

When It's Faster Than You Wanted

Perhaps you two conceived faster than you planned and are now coping with a pregnancy neither of you feel entirely ready for.

That was the story of when I was conceived. It took my parents six months to conceive my older brother, so they began "trying" for me when he was just ten months old, assuming they would conceive when he was closer to two years old. Surprise! It happened the first month! I suppose my little soul was ready and eager to come to earth.

My parents were shocked by the pregnancy—and felt some grief at already sharing their attention with baby number two while their firstborn was still so young.

A client of mine had a similar story. They conceived their second baby when their firstborn was only a year old. She shared with me:

> "I feel so guilty that my attention is already with a new baby, while my first baby is still so young and needs me so much. How am I going to juggle two babies so close in age?"

Of course, she was grateful for the baby growing in her belly, but she also was grappling with darker emotions like grief, guilt, and fear, which confused her.

On the other hand, maybe you conceived quickly and were delighted by the ease of the journey. If so, congratulations! Or perhaps you picked up this book having already conceived your baby. Perhaps it was a bit of an accident, or it simply happened quicker than expected.

When conception happens quickly, it can bring a whole host of emotions such as joy, excitement, nervousness, and tenderness. Conversely, if conception isn't happening as quickly as you'd like, that can also be quite challenging.

When It's Slower Than You Want

If you two have been trying for a while and not yet conceived, you may wonder, "Is there a problem? Are we both fertile? Is it my body? Is it your body? Is it the spirit baby? What's happening?"

A client of mine shares:

> "I've done all the right things, and I'm in great health. Why am I not conceiving? This is so frustrating and disheartening. Every month when I bleed, I curl up and cry for a couple of days, grieving the loss. It's hard to keep hoping for a baby when month after month, no baby comes.
>
> Worse, I feel so alone in this. My partner doesn't understand this grief. He just tells me we will try again next month and to stay hopeful. I try, but the grief is immense. I feel like I'm broken in some fundamental way."

Can you relate to aspects of her story?

Perhaps you've done the two-week waiting game (between ovulation and menstruation) for many months or years, hoping for those two little lines to pop up and indicate your pregnancy.

Perhaps you grieve every time you see the red blood of your period arriving, again.

Perhaps each cycle you go through feels like an emotional rollercoaster, waiting and hoping for a baby.

If this is your experience, I'm sending so much love to you through this tender and tumultuous time. This can be such a private heartbreak, something so few people see or truly understand.

If this is your story, I invite you to reach out for support. Do you know any women who can help hold you during this time? Perhaps you know another woman with a similar experience who you could talk to.

Also consider your relationship—What could your partner do to let you know that he is there for you?

While conception is a mystery happening solely in your body, you don't need to hold this burden alone. You deserve support through this journey. There are many physical and emotional resources you can turn to such as a naturopath, a holistic health practitioner, an acupuncturist specializing in fertility, a beloved therapist, a religious counselor, your doctor, and more.

Conceiving is a multifaceted journey that includes your body, mind, spirit, energetics, nutrition, relationship dynamics, and more. If you'd like to go deeper, I invite you to take a moment to slow down, tune in, and ask your womb these questions:

- What is my body and womb asking for right now?
- What type of support might help me in this conception journey? (Emotional, physical, energetic, relational, etc.)

- Do I know someone who can help in this area, or do I know where to find someone who can help?
- What would my future self say about this moment on the journey?

Remember that the answers lie within you. Your body knows both what she needs and what support would be best. You can trust your intuition.

When You Conceive

It's such a special moment when you discover that you conceived. Perhaps your journey was short and sudden, or long and full of emotions, yet either way, here you are! Looking down at those two iconic blue lines, or noticing your bleed has been missing for a while, or feeling the swelling of your breasts and belly.

However you discover the news, it is a blessing. And you may find a spectrum of emotions again for you and your partner. Many women expect their partners to be overjoyed with excitement, but in the case of a lot of the men I've talked to, the moment they hear that their partner is pregnant is complex.

As I mentioned earlier, men and women often respond to conception news differently.

When women talk about conception, it's usually the excitement and anticipation of having a baby. ("Ahh! I can't wait to cuddle those sweet squishy cheeks!")

When I hear men talk about conception, it's usually more, "Wow, we're going to have a child to support for the next eighteen years." It's almost like the men are envisioning from birth all the way through to that child becoming an adult.

So, when men hear the news, they see the long-term plan and realize that their whole life has just changed. Conception often feels heavy to the man. Not that he's not overjoyed and excited, it just might mean he needs a little time to acclimate to this big life change.

You can support him by letting him know it's okay for him to take all the time he needs to wrap his head around this.

Then notice your own emotions. If you're overjoyed, try not to let his lack of external joy dampen your joy. Who else can you celebrate with while he gets his head around this news? A friend or family member? Or perhaps you're feeling anxious about this news. Where can you turn for support at this moment?

However you're feeling, know that you're normal. Your life has just changed dramatically, and with change comes many feelings. I find it especially helpful to talk to other moms during this time. Women will likely understand you and what you're experiencing at this moment far more than your partner probably will.

Celebrate Conception

Finally, consider how you might want to celebrate conception together. Is there a ritual or way you can honor this life milestone?

For example, when James and I found out that we were pregnant with our firstborn, we had a special picnic in our garden that night. I will always remember looking around at the colorful flowers around us, a perfect place to acknowledge the new life inside me, our little rosebud. This moment marked the official start of our journey to becoming parents together.

Your ritual may be simple, like our garden picnic, or it can be more elaborate (a weekend away, a present, etc.).

If you did a ritual to "Open the Gates" to conception, this may be a time to metaphorically close the gates and acknowledge your pregnancy. So, you might again light a candle, say a prayer, or write a letter to your spirit baby to thank them for choosing you.

Thank your bodies for what you two have created, for the magic and the miracle of what your love is bringing to Earth. Your journey is just getting started!

Open: Our Conception Journey

The intense feelings around conception can drive you two apart or pull you closer together. By taking the time to talk through your feelings, you're creating a solid foundation for your future family.

Instructions:

1. If your partner is willing, each of you take ten minutes before your next date to download the PDF with these questions. Take time solo to each journal on the questions and then get ready to share.
2. Plan a special date where you two reflect on your conception journey so far.
3. These are the questions to discuss:
    - How has our conception journey been for you so far? What thoughts or feelings arise for you?
    - How connected to me do you feel on this journey? How connected to our spirit baby do you feel? What could help you feel more connected to me or to our future baby?
    - What's been the most beautiful moment for you so far?
    - What's been the hardest moment?
    - When we conceive, how would you like to celebrate?
    - Do we need any extra support or information in our conception journey?

4. As you share your thoughts on each of these questions, I recommend connecting your bodies physically in some way, such as holding hands or resting against each other. This helps your nervous systems sync up and feel connected as you explore the vulnerable terrain of conception.

5. Listen deeply to your partner without trying to correct or change their response. Just imagine you're seeing this journey through their eyes.

6. Share as vulnerably as you can about your experience so far.

7. Complete this with a kiss or a long hug, remembering that you two are on the same team, gently inviting new life in.

ECOSYSTEM

While conception is a mystery happening solely inside your body, it is also impacted by your broader ecosystem. Your body feels if you have adequate social support and signals that through relaxed hormones like estrogen and oxytocin, versus if you feel alone and unsupported, your body will be flooded with cortisol (stress hormone).

Similarly, the feeling and health of your home impacts your body. Do you feel safe here? Can your body soften and open in a beautiful cozy nest you've created, or does it feel cluttered and uncomfortable? Is the home as natural and toxin-free as possible, or is it full of chemicals that disrupt your hormone production and add stress to the body? Do you have access to nature?

It is all connected. Conceiving a baby happens inside your body, inside your ecosystem. Let's explore layer by layer.

Social Support

Conception can be a very private journey, *or* it can be an invitation into deeper sisterhood. A friend of mine created a text message thread while she was trying to conceive and shared her ovulation dates, updates on their lovemaking, and how she felt in her body. She found it so supportive to be surrounded by love and encouragement from her friends while on her conception journey.

Perhaps that feels far too public to you—that is okay! Is there another way you can rely on your social support in this phase? Are there any friends or family members you'd like to let in on this journey?

While conception is a private mystery inside your body, you may find it helpful to reach out to your social network for support, especially navigating the two-week waiting window and expressing any feelings that arise if your moon cycle comes.

Environment

This is a great time to bask in the fertility throughout all of nature. Maybe you take a walk and look for all the new budding life—flower buds, baby chicks, fresh sprigs of grass—breathe it in as you call on your own new little life that will form inside you.

Perhaps you want to plant a tree or a few seeds, water and watch the seeds grow, and witness the fertility of mother nature as a reflection of the fertility of your own body. This could even be the time you start a garden!

I started an organic garden just a few months before conceiving our firstborn. I suddenly felt a pull toward nature and the Earth in a way I had never experienced. It felt so good to get my hands dirty with damp earth, to watch the literal fruits of my labor come to life, to eat food I'd grown. I have many fond memories of relishing cherry tomatoes off the vine and delighting in our first eggplant "baby."

Three months later, we celebrated our conception with a picnic in this garden, and a year later, I sat in the garden, nursing our baby girl. Another year later, our baby girl waddled around the garden on her chubby unsteady legs, picking her own cherry tomatoes to eat. Such a full-circle moment.

Home

While it may be a bit soon to start decorating and painting the nursery (or not! You do you!), this is a great time to detoxify your home to prepare for a healthy pregnancy. Not to scare you, but our houses are riddled with toxins and hormone-disrupting chemicals that you definitely don't want around a baby or a pregnant woman. Luckily, natural swaps are easy!

For example, instead of a perfumed chemical floor cleaner, you can make your own with baking soda and apple cider vinegar. Instead of the mainstream laundry detergent with single-use dryer sheets, try out an unscented, eco-brand instead. There are hundreds of easy (and often cheaper!) natural swaps you can make to keep your home toxin-free.

My favorite resource on this is *Really Very Crunchy* by comedian Emily Morrow. She shares about "How to eliminate toxins from your life—without adding them to your personality." Great read!

I wonder if any of these ways of creating a supportive ecosystem around your conception appeal to you? What would you add?

CHAPTER 2 SUMMARY

You're officially ready for a new life! This is such an exciting and pivotal moment.

You can prepare your body physically for conception by connecting more deeply with your menstrual cycle and becoming aware of ovulation. Emotionally, you can prepare yourself by connecting deeply with your womb as the home of your future baby.

Conception was historically seen as the "strongest" sperm fighting off all the others to fertilize the passive egg, yet in this chapter, we revealed the patriarchal underpinnings of that story and learned a more empowered and scientific conception story instead.

I shared a way to deepen your lovemaking through awakening your sensuality through movement. I also offered suggestions for a ritual with your partner to consciously open the gates to new life. Lastly, we explored how to be with your conception journey, whether it's faster or slower than you expected.

To close the chapter, we looked at ways you can prepare your ecosystem and home for a healthy, supported pregnancy.

Ways to GROW

In this chapter, I shared the following invitations for you:

- **Go Do: Thanking Your Womb Meditation**—This meditation will help you connect with your womb, a future home for your baby, and acknowledge all it has done for your fertility thus far.
- **Go Do: Sensual Movement Class**—A powerful way to awaken your feminine sensual energy and feel the power in your erotic self as you welcome conception.
- **Go Do: Open the Gates Ritual**—A connecting experience for you and your partner to consciously welcome in new life in a sacred and ritualistic way.
- **Reflect: Conception Beliefs**—Journaling prompts to reveal your existing beliefs about conception to make space for new and empowering beliefs that will support your journey.
- **Open: Our Conception Journey**—An invitation for you and your partner to go deeper together by sharing your experiences of trying to conceive a baby.
- **Widen:** Here are the resources I recommended:
  - *Spirit Babies* by Walter Makichen—the spiritual nature of conception.
  - *Really Very Crunchy* by Emily Morrow—preparing a non-toxic home for a healthy pregnancy.
  - "The Egg and the Sperm" journal article by Emily Martin.
  - "Is the Sperm Race a Fairy Tale?" a podcast episode on *NPR* about conception.

Chapter 3

YOUR BODY AS A HOME FOR TWO (PREGNANCY)

I'm on the rollercoaster now,
Up, down, left, right.
Here we go!

My body takes over,
Swelling like a full moon.
Breasts round, nipples dark.
Puke, sleep, eat, sleep, cry, sleep.

I'm becoming pure animal, all needs.
Whose body is this?

Kick, kick, ouch.
Hey, that's my ribs!
There she is.
My little raspberry-mango-pineapple baby.

My heart flutters and eyes moisten.
It's just so absurdly precious.
Being one body with you.

Will I Regret This?

"What if I regret this?" I asked my coach shortly after I found out I was pregnant.

I continued, "Sometimes it feels like there's a parasite living inside me, this life that is not my own. And it's such a massive responsibility. What if I regret becoming a mom? I'm grateful, of course, I wanted this, and there's no going back now, but still . . . what if I regret it?"

My coach, a seasoned mom to a teenage girl, answered, "Oh, you will regret it at different points. The only question is if you'll tell anyone when you do."

I was shocked. And relieved.

So, is it normal to have mixed feelings like this? To be full of wonder, awe, and excitement—but also fear, dread, and anxiety? Yes, yes, it's normal, as many seasoned mamas told me.

It is not only normal but important to talk about with other mamas, to share this duality of being pregnant. If we don't share, these feelings can grow in isolation, hardening into shame of thinking we must be the only mama-to-be who feels this way.

We're culturally conditioned to believe that becoming mothers should be endlessly joyful and fulfilling, that creating life is our crowning achievement. Don't get me wrong, it is! It's beautiful and joyful, a massive achievement to celebrate, and a miraculous journey to delight in.

But it's not only that. It's also a loss of sovereignty. Our body is no longer our own.

It's a jump into the unknown: Will the pregnancy go well? Is the baby okay?

It's truly the end of one chapter (our life as a maiden) and the start of another (our life as a mother), a complete death-and-rebirth experience. Let's dive into the messy, beautiful nuances of pregnancy.

BODY

Most pregnancy books focus on the practical side of this phase (what to eat, what supplements to take, how to protect your growing bump, etc.) and while that is important, what about focusing on the spiritual miracle that you are, especially as you grow a new life?

You are a Goddess

Think about it. Every human on Earth has been gestated and nurtured inside of a woman's body. Our species would quite literally cease to exist without the incredible contribution of women's pregnancies. You are a miracle incarnate as the magic of creation unfolds inside your womb day by day.

There was this funny Instagram meme going around recently where a husband asks his pregnant wife what she did all day. She responds, as she lies on the couch, evidently doing nothing, "Oh, I grew a set of lungs, ten fingernails, and a beating heart. What did you do?"

I love that meme, because I struggled a lot with the sense of "doing nothing" while pregnant. I was exhausted and incredibly nauseous during the first trimester, so my professional career took a hearty backseat to my bodily needs. Sometimes I felt insecure about not earning as much money, having as many clients, or having many external accomplishments to show for my days.

Can you relate?

At the same time, I reminded myself that I was doing the most important work of my life—creating new life—while seemingly doing "nothing" (a.k.a. resting and eating).

Our culture often exalts external accomplishments and diminishes the incredible internal work of pregnancy. Many of us were conditioned to believe that our worth comes from what we do professionally and how successful we are "in the outside world." We become "girl bosses" and "go getters," chasing external achievements. But becoming a mother is an inside job, quite literally, and the journey asks us to embody a totally new type of energy.

So it's necessary and rebellious to remind yourself often: You are a miracle. Even if your days aren't full of "kicking ass" productivity, know that what is happening, deep inside the dark mystery of your body, is nothing short of awe-inspiring.

How do you keep this miracle top of mind while immersed in the everyday of your life or deep in challenging pregnancy symptoms? Let's explore ways to bring in ritual so you can keep a sense of awe and wonder in the journey.

Remembering the Wonder Through Ritual

You may know that you are a goddess incarnate while pregnant, and yet, in your daily life you might not *feel* like you are. You may feel the swollen feet and nausea a bit more readily than the awe and inspiration side of pregnancy. So, in order to remember the sacred in the mundane, I recommend creating a weekly ritual to mark your pregnancy.

Here is a simple ritual I loved in my first pregnancy: I would put on the same outfit each week, pose in the same place, and James would take a picture of my growing body. This was a sweet way for both of us to stop and really "see" the changes in my body through the lens of the camera, to create a moment of mindfulness and awe at my body's capacity.

After we took the photo, we would lay on the bed, cuddle, and read about this week in pregnancy on an app called Pregnancy+. We'd learn about the size of the baby ("She's a raspberry!") and imagine her in my womb. I will never forget those moments.

After my pregnancy, my husband made a little video of these week-by-week photos, and it felt so beautiful to honor the progression of my pregnancy and the miracle of the journey.

In my second pregnancy, time felt far busier as I was often running after a toddler. I didn't have the mental space to do this weekly photo ritual, but I did one big ritual. James surprised me with a belly casting kit at the end of my pregnancy and invited four of my friends over to help cast my belly. It was such a fun bonding event for us and it made me feel like a work of art.

What kind of pregnancy ritual would you like to create?

You might take a weekly flower-and-salt bath, using that time to meditate with your growing baby. Perhaps you'd like to draw the fruit that's the size of your baby, creating a new drawing for each week. Or maybe you'd like to do a pregnancy photo shoot to celebrate your curves! Maybe you want to do a weekly self-massage with coconut oil and soft music. Or perhaps you'd like to paint your belly, or have someone else paint your belly.

During my first pregnancy, I also took belly dancing and burlesque dancing classes. Each week I loved discovering how to move as my belly got bigger. My classmates celebrated my growing curves too, and as I danced, I felt sexy, feminine, and full.

I wonder how you would like to honor and celebrate your body as you navigate these changes?

Go Do: Create a Pregnancy Ritual

By intentionally creating one or two pregnancy rituals, you can feel the sacred awe, even during the ups and downs of pregnancy. These rituals can help you feel grounded, embodied, and connected to the bigger magic of growing life.

Instructions:

1. Reflect on your pregnancy journey so far. What moments have you felt most connected to your body, and most connected to awe of this journey?
    - Perhaps it was when someone took a photo of you, when you were dancing, reading about the baby's growth, receiving a loving massage from your partner, praying with the baby, decorating your growing bump, or something else.
2. Which of these activities would you like to make into a weekly pregnancy ritual? A photo, a dance class, a massage, something else?
3. Open your calendar and schedule in the time for your weekly pregnancy ritual. Remember that tending to the sacredness of your pregnancy through ritual is as important as any of the physical ways you may be tending to pregnancy (having an ultrasound, eating well, etc.). Our spiritual nourishment is as important as our physical one.

Your body is a miracle. Let these moments of ritual empower and nourish you, which will also help you uphold your sovereignty throughout pregnancy.

Who's Body is This?!

As soon as I was pregnant, it seemed that everyone and their mom had advice for me. I heard:

- "That's bad for the baby."
- "Watch out for spicy foods!"
- "Don't ride bicycles."
- "Are you sure you should be eating that?"
- And more.

I was inundated with this mix of well wishes and unsolicited advice.

Five months into my first pregnancy, rocking my cute little baby bump, James and I went out to eat at a fancy restaurant. I ordered the ahi tuna poke bowl. I had done my research on food safety while pregnant, and learned that generally it is safe for pregnant women to eat raw fish if it is fresh.

The waiter stared at me, glancing down at my belly. "Are you sure you want that?" he asked.

"Yes, I do," I assured him. Moments later, he returned. "We will just cook it for you a bit, as you're pregnant."

Furious, I replied, "No! I want it raw. Thank you."

He gave me a side-eyed look like I was a negligent mother, then left.

When the ahi tuna arrived, it was pretty heavily seared and no longer raw. I felt so frustrated because he treated me like a child who couldn't be trusted.

That moment always stuck with me because it's indicative of a shocking change that occurs when a woman becomes pregnant—people begin to treat her like her body is no longer hers.

Of course, your body is no longer *solely* yours, as it is also the home for this new little soul. And yet, you are solely responsible for this little baby. You get to decide what choices feel right to you, even though many people will not treat you that way.

> *Your body is no longer solely yours, as it is also the home for this new little soul. And yet, you are solely responsible for this little baby. You get to decide what choices feel right to you, even though many people will not treat you that way.*

Culturally, we treat pregnant women either in an infantilized way by over-caretaking her, *or* as a vessel to be controlled. This can be seen in the overturned Roe vs. Wade lawsuit in the USA, where a woman's right to choose abortion was denied. The justices dissenting to this decision wrote, "From the very moment of fertilization, a woman has no rights to speak of. A state can force her to bring a pregnancy to term even at the steepest personal and familial costs."

Yikes.

If you're reading this book, abortion is probably not your current plan (or may not be part of your belief system), and yet, the cultural attitude exists that, once pregnant, people will treat you like your body is no longer yours to make decisions for.

This stems from a patriarchal cultural view where women were traditionally seen as property of their fathers and husbands, with her primary role being breeding. If you're "property," of course people will have opinions about how you handle pregnancy, as the growing fetus is also seen as "theirs."

In Judeo-Christian tradition, mothers historically have been seen as "vessels of new life," placing the focus on the fetus rather than the woman, and reducing the woman's autonomy. In the 1900s, pregnancy care across the world shifted from female-led midwifery to male-led medicine institutions, which reduced pregnant women's autonomy and placed (often male) doctors as the ultimate authority.

You may notice that even strangers feel entitled to comment on, or sometimes even touch, a pregnant woman's body. Have you experienced that? This reflects the societal tendency to view her as a shared, public entity, rather than an individual with personal boundaries. This objectification is even more true for marginalized groups or lower-income women who historically have been exploited for reproduction, undergone forced sterilization, or denied basic healthcare.

Phew, let's take a breath. Can you relate to any of these cultural narratives?

There are deep, intergenerational cultural patterns at play around pregnancy, and if you are trying to have an empowering, sovereign pregnancy experience, there may be a lot to unravel.

While pregnant, many "authorities" will have opinions about what you should and shouldn't do. The authority could be your doctor, your mother-in-law, or even just a random waiter at the restaurant like in my story.

Some examples of how this lack of autonomy could show up:

- You attend a challenging yoga or Pilates class and someone asks, "Are you sure you can still do that while pregnant?"
- On a trip you're taking, someone asks if it's really healthy for a baby to be on a plane.
- While at the dentist, he asks about your birth plan, then gives unsolicited advice about the safety of your plan. "That sounds dangerous. Have you looked at health statistics?"
- When meeting an acquaintance, they reach out and touch your belly (without asking), cooing at the baby before saying hello to you.

- Your mother-in-law cooks a spicy dinner for everyone but makes your dish bland without asking for your preferences. "Spicy isn't good for the baby!" she cries.

Have you experienced any moments like that, or something similar?

If you have, I am sending you so much love. It is painful to be objectified, infantilized, or dismissed like that.

Here is the truth: No one gets to choose what happens to your body except you. You are not a child, and you don't need to be treated like one, even though you are now "with child."

> No one gets to choose what happens to your body except you. You are not a child, and you don't need to be treated like one, even though you are now "with child."

How do you assert your autonomy? Let's equip you with a few ready-made boundaries for when these awkward moments of pregnancy arise:

- When asked "Can you do that with a baby?" ---> *"Yes, I've done my research, and I feel safe doing this."* Then continue what you're doing.
- When you get unsolicited advice about your body, pregnancy, or birth plan, set a clear boundary and then redirect the conversation toward subjects that would connect you two: *"Thanks for your interest, but I feel good with my choices, and I'm not open to talking about them right now. Would you like to talk about X instead?"*
- When a stranger tries to touch you without asking, shift your body away from their reaching hands, and usually people get the hint. You can also say: *"I appreciate that you are excited about the baby, but I'd like you to ask before touching my body. Thank you."*

- When someone (incorrectly) assumes your preferences or needs: *"I appreciate you for thinking of me, but I actually want X instead. Thank you."*

As you read these statements, breathe into your body. How do they make you feel? Do you stand up taller, breathe deeper, hold your head higher?

Or perhaps the idea of saying these things feels scary, confrontational, and uncomfortable. That is okay! Clear, loving, unapologetic boundaries may be a new skill for you (it is for many women). You can ask your higher power to give you courage as you practice this new skill of self-advocacy and clearer boundaries.

Remember, you are your own authority. Do your research (most pregnancy advice is outdated) and take pride in what you learn. Information is power. It will give you the confidence to advocate for yourself and your unborn baby. I love the book *Expecting Better* by Emily Oster, as she reviewed many studies to give the most realistic pregnancy advice I've found yet.

As you navigate the waters of unsolicited advice and objectification, know that you are rebelliously, courageously carving new paths of pregnancy, paths that honor the woman as well as the baby.

Now let's look at who is actually an authority here—your very own body and the innate wisdom that it carries.

Nausea as My Great Embodiment Teacher

I was utterly *shocked* by the nausea of my first pregnancy. Leaning over the toilet, puking for the umpteenth time that day, I felt betrayed by my body in a way I never had before.

I was an embodiment teacher, for goodness' sake! Why did I suddenly feel so out of touch with my body? Why could I not prevent or even understand this nausea? Why did I feel so completely out of control?

Before getting pregnant, I thought I was already listening to my body. I expressed my emotions, I moved and danced intuitively, I synced my business activities with my menstrual cycle, I meditated on bodily sensations, I asked my gut for guidance. I did many of the "maiden" forms of embodiment.

Yet each of my pregnancies showed me—gently, fiercely, wildly—that there are more layers to my body's wisdom. That I can surrender even deeper, listen even more subtly, to my body, and in that listening, I'd find a well of profound guidance.

So, here I am, pregnant for the first time, and all I can eat is kid's breakfast cereal, crackers, and plain pasta. Of course, that would spike my blood sugar, crash it, and start the cycle of feeling nauseous again. It was torturous. No joke, I puked every day during my first pregnancy and spent most of the day feeling like I was in a car driven by a drunk person on a windy road.

While I knew this was common, I was still shocked by how sick I felt. Anything could set it off—the smell of toothpaste, the smell of hot sauce, being too hot, and so on. It was so overwhelming. I asked myself, *How do women do this?! How do women all over the world just deal with this level of nausea and sickness? How have I not heard about this before?*

Now, not every woman gets this nauseous. My own mother, bless her, experienced *zero* nausea in any of her three pregnancies. Lucky woman! Your story may be different, with unique symptoms, and yet, the common thread is: What is my body communicating with these symptoms? What is the message?

Looking back, I realized my body was sending me some important messages through this nausea.

First, and most practically, my body was telling me to eat more protein more often. During my second pregnancy, I had a protein snack (like chicken, eggs, cheese, peanut butter, chickpeas, or yogurt) every two hours (before nausea hit) to help stabilize my blood sugar and keep the nausea at bay. The trick was to eat before I felt hungry, because once my blood sugar dropped enough to feel hungry, I felt too nauseous to eat. I was like a squirrel, tucking away snacks everywhere—in my bedside table, in my bag, at my desk. This helped a lot.

Physically, I saw how my blood sugar caused nausea, yet I knew this wasn't the whole picture. There were emotional and spiritual causes as well.

During my first pregnancy, while I felt so excited, I also had an underlying current of anxiety. This little life was growing inside of me that I had no control over. I couldn't manage it in any way, and this made me feel intensely vulnerable. Looking back, I realized this vulnerability caused me to often clench my stomach and breathe more shallowly. The clenched stomach and shallow breathing invited any food I ate to come up and out through vomiting.

I wonder if you can relate to that emotional aspect of nausea?

There is an interesting cycle between emotional triggers, like anxiety, prompting physical and hormonal changes, like holding my breath, that result in physical symptoms, like nausea and vomiting. Conventional medicine often separates out emotional, physical, and hormonal factors for simplicity, but this view is reductionist at best, or blatantly harmful at worst.

> *Conventional medicine often separates out emotional, physical, and hormonal factors for simplicity, but this view is reductionist at best, or blatantly harmful at worst.*

Pregnancy reminds us we are one interconnected, multifaceted being, and our bodies are beautifully complex systems. To understand a symptom like nausea, we need to look at it from many different angles, to see the dynamics between our emotional, physical, and spiritual selves, as well as the broader ecosystem that holds us.

> *Pregnancy reminds us we are one interconnected, multifaceted being, and our bodies are beautifully complex systems.*

With my second baby, I took a more interconnected approach to nausea. When I noticed I was anxious, I would practice taking deep breaths into my belly, softening and opening my body. I imagined welcoming in nausea and the vulnerability of pregnancy. I prayed to higher power and surrendered to the process, feeling my nervous system relax. I imagined making space for my body to receive this baby with ease and grace. As a result, I kept more food down and threw up far less often and experienced a more enjoyable first trimester.

Third, while I am a bit embarrassed to say this, I also believe that a part of the nausea in my first pregnancy was my body signaling to my partner that I needed help. He was so sweet after I'd puke—bringing me water, holding my hair, telling me how proud of me he was. A part of me loved that support, but I didn't know how to ask for it directly. Nausea invited me to learn how to receive support and attention in a whole new way.

Fourth, I noticed that, when I slowed down and rested, I felt less nauseous. I had a big program launch planned in the first trimester of my first pregnancy, but every time I started working on writing content for it, I wanted to puke. Rather than "push through," I listened to my body, changed the program to a self-paced course, and took the extra time to rest. Immediately, I felt less nauseous and more at ease in my body, and you know what? I deeply enjoyed that break as well.

The last thing that helped me with nausea was having a sense of humor about it. I remember feeling so grossed out by my partner's body, his breath, and even the smell of his toothpaste when he brushed his teeth. It was hard to feel disgusted by the man that I loved—and it wasn't his fault! Luckily, he didn't take it personally.

Being honest and joking about the nausea helped. I would even jokingly say, "Hey, baby, I'm not nauseous right now," with a wink, which meant, "Let's get intimate." The moments when I was not nauseous were few and farbetween, but they were golden moments in our intimacy.

So, all in all, nausea taught me five big lessons:

1. How to nourish my body by eating well and often;
2. How to surrender to uncertainty through deep-belly breaths and prayer;
3. How to ask for help;
4. How to slow down and do less;
5. And how to find humor in uncomfortable situations.

Each of these lessons from my nausea served me immensely in the rest of my pregnancy, birth, and beyond. If you are also nauseous in pregnancy, I wonder what your nausea wants to teach you? What lessons might your body hold for you?

Maybe you're not experiencing much nausea, but you are noticing other symptoms, such as food cravings, back pain, swollen ankles, or heartburn. What do you believe the deeper or hidden message in these symptoms are? What might your body be asking for? Your body speaks to you through pregnancy, guiding you in an ancient and primordial way toward what you need and away from what might harm you. It's the most primal guidance you'll ever receive, if you're willing to slow down and listen deeply to your symptoms.

I've heard that listening to the quiet voice of your body over the loud voice of your mind is like trying to hear a friend whispering in your ear during a rock concert. What she is saying is very important, but the music is blaring, you're dancing up a storm, and it's easy to miss what your friend is saying. The antidote? Find a quiet corner where you and your "friend" (a.k.a. your body) can talk in peace. The following practice will help with that.

Reflect: What's My Body Telling Me?

By taking a quiet moment to reflect on your body, you will access the deeper wisdom in any pregnancy symptoms that arise.

> **Bonus:** I have a beautiful playlist I like to put on during quiet, reflective moments like this. You can find it on my website at www.megandlambert.com/emresources.

Instructions:

1. Create a cocoon for reflection. Perhaps you get your favorite warm beverage or snack, put on a special playlist, and find a comfortable place to sit and journal.
2. Start by closing your eyes and taking three deep breaths. You might like to scan your body, gently inviting any tense areas to relax and soften.
3. Grab your journal and respond to these questions:
    a. What pregnancy symptoms am I noticing right now? (e.g., swollen feet, aching back, headaches.)

> b. What is my reaction to these symptoms? Am I trying to "get rid" of them, control them, or welcome them in?
>
> c. What might my body be communicating through these symptoms? Is there something I need more of? Less of? Is there a message for me?
>
> d. What would it look like to be in greater harmony with my body here? Even if these symptoms don't "go away," what would it look and feel like to come to peace with them? To welcome these symptoms as messengers?
>
> 4. When you finish this practice, close your eyes again and take one more deep breath as you thank your body for all that it is doing.

SENSUALITY

How connected to your body and sensuality are you feeling right now? Do you feel juicy, lush, and full—or do you feel heavy, sore, and cranky? Likely a mix of both at different times!

Sensuality during pregnancy can be extra challenging, but it can also be extra rewarding. Everything becomes amplified during pregnancy, and with the right guidance, this could be one of the sexiest, juiciest times of your life.

Maybe you're reading this, rolling your eyes like, "Yeah, right! How am I supposed to feel sexy when I'm fifty-pounds heavier and get shooting pain down my legs every time I walk?" (That was me during my third trimester in my second pregnancy.)

If you feel like your sexy self could not be farther away, I see you! And I want you to know that your sexiness and desire might be closer than you think. In this section, we will walk together trimester by trimester through powerful ways to get turned-on and to reignite your sensuality.

But first, why is it important to connect with your sensuality while pregnant?

Here are eight reasons . . .

1. **Body enjoyment:** Feeling sensual helps you enjoy your body and this life phase more, relishing in your curves and bodily changes.
2. **Heart connection:** Connecting with your sexuality also helps you connect with your emotions and heart, to understand the deeper layers of what's happening inside you.
3. **Stress relief:** Pleasure is amazing stress relief! Fun fact: You can't make sex hormones and stress hormones at the same time. So, if you're stressed and start experiencing pleasure, it literally shuts off the production of stress hormones.
4. **Relationship strengthening:** Making love makes love. By getting intimate with your partner, you two will feel closer and more connected.
5. **Family unity:** When you and your partner are feeling close, the foundation of your budding family is stronger and more resilient, which benefits your children (born or unborn).
6. **Playfulness**: Sensuality can be a great way to bring play and exploration back into your day through spicy erotic games or exploratory touch. (More ideas below!)

7. **Easeful communication:** If you're making love with a partner, it can help you two communicate better. I've seen time and again how when couples are making love frequently, their everyday communication becomes more loving, kind, and considerate. If they aren't making love, minor irritations are more common and often become big fights. Have you noticed that connection, too?

8. **Health boost:** Pleasure lowers cortisol (the stress hormone) and increases oxytocin (the bonding hormone) and serotonin (the happiness hormone), which help your body repair and stay healthier.

So are you convinced sensuality is important? Great! Now, how do you feel sensual?

First, start by embracing your own erotic self—your desires, your turn-ons, your fantasies, your pleasure. Then, if you'd like to share that juiciness with a partner, I'll share ideas on how to do that as well. Remember that getting turned-on is an inside game. It starts with you!

Bringing All of You Into the Erotic

What comes to mind when I say a "sexy woman"? Is it someone who is happy, horny, and beautiful?

I want to invite you to broaden your perspective on what "sexy" is. Sexy can be your tear-stained cheeks as you cry with grief. Sexy can be your growls of anger as you claw at your partner. Sexy can be your shyness and timid fear of revealing your changing body. All of this can be sexy.

What truly makes a woman sexy is her ability to be in her body and to move with the authentic energy that arises inside of her. Moving with her emotions. Moving with the sensations of her body. Moving with her internal voices, self-doubts, and fears. Letting all of that coexist inside of her, welcoming it, and moving it through in the act of lovemaking.

> *What truly makes a woman sexy is her ability to be in her body and to move with the authentic energy that arises inside of her.*

This is a liberating perspective because it means **all of you are welcome inside the erotic**. You don't need to push away your feelings or thoughts in order to be turned-on. You can bring *all* of it into the erotic experience, and let the arousal of the moment move it through.

You don't need to wait for a perfect moment when you're feeling happy, horny, and beautiful. No. You can show up for your love dates or solo practice as you are, with all your emotions and energies and thoughts, and let them bring unique color and texture into your erotic experiences.

When you bring whatever energy is authentically inside you, plus the heat of arousal, something alchemical and magical happens. The energy or emotions might shift, change form, reveal new insights, or deepen inside you. Your sex is magic, and by bringing all of you in, you become the alchemist of your inner world.

Sounds good? Okay, let's go trimester by trimester on how to awaken your sensuality through your pregnancy. Stay tuned for two of my all-time favorite practices on connecting with your body and pleasure.

First Trimester

Congratulations! You've just begun your pregnancy journey. For many women, the first trimester signals a significant dip in their eroticism and desire to connect intimately with their partners.

Why? Primarily due to these four factors:

1. Nausea
2. Exhaustion
3. Anxiety about the baby
4. Deep emotional processing

Nausea signals disgust, which can be difficult to transition into lust. Disgust, lust, disgust, lust—it sounds like a riddle, doesn't it? Sometimes your erotic self can feel as challenging as a riddle in this phase. Are you really going to squeeze intimacy in between puking sessions? How do you find the erotic pleasure in nausea? What if your partner's body smells really turn you off? Don't worry, love, we will get there.

The first trimester also brings very real exhaustion. Your body is doing immense work in the first trimester, and you likely don't have much extra energy for socializing or overworking, much less putting on that sexy lingerie or planning a self-pleasure session. I remember feeling like such a couch potato in my first trimester, spending hours laying on the couch reading or doing work on my phone. It was like everything in my body was asking to be as horizontal as possible—and not in the sexy way.

Third, some women feel afraid that having sex or having an orgasm may contribute to a miscarriage, which is a fearful myth that has been passed down through the ages. If that's you, I'd like to reassure you that there is absolutely no evidence that sex during a healthy pregnancy increases risk of miscarriage. Miscarriage is often caused by chromosomal abnormality or other issues that are not related to activities like sex. Of course, if you're truly worried, talk to your midwife or doctor for guidance.

Last, you may be going through a deep emotional process while being pregnant. Carrying new life is an incredibly vulnerable and tender time with possibly turbulent emotional waters. If you're navigating deep emotions during this time, reaching for sensuality can be challenging but also incredibly healing. As always, go slowly, go gently, and listen to your body about what you're available for.

Now with all these obstacles, how do you realistically still feel sexy during the first trimester, and if partnered, find an intimate moment with your lover?

Let's dive in. Here are four tips for you:

1. Go slow, remove the goal.

For many women, being pregnant feels incredibly vulnerable, tender, and intimate. For this reason, your sensuality may feel more "slow" or "shy" than before (or maybe you have the opposite experience! The erotic is unpredictable like that.)

If you're feeling tender, I encourage you to go slow during self-pleasure or lovemaking, to allow your body and pussy to bloom in its own time, without pressure or hurry. Taking the "goal" off the table helps a lot in creating a slow, exploratory ambiance.

For example, in a self-pleasure session, can you remove the aim to climax and, instead, simply seek to find pleasure in the moment? In a love date, can you take sex off the table and explore various erotic activities instead? Removing the usual "goal" changes the erotic from a destination-based activity to curious, exploratory play.

2. Communicate what you want.

Your body is changing rapidly right now, so it makes sense that your desires and needs may also be changing. If you have a partner, it's important to communicate freely about these changes and to ask for what you want.

This is a big challenge for many women, pregnant or not, because it requires a) noticing what you want, b) having the courage to ask for it, and c) being present with your partner, even if they get defensive or confused.

How do you skillfully ask for what you want?

Later on I will share a powerful way to do this called "The Adjustment Sandwich." This seemingly simple tool is incredibly skillful at guiding your partner toward touch that is more pleasurable—without making your partner feel criticized or like they are "doing it wrong." Instructions are below.

As a reminder, great intimacy always begins with great communication. You two will never just magically know each other's bodies. It is only through honesty and a willingness to learn each other's desires that your lovemaking will become truly magnificent. Yes, this takes immense courage and vulnerability, and yes, it is 1,000 percent worth it.

3. Find a moment when you're not nauseous.

It's no secret that nausea and lust don't go well together. What's a queasy girl to do if she wants to also stay connected to her pleasure? Find windows of opportunity.

As I mentioned above, my pickup line during this trimester was "Hey, baby, I'm not nauseous" because it was a rare window when I wasn't feeling queasy. When the window arrived, I knew it was a golden moment to connect with my partner, so we would jump on the opportunity. Our intimacy matters to me, and I refused to let it die, so we prioritized connection in those rare nausea-free moments.

For you, I wonder how you can use those precious nausea-free windows to connect with your pleasure, and if you'd like, with your partner? Are you regularly not nauseous at a particular time (e.g., an hour after dinner) and could plan on a scheduled self-pleasure session or love date then? These pockets of pleasure can help you remember that you are an erotic being as well as a pregnant one.

If you're in a relationship, what if the smell of your partner turns you off? First off, know that you are not alone. This is so common! As I shared my experience of this with a pregnant friend, she sighed with relief.

"Thank goodness! I thought it was just me who sometimes felt disgusted by my partner's smell, and I felt so embarrassed."

See, love, you're not alone.

This is an opportunity to be creative about ways to connect with your partner without getting your nose all up in their armpits or mouth. For example, he can sit behind you and stroke your breasts. Or you two can explore lovemaking from behind. Or try spooning sex. If being face-to-face (a.k.a. breath-to-breath) is just a little too much for you at this moment, these are all great options.

Last, know that this, too, shall pass. One day, in the not-too-distant future, you will once again love the smell and taste of your partner, I promise!

4. Practice "Active Surrender."

You're likely quite tired in this phase, so it's a perfect time to try what I call "Active Surrender," which is a (surprisingly) deeply spiritual exercise. Below you will find instructions for this practice.

Pregnancy requires an immense expenditure of energy, so it can feel nourishing to receive pleasure without having to "do" anything for it. With "Active Surrender," it is about being in a truly surrendered state, receiving your partner's touch without having to give anything in return.

For many women, receiving without giving back can be a vulnerable and powerful exercise because it takes away a level of control and external activity, and instead, invites you to deeply feel the sensations in your own body.

You may worry that you're not "doing enough" or "giving enough." That is okay. As you engage in "Active Surrender," just continue to feel and expand your capacity to receive. As you feel into the sensations, express (honestly) through sound, breath, and movement how it feels. Ask for what you want (e.g., slower, faster, lighter, harder), then continue receiving the sensation on deeper and deeper levels.

This is profound because it unravels much of the erotic conditioning we inherit as women that tells us to make it sexy, to put on a performance, or to make sure he "gets his." Instead, we lay like a goddess, embodying our worthiness to receive pleasure.

Your Turn!

Now that you have a roadmap, try these practices in your erotic life:

Open: The Adjustment Sandwich

Great intimacy begins with great communication. This simple communication tool will help you communicate your desires in a way that your partner can truly hear them.

Instructions:

The Adjustment Sandwich has three parts:
1. **Love:** Emphasize what you love about what your partner is doing.
    a. E.g. "I love that you're going down on me" or "Those slow kisses feel so good."

b. This builds connection and highlights what is going well.
2. **Adjust:** Ask for the adjustment you want. Be as specific as you can.
   a. E.g. "Would you go a bit softer?" or "I'd love a little to the right," or "Can we slow down a bit?"
   b. Avoid saying something vague and judgy like, "Can you do it better?" or "Be more present!" or "Ouch, I don't like that," as this often puts partners on the defensive and closes them down to the moment.
   c. Specific direct requests give your partner the information they need to provide more pleasurable touch.
3. **Express:** When your partner responds with the new touch, if it genuinely feels good, express to them through your breath, body, and sounds that they are on the right track.
   a. You might do a long sigh, a moan, or a melting if it feels good.
   b. If the touch does not quite hit the spot, adjust again, and then express how it feels. It's ok to ask for a few adjustments to get the touch just right! Just provide encouragement along the way like "That is closer. Can you go even slower?"

Let me give you an example of putting this all together. Imagine he's going down on you, and his tongue is a bit rough on your clitoris. You might say something like, "Mmm, I love you going down on me. Can you go a bit softer? . . . (Wait for the change) . . . "Ah, yes! Just like that."

Give it a try and notice how small adjustments can enhance your connection.

Open: Active Surrender

This practice is about deepening your capacity to receive pleasure and releasing the need to "do" something, letting your body experience fully.

Instructions:

1. Share this game with your partner first to make sure you both understand the parameters and, together, set a timer for fifteen minutes.

2. Lay on your back on the bed with your arms by your sides. This is the same pose you might do at the end of a yoga class (savasana pose) or during yoga nidra.

3. Invite your partner to touch your body, experimenting with different ways to bring you pleasure. Kissing your breasts, massaging your neck, going down on you, etc.

4. Notice which touch feels good. Communicate with your body which types of touch feel good with a sigh, moan, or "mmm" sound. Conversely, if a type of touch doesn't feel good, then also let that show through your body with a wince or tension. If you want a different type of touch, feel free to ask for it.

5. Your goal through this exercise is to completely receive your partner's touch without trying to figure out what's next or how to make it "sexy." No forced vocalizations or moans, no performance, no "tit-for-tat" oral sex. Just lay back and receive.

6. When the timer goes off, complete the exercise. It does not need to get to sex or orgasm.

7. Afterward, share what you noticed during the exercise.

Second Trimester

Welcome to your golden era! For many women, the second trimester is their favorite part of pregnancy, because the first trimester nausea may have faded a bit, and you likely don't feel as huge and ungainly now as you might in the third trimester.

The second trimester is like spring or summer in a pregnant woman's body. The hibernation of the first trimester may have lifted, bringing a bit more social energy into your body. While the third trimester is a bit more like autumn, with cozy cocooning and leaves (or babies!) dropping. You probably have a cute baby bump, are enjoying the baby's first kicks, and may feel like celebrating a bit more.

When I did my pregnancy and sex research study, almost all women reported feeling more desire, more arousal, and having more sex in the second trimester as compared to the first and third. Many described it as the sexiest time of their pregnancy, which makes this a great time to explore some new sensual exercises!

(Not feeling so sexy? Not to worry, we will do some troubleshooting to support you with this after these exercises).

Here are a few sensual exercises you might enjoy exploring during your second trimester.

Go Do: Breast Massage

Your breasts may feel increasingly sensitive, tender, and possibly erotic at this time. Massaging your changed breasts with love is an amazing way to honor all the shifts happening there as your body prepares to feed your growing baby.

In Tantra, breasts are also believed to awaken feminine energy and open the heart, and so they are seen as a potent portal to female eroticism.

> **Bonus:** I highly recommend doing the audio version of this meditation so you can relax completely. Find it here: www.megandlambert.com/emresources.

Instructions:

You can do this solo or partnered. You'll need:
- Soft music
- Incense or a candle
- Coconut oil
- A towel or sarong
- At least fifteen or twenty minutes uninterrupted

If you're solo, lay comfortably on your bed, perhaps propped up on a few pillows. If you're with your partner, I recommend that they sit up against the wall or headboard, and you sit between their legs, leaning your back against their chest. Share this with them ahead of time, and they will do the touching while you simply receive.

1. Begin by taking five deep breaths, breathing down into your belly. Close your eyes and simply feel. This is your chance to settle into your body and into this moment. Do your best to release any to-do list or other thoughts that may try to pop into your head.

2. Then take the coconut oil and warm it between your hands (or between your partner's hands, if they will be doing the massage). Cup your breasts with both hands, taking a deep breath as you feel the warmth of the hands seeping into your breasts.

3. With your fingertips, trace circles around your breasts, starting at the center of your chest and moving up and outwards. Avoid contact with your nipples for now. (We will get there later!) Make perhaps five to seven circles.

4. Then cup your hands on the outside of each breast and slowly bring your breasts together. Move them as if you are creating cleavage, releasing at the center and repeating, without touching your nipples. Repeat a few more times.

5. Massage around your breasts and chest intuitively, pressing into any tight areas as you breathe deeply. Continue for five to ten minutes.

6. When you feel ready, begin circling your areola with your fingertips, not yet touching your nipple. You want to build desire or longing here before you touch your nipples. (This is true for many erotic areas of the female body. Build desire first, satiate next.)

7. Let the circles get smaller and smaller until you're tracing the outside of your nipples. Finally, touch your nipples and play with them as you desire. You can try touching just the tip, pinching them, or squeezing them lightly.

8. Another touch to explore: Open your hands and fingers wide, covering your breasts, then draw your fingers in toward your nipples. This can be a very arousing touch!

9. Continue exploring for at least ten minutes. Female arousal comes to a boil much slower than male arousal but can stay boiling for much longer. Take your time.

If you feel the desire, you can move to touching your pussy or inviting your partner to touch your pussy and your breasts at the same time.

Let this be an erotic exploration with no goal but to feel deeply. This means resisting the urge to push for an orgasm, sex, or a destination.

If your partner is doing the breast massage, I invite you to simply receive this touch, without thinking about "paying them back" in some way. Often as a woman, you may struggle to receive sensual touch without feeling like you owe your partner something. It may feel "selfish" to the part of you that is conditioned to always be giving (as many women are taught to be).

That is okay! Be selfish for a moment. I promise it feels better to your partner, too, if you're deeply in your pleasure rather than in your head about when it might be "his turn."

When you feel complete, cup your hands around your breasts and take five deep breaths together. Thank your beautiful body for all it is doing.

Sexy Troubleshooting

Not feeling so sexy this trimester? You're not alone, love. It's normal during such an intense journey like pregnancy for your libido to have ebbs and flows.

I invite you to not judge yourself or your experience, and instead, bring deep compassion to yourself. Self-judgment is one of the biggest buzzkills of all time.

I wonder if you can relate to any of these three (very common!) experiences?

1. I feel HUGE and am struggling with body image issues.

I hear you, love! You are not alone.

We live in a culture that (still!) teaches women that their worth comes from their weight and that their sexiness depends on a slender, youthful physique. Our culture prizes the body of the maiden, while condemning the body of the mother and crone (the two other archetypical phases of a woman's life). Unrealistic beauty standards abound (WTF is a "basketball pregnancy?!" Um, no thanks).

In reality, all this conditioning? It's total bullshit. This view of women's bodies is not real, it's a cultural trope, an indoctrination. We can shed that view like an ugly, itchy sweater—take it off, sister.

Can you imagine if we lived in a culture where a pregnant woman was seen as the Goddess embodied? In fact, in so many ancient cultures, we find many images in art and temples of a birthing woman being applauded as sacred and divine. So why is it that, today, this image of pregnancy and birth scares us as a culture, and we try to hide it as much as possible?

I remember I was at the beach, hugely pregnant with my second baby, feeling like a total whale in my bikini, when a French man told me (in a very thick, sexy accent), "I love pregnant women! All those curves, it is a woman in full bloom!"

I'll never forget that statement because it's also true. Yes, I felt like a whale. But also? I could see that I was curvy in a way I've never been before, with my swelling breasts, rounded hips, and full-moon belly. That viewpoint—of being a woman in full bloom, lush in her radiant femininity—is certainly more empowering than telling myself I look like a whale.

I wonder if this helps you too? To let go of any negative images and create a new narrative about your blooming body?

If not, consider the miracle that your body is creating. Your body is growing new life! What an amazing feat. Resting in awe around what your body is capable of can alleviate some anxiety of what your body *looks* like. It moves the focus from how you look to all that your body is capable of.

Notice all the changes happening in your body—the darkening nipples, the bigger hips, the growing breasts, the growing bump—and speak kind words to yourself. Your baby is listening to each word you speak to yourself, and by gently celebrating yourself, you're teaching your baby to do the same.

Last, if you're in a relationship, I *highly* recommend asking your partner to compliment your body, perhaps every day. (And if that feels like it's too much? Oh well, then let it be too much!) My husband told me I was beautiful most days while pregnant, and honestly? It never got old. Sometimes it truly helps when others remind us how beautiful we are.

Finally, if you still feel unsexy and huge, full of self doubt - can you let that be okay? Can you sit with those harsh voices and tender feelings without them needing to go away? Can you breathe with those feelings? Sometimes those voices just need space and acceptance (like we all do!)

2. What if my partner isn't attracted to my pregnant body?

Occasionally, a woman's partner is not attracted to her changing body. If that is your situation, know that you're not alone. Many women have this experience. It can be heartbreaking to see a lack of desire or arousal in your partner as they look at you.

If this is your situation, I recommend a couple of things:

1. Know that your partner likely has similar cultural indoctrination to you—a.k.a. feminine beauty is slim and young,

rather than full and mature. Remember that this indoctrination was not their choice and does not reflect their deepest self. It's the way we've been brainwashed to see beauty by media and culture.

2. Feel the feels. Rage, grieve, cry it out. The way our partner sees us can heal us or hurt us, and to not be seen as beautiful right now can be painful. Welcome the pain and let it move through you.

3. Realize that you can feel beautiful *even if* your partner can't see you that way. You can choose to celebrate your changes with or without them. If you have supportive friends, maybe you ask them to praise your body as well.

3. I don't feel emotionally close to my partner, so I don't want to be sexual with them.

Aw, love, I get it. It is so painful to be disconnected from your partner. For many women, they need to feel loved to want to get intimate, so if there is emotional disconnection, there is often erotic disconnection too.

So, what can you do?

The pathway ahead includes three basic steps. They are simple but not always easy.

1. **Clear** emotional baggage.
    - Did your feelings get hurt somewhere? Are there any truths you haven't shared yet? Any fears you want to put words to?
    - When we don't feel like connecting intimately, it's often because our heart got hurt. So slow down, tune in, and see if there is anything you need to share or ask for (as vulnerably and blame-free as you can!)

- Nonviolent communication (NVC) can be a helpful tool in clearing resentment and opening the channels of communication.
- A couples' coach or therapist can be useful here in helping you two hear each other.

2. **Play** with and rediscover each other.
   - Once the channels of communication are clean and open, it's a great time to bring in some laughter, fun, or play. What do you two like to do together? Dance, tennis, card games, nature walks? How did you two enjoy each other's company when you felt most connected?
   - Spend nonsexual time together, just enjoying each other's company. Rediscover your friendship with each other first.

3. **Ignite** the spark.
   - Once you feel more connected, you may feel more open to exploring desire together. Ask yourself: What type of touch would be fun? What is my body craving? What would feel pleasurable?
   - Practice each of you asking for a desire and see where it takes you.

These are the basic steps I guide couples through who are looking to reconnect erotically, and I hope it gives you an idea about the next step on your journey. If you need support reconnecting (and what couple doesn't at some point?), I highly recommend working with a coach or therapist.

4. Help! My baby kicks during lovemaking, and it takes us out of the mood.

I distinctly remember during my first pregnancy, there was a moment when James and I were making love with him on top, and we both felt the baby kick. We burst into laughter. It was such a strange feeling to sense a third soul in the room with us! It felt like such a private, intimate moment—and then, bam! Our baby made her presence known.

Has this ever happened to you?

This is so natural! It happens to nearly every pregnant couple I work with. I joke that the baby can feel all those feel-good hormones from the lovemaking, and the happy hormones make him or her want to dance!

When this happens to you, I highly recommend bringing in laughter. Think about how hilariously absurd it is that there is a whole other human hanging out with you two while you're trying to make love. What kind of ridiculous awkwardness is that?!

Humor will help you two feel more connected. In that connection, you may feel less resistant to the natural, awkward kicks of a baby during an intimate moment. After a bit of laughter and levity, you may feel up for continuing to connect sensually. Or not—either is okay.

I hope these four troubleshooting spots help you feel perhaps 10 percent closer to your own sensuality. We aren't looking for you to go from feeling like a couch-ridden whale with a distant relationship to straddling your partner like a preggy porn star, belly bouncing up and down. That's a big jump! But if you can take steps toward your erotic self, even tiny 10 percent steps, that can make a huge difference in how you feel and how connected to yourself and your intimacy you are.

Let's carry on now to the last trimester . . .

Third Trimester

You're here! You're almost ready to meet your baby.

At this point, you may be discovering all kinds of aches and pains you never realized were possible. A sore sacrum, tender lower back, and tight neck—ouch!

In my first pregnancy, my hands and feet swelled up significantly. All my fingers and toes were so pudgy, they felt stiff and hard to walk. I was also *so* sweaty and hot. I could never get to a comfortable temperature. (I was in Bali, so hot and humid was to be expected, but still!) In my second pregnancy, I had those symptoms, plus sciatica with shooting pain down my legs every time I walked.

So, yes, I was in awe of my body and this miracle happening inside me, and still, by the third trimester, I felt so uncomfortable that I wanted to crawl out of my own skin.

Or, conversely, you may feel great! If that's the case, I'm so happy for you. What a joy to experience your body so deliciously.

In either case, how can you continue to nourish your sensuality, even while feeling big and full of baby? What unique challenges or opportunities does this trimester bring?

The third trimester is a great time to adopt a gentle movement practice that helps you deeply tune in and listen to your body, which is excellent birth prep. I did this movement practice every single day toward the end of both pregnancies, and it helped clear the creakiness out and lubricate my body for birth.

Go Do: Intuitive Movement

This gentle practice helps you listen deeply to your body (which is amazing birth prep) and clear out any creakiness or stiffness that may have arisen from carrying all the extra pregnancy weight.

This movement practice is inspired by Michaela Boehm's non-linear movement method, but I've changed a bit of it. If you want to go deeper, check out her work, which is referenced at the end of the chapter.

> **Bonus:** I created a special playlist for this practice that you can access on my website: www.megandlambert.com/emresources.

Instructions:

For this practice, you'll need:

- A speaker
- A playlist with instrumental, tribal music
- A yoga mat or towel
- Clothes you can move freely in
- At least ten or fifteen minutes of uninterrupted time

Begin by preparing your space—lay out your yoga mat, turn on your playlist, and dim your lights. Be sure to let anyone else in the home know not to interrupt you during this time.

Start on your hands and knees (tabletop position) and take a few breaths into your side ribs. This side-rib breathing helps you move into a parasympathetic (rest and digest) state. Begin moving slowly, intuitively, listening to how your body wants to move.

Now here's the clincher—there is no set sequence here. It's a moment-to-moment listening of what would feel good to your body, a chance to deeply tune in and sense where your body wants to lead you.

You might do some cat-cow arches of your spine, a circling of your rib cage, swiveling of your hips . . . you might stretch one arm up, then the other. You might shake your hips or head, rock side to side, or lay on your back. Your body has full permission to take you anywhere she wants to go.

If you have a practice like yoga or dance, resist doing the moves or sequences you know, and instead, listen to your body.

Explore different speeds. How does it feel to move fast? Or slow?

Explore moving in fluid, soft, languid ways . . . and then in jerky, jagged ways. How does each feel?

Explore moving up and down versus side to side. What do you notice?

Explore softening your muscles fully to feel their suppleness or tightening them to feel their strength. Notice how each movement impacts your body and breath. Notice. Feel. Breathe.

Like many practices in this book, this is a deceptively simple yet profoundly deep exercise. Taking time each day to practice listening deeply to your body and sensations is the best birth prep you can do. No book or teacher can tell you how to birth your baby—only your body can, moment-to-moment.

> This practice can help you feel more supple, fluid, and perhaps even sensually alive.
>
> Now let's imagine that you'd like to share this sensuality and make love with your partner in the third trimester. How do you do this with a big belly? Let's talk about it.

Third Trimester Lovemaking

All the erotic teachings from earlier in the pregnancy apply here—asking for what you want, making adjustments, moving slowly, scheduling intimacy, etc. Now in this phase, you also have another unique challenge—namely, your big ol' belly!

You may have noticed tried-and-true favorite positions no longer cut it now that your belly has grown.

This is a great time to try some new lovemaking positions! Here are a few of my favorite positions for third trimester:

- **Bent over** (a.k.a. doggy style): Bent over a table or the bed as your partner enters you from behind. This can be quite deep penetration for your cervix though, so only try once you're fully aroused and move slowly.
- **Spooning sex**: Both laying on the bed, on your sides, as your partner enters you from behind. This is a cozy, lazy position that is great for emotional closeness, with minimal effort on your part.
- **Upright woman on top** (a.k.a. cowgirl--who gives the positions these names?!): Straddling your partner while they lay down. This is an empowering pose that many women also find is best for orgasming, as your partner's pubic bone can rub nicely against your clitoris (try leaning forward to feel this).

- **Legs up**: Laying on your back at the edge of the bed while your partner is standing and holding your legs straight up in the air as they enter you. This works great with a big belly, and it can stimulate your G-spot (or groove tube, as the area is more accurately called) with each thrust. Just be mindful with your movements, as penetration can be quite deep, and some women find it too intense.

Which position do you like? Do you have others you prefer?

You're in a rare and beautiful phase of life right now with your big belly. This can create an invitation for tender exploration between you two—if you're both willing to bring a sense of humor and a willingness to try new things.

RELATIONSHIP

How does being pregnant affect your relationship? In so many ways! Where do I even begin?

Being pregnant is a raw, vulnerable time, and you may notice waves of emotion through your relationship. You may feel the joy of creating life together and excitement for what lies ahead. You may possibly feel resentment if your partner doesn't seem as into the pregnancy as you hope. (Hint: they rarely are!) Or perhaps you feel grief for the days when it was just the two of you. You may also feel anxiety and nervousness ("Is my partner really the right person?") as you two deepen your commitment together through becoming parents.

Pregnancy is a *big* time for your relationship, so be gentle with yourself and with your partner as you navigate these turbulent waters.

One common point of tension I hear again and again from couples is that while pregnant, she is craving closeness and nesting, while her partner is pushing to provide for the family. Let me tell you our story on this . . .

James and I went through this spot several times toward the end of each pregnancy.

I wanted to cuddle, connect, and talk about our feelings with this big change coming. I felt vulnerable moving toward birth, and I was reaching for our relationship to gain a sense of security.

Meanwhile, James was deep in his own version of preparation for the baby. If he wasn't working, he was down a research rabbit hole on the best stroller, or on how to babyproof our house.

It isn't that James wasn't excited about the baby coming; it's just that he's a man, and the masculine way to prepare tends to be related to practicalities, logistics, and getting the space set up. (This tends to be true for the more masculine-oriented partner, no matter what gender they are.) He felt like it was his role to provide in a tangible way with the baby coming, which meant making sure we had all the supplies we needed, that the space was ready, and that our finances were in order.

Meanwhile, I was craving emotional connection and reassurance that we wouldn't grow apart once we became co-parents. I wanted to feel that cozy sense of being united as we move toward the deep unknown that is birth and early postpartum. My focus was more on emotional preparation, while his was on practical preparation.

Can you relate to this dynamic? It is one of the most common tender spots couples bring up while pregnant.

We moved through this dynamic (and many tough spots later!) by seeking to understand each other's world more deeply. To do that, we asked each other questions like:

- What's really important to you right now? What's on your mind these days?
- What are you afraid of? What are you excited about?
- What do you need right now?
- How do you want to be supported by me? (Make clear, specific requests.)

These questions help you slow down enough to really "see" into the other person's world and experience. (More on that in the exercise at the end of this section.)

Pregnancy is the start of a major divergence in both of your experiences. As you move through pregnancy, birth, and early postpartum, your body is undergoing massive change—hormonally, emotionally, socially—which can be quite a mystery to your partner.

It can be hard for your partner, who is on the outside of the experience, to really understand what this portal is like for you. And the truth is, this birthing portal is not supposed to be the same for both partners. Indeed, each is being initiated in their own unique way.

Pregnant women often want their partners to understand their experience. Of course she does! There is a funny Instagram meme of a man trying to get out of bed with a watermelon strapped to his belly in an attempt to empathize with his pregnant wife. Even with funny exercises like this, though, your partner rarely has a clue what your inner experience is like. They simply can't relate to it as it's not in their body or their reality.

Similarly, you're deep inside the pregnancy experience, and it can be hard to understand what it's like for your partner to watch this massive unfolding, and yet not know exactly their place in the process. They're trying to figure it out, show up for you and the family, and like you, they're new to this experience.

Simply understanding that can help bring compassion. You two are doing the best you can as parents-to-be navigating this new terrain without a map or, often, any guides. You're both undergoing massive transitions but in completely different ways.

One way to bridge the gap a little is to let your partner into your experience, and then to make clear requests of ways they could help you. Let them in by sharing how you feel (emotions and sensations) and specific ways they can help.

For example:

- "My feet are so sore from carrying all this extra belly weight. Would you be up for giving me a foot massage later?"
- "I'm totally overwhelmed with decorating the nursery. Could you help me put together the furniture later while I hang the paintings?"
- "I keep forgetting to snack, and then I get so nauseous! Can you remind me to eat when you see me?"

This is so powerful because it a) reveals your experience to your partner and b) invites them into being a team with you. It gives them a clear way to "win" with you, to support you, and to ease the (literal) load of pregnancy.

Ultimately, this phase invites you to trust more completely.

Trust that your partner wants to help you, even if they seem bumbling and clueless. Trust that your partner is devoted to you and to your budding family, even if they seem distracted and busy. Trust that your partner is undergoing their own inner transformation, even if they appear to be the same person on the surface. Trust that you two are a united team, even when you feel like your realities are miles apart.

Your trust is the key to feeling connected through this transition.

How deeply can you trust your partner? How deeply can you trust your relationship? How fully can you let them in?

Open: See into My World

This process will help you and your partner stay connected, even while your experiences of pregnancy are wildly different. This journey is about "seeing into each other's world," as if you could put on their glasses for a bit and really understand what's happening for them.

This is also a powerful practice to come back to during the chaotic days of early parenthood. It can take as little as twenty minutes and can be done during a baby's nap.

Instructions:

1. Carve out time to connect where you can give each other your full, undivided attention. Perhaps you two go out to dinner together, or maybe you simply cuddle on the couch.

2. Start by connecting your bodies physically and taking a few breaths together. Maybe you hold hands, lean your back against his chest, or hug each other. By doing this, you are syncing your nervous systems and reminding your bodies that you two are on the same team.

3. Once you feel connected, ask each other the following questions, like the ones James and I shared earlier:
   a. What's really important to you right now? What's on your mind these days?
   b. What are you afraid of? What are you excited about?
   c. What do you need right now?
   d. What do you want me to understand about your experience right now?
   e. How do you want to be supported by me? (Clear, specific requests!)
4. As you listen to your partner, imagine being them, with these thoughts, feelings, fears, and desires. What would it be like to be in their shoes, to see through their eyes?
5. At the end of these questions, share a commitment you're willing to make. Perhaps it's offering to support your partner in the specific way they asked, or committing to doing this practice each week, or committing to listening more deeply. What change are you open to making? Share it now.
6. End the practice with a long hug, taking three big breaths together.

ECOSYSTEM

Your body is your baby's home, just as our earth is your home. Nested ecosystems, providing all the nourishment you both need to thrive.

How can we help create the healthiest ecosystem for ourselves and our baby?

It starts with our home, then ripples out into community and nature. Let's explore each of those now.

Home

Are you feeling nest-y yet? If yes, you're not alone! There is often a deep urge in pregnancy to prepare a safe and cozy place for your little bubba to thrive. Whether that's a dedicated nursery or a part of your own bedroom, it can feel so rewarding to create a little nest for your baby.

Preparing a physical space for your baby is an alchemical, magical process. By hanging paintings, building furniture, painting, or whatever else you're doing, you're consciously creating a physical and emotional space in your home for new life. It may seem mundane, but it's actually quite sacred.

Your setup doesn't have to be fancy! Ours certainly was not. We planned to co-sleep with the baby in our bed, so we never made a nursery or separate room for the baby. Instead, we took time to make our bedroom extra comfortable for the postpartum period.

We cleared out the clutter, got new indoor plants to purify the air, made a cushy round chair perfect for breastfeeding, and got a soft throw blanket to keep us cozy. I colored pictures with birth mantras, painted art for the baby, and added flowers to the room. We also set up an herbal tea station, plus arranged all the breastfeeding and diaper changing supplies in a visually appealing way.

Making a beautiful space was one of my favorite pregnancy activities because it felt like such a devotional way to welcome this new soul.

My favorite ways to prepare a space for a baby:

- Deep clean with natural cleaning products (vinegar and baking soda is all you need.)
- Get rid of clutter.
- Draw and hang your own artwork.
- Bring new plants into the space (many can be bought cheaply at a plant nursery.)
- Set up a cozy spot for breastfeeding with wipes, water, and snacks.
- Hang photos of your family or community.

These ways to prepare your home are low-cost or free, yet bring extra love, attention, and coziness into your space. I promise, all the extra love you put into your space will pay off big-time when you are postpartum and spending all day in your room!

Rather than adding more into your space, I recommend putting most of your attention into cleaning and clearing what you already have. Decluttering is a spiritual practice that makes literal space to welcome in new life and creates physical space for your family's expansion.

To do this, take one corner of your home that feels a little "icky" — Maybe a basket of old toiletries you never use, a desk drawer full of junk, an overstuffed closet, etc. Trust where you are guided to begin. Then, clean and clear. As you go, imagine offering this stuff up to your higher power as you consciously make space for your baby. Keep going, tackling one "icky" area at a time.

Once the space feels clear, you can start to add in elements. When it comes to nesting, fancy or extravagant does not equal better. A house becomes a home not from what you buy, but from the love you put into it. You need very little actual equipment for a baby—truly, just a place for the little one to sleep, a blanket, and a couple of outfits is all you need.

Don't buy the media hype that pushes parents-to-be into a frenzied overconsumption! Trust me, you don't need the latest baby crib that swings itself, the glitzy mobile, or the fancy changing table. These things won't add to your enjoyment of the baby the way that a space created with love will. This hype may sell products, but it also hurts the earth and our wallets.

So, my recommendation? Keep it simple, get hand-me-downs where you can, and focus on putting your love into the space rather than buying the fanciest new gadgets.

Your home is nestled on a particular piece of land—the natural world that surrounds you. Let's continue expanding outward to explore the nature around you.

Nature

After my babies were born, I was surprised by my intense desire to be around nature. I wanted to sit under trees, be surrounded by flowers, and walk through meadows. I've always loved nature, but this felt different—my pull toward it felt primal, urgent, ancestral.

It was like in the process of creating life, I felt how deeply connected to life I am. I felt how unnatural it is to be surrounded by four walls, indoors, in climate-controlled spaces with right angles and hard edges all day. My spirit longed to be in the wide outdoors, surrounded by flowers and trees, organic shapes, fresh air, soft textures, and wild beauty. I felt a "coming home" as I found my way to nature.

Have you felt this pull toward nature too?

There is a way that pregnancy invites us back into a relationship with the wild mystery of our body, and in the same way, connecting with wild nature invites us back into appreciation for the great feminine mystery. It's a rewilding, a reclaiming of our true nature, and I believe that process has to happen *in* nature (or as close to it as we can get).

The irony is that, even by using the word "nature," we create an us versus them, a separation from nature, whereas **we are nature**. You, me, our babies, our gardens, our parks, and even our homes are all part of nature. When we feel this connection, it nourishes our soul. It reminds us that we are not alone, that we are held by a vast network of living creatures.

Yet this deep interconnectedness can be simply a heady experience if our bodies don't have access to wild spaces. When surrounded by white walls, stuck in air conditioning or central heating, looking at screens or other man-made items ... our deepest, primal nature can feel far away. While comfortable here, a part of us may feel trapped, domesticated, or like something is missing.

It is! Wild, lush nature is the missing ingredient. Being in a wild space, surrounded by plants and animals, helps us remember our own wildness. As one of my yoga teachers said, "If you want to feel more alive, spend time with things that are alive."

This is true, always, but it feels extra true while you're carrying and nurturing life. Pregnancy, birth, and postpartum are primal, wild experiences—an embodied journey we share with all mammals. So, of course, you may instinctively seek out more wild spaces or living things as you embark on this very animal journey of reproduction.

So consider: How can you nourish your soul with nature during pregnancy and postpartum? Is there a park nearby? A balcony you can make into an herb garden? Walking trails you can drive to? Scope out what's available now and maybe add more greenery to your home.

I planted a garden just before getting pregnant and drew great joy from tending to our "plant babies" while growing our baby in my belly. Each day when I watered the plants, pulled the weeds, and enjoyed the fruits, I felt so nourished. It felt so natural, so right to my soul.

I wonder if you've felt this as well?

In addition to plants and animals around you, let's look at the people you surround yourself with.

Community

Pregnancy is a beautiful time to draw your community closer, to invite them into this journey, and to fortify the network that holds you. You can gather real strength by being supported by others during this journey.

While pregnant, you may notice your social connections beginning to shift. I remember feeling closer to my friends who had children or were pregnant, while struggling a bit to connect with my friends who weren't interested in motherhood—because becoming a mama was such a central aspect of my life at the time. I've heard the same from many clients, that pregnancy brings a natural ebb and flow to friendships, drawing some people closer and creating a bit more space in other friendships.

It's also a moment to notice your desire to socialize vs. enjoy solitude. Where do you feel most recharged and re-energized?

Being pregnant is already such a draw on your vitality, and with so much of your energy going into creating new life, you may find you have less energy to invest in relationships and endeavors that don't feel energizing to you. *That's a good thing*. As harsh as it may sound, pregnancy can be a potent time to reevaluate your relationships and cut any that are repeatedly draining you.

You deserve friendships that are supportive, easeful, and nourishing. You can look for a give-and-take of support, of listening, of caring for each other. If a relationship feels too lopsided (say you're always taking care of the other person or always listening to their drama), it may be time to either a) try to shift the dynamic (e.g., interrupt a dramatic monologue) or b) allow more distance to develop in the relationship. It's okay to let a relationship drift apart if it isn't serving both of you.

While interacting with your community can be beautiful, it can also be draining, particularly for introverted people. If you find this to be the case for you, ask yourself if there are any practical shifts you can make so that being around the community feels more nourishing.

For example, would meeting in a quieter, less stimulating setting feel better than a loud café? Maybe you prefer one-on-one heart-to-hearts over big birthdays? Or maybe you enjoy doing an activity with people (e.g., a yoga class or dance) rather than sitting and talking? Or maybe you can stop by the party for a shorter period of time? Or maybe you can bring some structure to the socializing, such as meeting about a topic you want to talk about?

The moral of the story is, your energy is precious, and if something is draining you, it's time to shift the way you're socializing.

Last, pregnancy marks the beginning of a "high-need" stage of your life. You will need extra love, attention, and nourishment during this time, and that is 100 percent okay! Not only is it okay, your

> *Your energy is precious, and if something is draining you, it's time to shift the way you're socializing.*

receptivity is a gift to your community, as it gives people a chance to pour love into you.

This is an amazing time to practice asking for support. Not sure which brand of diapers to stock? Ask a friend who is an experienced mom. Confused on how to nourish your body while pregnant? Ask a friend who rocks at cooking. Feeling emotional and needing a cuddle? Reach out to your own mom, if possible, or a loving friend. People *want* to help you in this phase. You just need to ask for it. Be specific, be concrete, and lean on other people's expertise or wisdom.

As I write this, one of my closest friends is thirty-five weeks pregnant with her first baby. She admitted that she feels vulnerable, uncertain, and in need of support, so I made an extra effort to create a special birthday breakfast for her. I also surprised her with a cooking party, where we made a bunch of postpartum recipes to freeze, and I'm about to send her Epsom salts with herbs for a sitz bath postpartum. It's been so much fun to pour love into her this way—it feels good to me! The bottom line is, asking for help gives people an opportunity to be generous and love you, which feels amazing.

CHAPTER 3 SUMMARY

You're pregnant! Suddenly your body is a home for two. We explored the beautiful, awe-inspiring nature of this, and how to keep the sacred through ritual. We also looked at the challenges—loss of sovereignty, unsolicited opinions, and pregnancy symptoms.

I invited you to go deeper into any pregnancy symptoms to listen to your body's wisdom here, and trust your instinctive nature.

Your sensuality can be a haven of rejuvenation and restoration for you, as your body undergoes rapid changes. We explored how to keep your sensuality alive, trimester by trimester, with specific practices such as the Breast Massage and Active Surrender.

Men and women prepare for a baby in vastly different ways. In this chapter, we covered some of these differences, and how to "see into" each other's worlds so you two can better understand each other.

Finally, your baby's ecosystem is your body, and your ecosystem is your home, the natural world, and your community. We looked at ways to strengthen this larger ecosystem that holds you, so you can nourish your baby.

Ways to GROW

In this chapter, I shared the following invitations for you:

- **Go Do: Create a Pregnancy Ritual.** Take the time to deliberately design a ritual to honor your pregnancy and stay connected to the wonder of growing a new life.
- **Reflect: What's My Body Telling Me?** An invitation to explore pregnancy symptoms as portals to deeper bodily wisdom and gut messages.
- **Open: The Adjustment Sandwich.** A powerful way to communicate what you want in a way that your partner can hear and "win" with you.
- **Open: Active Surrender.** A deceptively simple practice with profoundly deep insights on your capacity to receive pleasure.

- **Go Do: Breast Massage.** A beautiful way to honor your changing form and awaken your feminine erotic energy. Can be done solo or partnered.
- **Open: See into My World.** A twenty-minute practice with your partner to help you two understand each other's perspective and needs more deeply. You can do this while pregnant or in the chaotic early days of parenthood.
- **Widen.** Here are the books I recommend to enhance your pregnancy:
    - *Nurture: A Modern Guide to Pregnancy, Birth, Early Motherhood—and Trusting Yourself and Your Body* by Erica Chidi is the best pregnancy prep book I found.
    - *Ten Moons: The Inner Journey of Pregnancy* by Jane Hardwicke Collings - great info on the inner, witchy aspects of pregnancy.
    - *Expecting Better: Why the Conventional Pregnancy Wisdom Is Wrong--and What You Really Need to Know* by Emily Oster - Practical, research-driven do's and don'ts of pregnancy.
    - *Wild Woman's Way: Unlock Your Full Potential for Pleasure, Power, and Fulfillment* by Michaela Boehm: The inspiration behind the Intuitive Movement practice I shared in this chapter.
    - *Baby Bomb: A Relationship Survival Guide for New Parents* by Kara Hoppe and Stan Tatkin.

Chapter 4

THE UNDERWORLD JOURNEY (BIRTH)

Shedding, shedding.
Goodbye, control.
Goodbye, mind.
It goes, goes, goes.
Down we go.
The waves are big, terrifying.
I stumble and lose focus, ouch! It fucking hurts.
Wait, drop in.
Breathe.
Slipping below the surface.
Sinking to the bottom of the ocean.
Cool, dark, timeless.
I AM the ocean.

Wave comes.
Yes. YES. YES!
I rise with the wave,
Letting it break me open.
I shatter apart.
A million little pieces.
Nothing left of me, just God.
Then I catch her, crying, crying, crying,
"We have a baby!!"

BODY

How do you feel when you think about birth? Do you feel excited, scared, nervous, overwhelmed? All of those feelings are so normal and natural—birth is *big!*

When I was a little girl, my dad invented a rating system for our adventures like water skiing, snow skiing, and roller coasters. Each time we embarked on a new challenge, he would have me rate the adventure one through four, which means this adventure is:

1. 100 percent fun
2. 100 percent scary
3. Both fun and scary
4. Fun *because* it's scary (or challenging)

I distinctly remember my first black diamond ski run at eight years old. I stood in my pink puffy snowsuit, facing the hill, absolutely terrified (I was at two on the scale! Just scared). My dad gently coaxed me to nudge off and down the hill. Once I started, I felt exhilarated, terrified, and totally alive. I couldn't believe I could do something so challenging, and yet, here I was, rocking it.

At the bottom, he asked me for my number. Definitely a four! Fun *because* it was scary, novel, and incredibly expansive. I was far more capable than I realized!

I share this because *birth* can be a four, too. It can be incredibly "fun"—a.k.a. empowering, transcendental, awe-inspiring—as well as "scary"—a.k.a. intense and challenging.

Birth transforms us. It requires us to face our fears and meet intensity.

Birth is not for sissies, but it is for pussies. (See what I did there?)

There are two camps of people around birth. One camp says, "Birth is so scary that you have to control and medicalize it. You have to manage birth, or it will rip you apart." Most of the mainstream media follows this camp, spreading fear about the unpredictability of birth. Many, many women are terrified of birth because they have never learned how joyful, empowering, and transcendent it can truly be. (This would be a two on my dad's scale!)

The other camp is the alternative one, the orgasmic birth, and hypnobirthing movement that (sometimes) says things like "Just breathe your baby out, and let it be pleasurable," as if it's just one long sigh and out comes the baby. While the intention of this movement is to show the beauty of birth, I believe at times it minimizes the intensity that birth brings. (This would be a one on my dad's scale!)

In my experience? There is a middle spot where you acknowledge birth is mind-blowingly intense, yet it can be the most empowering, transcendental experience of your life. In fact, **the intensity of birth serves a sacred purpose—it initiates you into your deepest feminine power.**

> *Birth will bring you to your edge, and then push you past your edge, until you realize that your edge was just a myth and that you're actually far vaster and far deeper than you ever thought you were.*

Birth will bring you to your edge, and then push you past your edge, until you realize that your edge was just a myth and that you're actually far vaster and far deeper than you ever thought you were. That's the potential of birth. Birth asks . . .

- What happens when we don't run from intensity?
- What happens if we don't try to control or numb the sensations?
- How can we work with our mind to embrace intense sensations and open into them?
- What if we don't try to breathe intensity away, or meditate out of the moment?
- What if we turn and welcome the intensity of birth, only to realize that the intensity is not outside of us—it *is* us?

We realize that *we* are that intense.

Then we realize what a badass we are, how powerful we women truly are. When we surrender and trust our bodies - we are so much more capable and powerful than we ever imagined.

We are witches, portals between heaven and earth, bringing souls down between our legs into this plane of reality. Of course it's intense. How could it be any other way?

> *We are witches, portals between heaven and earth, bringing souls down between our legs into this plane of reality. Of course it's intense. How could it be any other way?*

There is a kindness in the intensity of birth. It's training us to become fierce mama bears who are deep, grounded, and surrendered.

> Mamas who know in our bones how wise our bodies are.
>
> Mamas who can't be pushed around because we know the truth when we feel it.
>
> Mamas who welcome intensity because we know our inner strength.

Birth trains us for motherhood. It leaves us with a bodily imprint of how vast and capable we are.

That is the potential of birth, but it isn't every woman's reality.

The truth is, many of us live in a culture that distrusts women's bodies, that believes birth needs to be "managed," that babies need to be "delivered" by an authority. We grow up watching movies where birth is a scary emergency of panicked people and screaming women. We hear horror stories of births gone wrong, and how (mostly male) doctors swooped in to save the women at the last minute. (Notice any patriarchal undertones there?)

Many women I talk to are straight-up terrified of birth. And no wonder, with that diet of media and messaging! Let's take a look at what we need to unlearn in order to have an empowering birth.

My Unlearning

Growing up, I knew I wanted children, but I was so afraid of getting pregnant because birth sounded terrifying. Once I conceived, I'd have to get the baby out somehow - eek!

Why was I so afraid of doing what my body was born to do: create life?

Because of the cultural context I lived in.

For example, I did not hear empowering birth stories. I didn't see women exclaim joyfully about the power of their bodies. I didn't see a system that trusts women's innate wisdom.

Instead, I saw a medical system that saw birth as an emergency to manage, that the best I could hope for was a "healthy mama, healthy baby," no matter how traumatizing the birth journey was.

I saw movies where women are screaming through labor and everyone is panicking. I read books where women die in childbirth. Yikes! Of course I was scared.

When I moved to Bali, I learned about natural birth. I became friends with two women who'd both had smooth, empowering home births. I soaked up their stories like a thirsty woman at the well of feminine wisdom. I sat in on a few Mama's Blessing Way (a ritual to honor mama before birth), and listened to their visions for birth. I began to see that birth could be different than I heard while I was growing up.

Following my curiosity, I also stumbled across a few Instagram accounts (@Petajean was first) that shared about their home births. I was in awe! Having a home birth still felt risky to me as it was so different from the birthing environment I grew up with in the US, where 98 percent of women give birth in the hospital. The hospital felt safe and familiar, comforted by the beeps and dings of authorities who could help me.

Yet, the more beautiful birth stories I heard, the more something deep within me woke up. I imagined that maybe I, too, could have an empowering birth.

I was in the process of unraveling deeply held, mostly unconscious beliefs about birth. Hearing women's stories and talking to natural birth experts helped me unlearn what the dominant culture had taught me and become open to a new view of birth.

When James and I were talking about conceiving, we met with a midwife to gather information. I grilled her, sharing all my fears and asking what she would do in each worst-case scenario. She patiently outlined the facts for me—birth often goes smoothly when a woman feels safe. I saw how deeply the emotional state of the mother impacts the physical process of birth.

Once pregnant, I went down a rabbit hole of reading birth books and listening to birth stories, filling my mind with new, empowering information while letting go of limiting beliefs. I imagined I was preparing for the most important marathon of my life: birth.

Here is the truth: an empowering birth rarely happens by accident. If you desire a birth that is empowering and transcendental, this requires examining and unraveling conditioned beliefs that stand in the way of that vision. If you're like many of us, there will be a lot of beliefs to examine.

Mining Your Beliefs

We come into pregnancy and birth with a ready set of beliefs and ideas, many of which we never consciously chose. Instead, these stories are from a steady diet of media, parental influence, stories we've heard, and images we've seen. You may be aware of these cultural narratives, or they may rest in your unconscious, emerging only as vague feelings around birth.

Have you heard the story of the fishes swimming in the water? Here's how it goes:

> Two young fishes were swimming along one day when they bumped into an older fish. The older fish goes, "How's the water today, kiddos?" The younger fishes turn to each other, confused, and ask, "Wait, what is water?"

Your cultural conditioning around birth is that water. You're seeped in it from the time you were born, but you may not be able to see it, at least until you take time to look closer.

The following exercise will help you find these unconscious beliefs.

Reflect: Your Birth Beliefs

This process makes unconscious beliefs conscious, and in doing so, allows you to have some influence over what beliefs you keep and bring with you into your own birth experience.

Instructions:

Get out a notebook and a pen, set a timer for twenty minutes, and respond to these questions:

- What images of birth did I see in movies, TV, or media growing up?
- When I imagine birth, what sounds, sights, or textures do I sense? What is the emotional texture of the scene (e.g. peaceful, stressed, scary, uplifting, etc.)?
- What birth stories have I heard? What about these stories stuck with me or impacted me? (These can be particularly scary or beautiful moments.)
- What fears do I have about giving birth?
- What do I believe my birth will look like?

After you complete the journaling, read back through your responses. The first three questions draw on the images and stories that lay dormant in your unconscious mind, while the final two questions draw on your conscious mind.

Note that we aren't yet talking about your dream birth - that will come. First, we need to clear space and get rid of beliefs you no longer need.

Notice what recurring messages or beliefs are woven through your responses. What beliefs are empowering and enlivening? What beliefs are scary and limiting?

Remember that you hold the power to work with beliefs that are scary and limiting. Simply acknowledging these beliefs, as you've just done, is the first step. Now let's look at how to unravel beliefs you're ready to shed.

Before we dive in, know that **this is brave work**. There is a reason this chapter is called the Underworld Journey! When most people encounter their deepest fears, they run in the opposite direction. It's as if the little girl inside of us closes her eyes, sticks her fingers in her ears, and declares "If I don't see you, you don't exist!" to the fear.

Unfortunately, the adult version of you knows that this won't work. The fear still exists. So imagine the adult you hugging the scared little girl inside. She needs your reassurance that you two can face this fear together and be okay. If you feel afraid to do this work, praying to your higher power and asking for courage can be very powerful.

Once you feel ready to face your fears, continue reading.

Unraveling Your Beliefs

Once you discover a limiting or scary belief, what do you do with it? Here are four steps:

1. Gather information.
2. Hear stories.
3. Practice affirmations.
4. Connect with your baby and with Higher Power.

I'll share a real example from my second birth. After having my first baby, there was a baby born in our community that struggled to breathe at first. This baby was transported to the hospital and had further complications. This story scared me deeply as I prepared for my next baby, and a fear repeated in my mind: *What if my baby is born not breathing?*

That thought terrified me, so I knew it was a good one to work with. Rather than ignore the scary thought and hope it goes away-- Hint: It doesn't -- I decided to face the fear head-on.

1. Gather Information

First, I gathered information. I asked my midwife to explain the steps we would take if the baby was not breathing at birth. If needed, I learned that we would (in order) 1) Suction out his nose and mouth, 2) Rub his feet, 3) Connect him to the oxygen tank, 4) Go to the hospital. Knowing the protocol helped me feel more relaxed (I am a Capricorn 7 times over! Ha).

I also learned that many babies don't take their first breath right away, but they're just fine if the umbilical cord is still pulsing. Oxygen travels into the baby through their bloodstream via the cord. Having this information helped me feel more confident.

I also asked questions about the scary story I'd heard from our community. I learned what factors had caused the situation so I could prepare differently (as much as possible! There is always an element that is up to God). Information helped calm my overactive, fearful brain that wanted to prepare for every situation possible.

2. Listen to Stories

Before my first birth, I attended a birth workshop, where I met a heavily pregnant mama of four. She said, "I'm so excited to give birth! I love giving birth. If I could birth all your babies, I would!"

I was shocked. Someone *loves* giving birth? How strange. I had never met someone who loved giving birth.

Up to that point, every woman I'd met emphasized how painful it was, how difficult, so I saw birth at best as a challenge to endure. Yet to imagine it could be pleasurable? Fun? Something I might love? It was a radical idea.

I highly recommend seeking out women who can role model to you a love of birth. There is no birth prep better than feeling surrounded by your soul sisters—other women who have walked this path before you and can show you the way.

During my second pregnancy, one of my favorite activities was to go on a long walk and listen to birth stories from Ina May's book *Spiritual Midwifery*. Hearing all these women's varied stories and experiences opened my eyes to different ways to cope with the sensations, mindsets that would help me, and an embodied knowing that I could do this.

When I went into labor with my second baby, I felt those women's stories echoing through my mind and body. I read somewhere that when you give birth, there are 300,000 women birthing with you at the same time. I felt all those women in the room with me, meeting each sensation together, as a sisterhood—a tribe of feminine power.

A Quick Caveat: Make sure to filter out any stories that are scary or traumatizing. It's important for women to share their birth stories as a way to process the experience, but when you're pregnant, it's 100 percent okay to not be available to listen to any birth story that was scary, disempowering, or traumatizing, because all birth stories you listen to will imprint your unconscious mind and can affect your birth.

3. Practice Affirmations

Lastly, I practiced affirmations. My favorite was "I trust God, I trust my body, I trust our baby." Every time I felt the fearful belief pop up, I said this to myself (including during the birth, as you will read later in the birth story).

Here's the crazy part—my fear actually happened. My second baby didn't breathe right away, but because of the prep I'd done to gather information, listen to stories, and practice trust, I felt calm and grounded while we waited for his first breath. I knew we could handle this, and within a few minutes, he was breathing just fine.

That's the power of working directly with your scary beliefs. It helps you move from fear and uncertainty to a grounded knowing and trust.

4. Connect with Your Baby and Higher Power

When I felt fear, I would touch my belly and sense into my baby. I'd remember that we are doing this together and that neither of us are alone. Singing and talking to my baby often comforted me when I felt afraid.

I also prayed to my higher power frequently. When I felt a wave of fear, I'd write down my fear on a slip of paper and put it into a special wooden box I call the God Box. As I placed the fear inside the box, I imagined that I was handing over my fears to Higher Power and trusting Her to hold them.

These dual connections - to Higher Power and to my baby - helped ground and anchor me, reminding me that I am not alone, that I am held in a network of support and love.

Reflect: Unraveling Your Beliefs

The following exercise will help you unravel scary beliefs so they have less hold over you and you have more conscious control over what you believe. Remember to hold the little girl inside you and pray for courage if you feel afraid.

Instructions:

1. Look at your journaling from before, and choose one scary or limiting belief that feels most potent to work with. If you're having trouble finding one, below is a chart with some common beliefs that you can choose from. Circle the one that feels most potent.

Common Limiting Beliefs
Birth is dangerous.
Someone needs to manage my birth; I can't do this.
Birth will rip me apart or damage my body forever.
I won't be able to handle the pain.
My baby will be hurt during birth.

   Breathe deeply as you face your fears, and choose one fear to work with for this exercise.

2. Ask yourself, "What information do I need to feel more grounded here? What do I need to know?"

   For example, if you're afraid that birth will damage your body forever, perhaps you'd like to learn about common birth injuries and what the recovery process looks like.

   Or if you're afraid you won't be able to handle the pain, maybe you'd like to explore pain-management techniques and what your options are during labor.

Or if you are worried that birth is dangerous, you might look up statistics around maternal mortality and the factors that contribute to it.

3. Discover what stories would be most helpful for you here.

   Again, if you're afraid that birth will damage your body forever, maybe you'd like to talk to mamas about how birth impacted their bodies, and what their recovery looked like. Maybe you could listen to podcast stories from mamas who had an amazing recovery.

   If you're afraid of not managing pain, maybe you want to ask your mama friends how they managed their pain during birth and what techniques they used. Perhaps you'd even like to practice a few of these techniques together (Pam England and Rob Horowitz's book *Birthing from Within* has great exercises for this).

4. To challenge your limiting beliefs, try on a new affirmation. Here are a few examples:

Common Limiting Beliefs	Affirmations to Try Instead
Birth is dangerous.	Birth is far less dangerous than driving a car, which many of us do every day. (It's true! Risk of mortality in the US from driving a car is 1 in 93, while birth is 2 in 10,000.)
Someone needs to manage my birth; I can't do this.	I lean on the wisdom of women who have birthed before me, yet ultimately, my body is my teacher. She knows what to do.

Common Limiting Beliefs	Affirmations to Try Instead
Birth will rip me apart or damage my body forever.	My body was perfectly designed to stretch and flex for birth. If any birth injuries happen, I am resilient, and I will heal.
I won't be able to handle the pain.	My body releases natural endorphins to manage pain. All I have to do is breathe and meet each sensation.
My baby will be hurt during birth.	I trust my higher power, and I trust my baby. Babies instinctively know how to be born.

How does it feel to read these statements? Feel free to highlight or make notes on ones that resonate with you.

As you work with your limiting belief, ask yourself, "What would the wisest, most loving part of me say about this fear? What part of me knows everything will be okay?" By consciously calling on your inner "wise woman," you cultivate a deep inner relationship that will serve you well.

5. Connect to your baby and higher power.

What could you do to connect to your baby right now? Singing, talking, meditating with him or her? Simply imaging them inside you and feeling your heart swell with love? These are powerful ways to soothe your fears.

Similarly, how can you release these fears to Higher Power? Would you like to meditate or pray? Make a God Box like I did? Your higher power is ready and willing to hold these fears for you - you just need to ask.

Now that we've talked about how to prepare your mind for birth, let's talk about how to prepare your body for the birth through sensuality and meeting sensation.

SENSUALITY

Your body's primary role during birth is to welcome all the sensations. That's it. Everything else happens automatically as long as you don't resist or brace against the sensations. How do you help your body learn to welcome sensation? You practice it!

Before my second birth, I did a daily ice bath (midwife approved) of three minutes. When I first dipped into the ice bath, I felt like I was dying—I'd shriek or shout or cry. I practiced meeting that intensity, and then consciously calming my nervous system with different techniques like long exhales, deep breaths, making sounds, and relaxing my shoulders and neck. This practice gave my body a template of how to welcome intense sensations while regulating my nervous system.

How can you practice meeting intense sensations?

Another favorite practice is from the book *Birthing from Within*, where the author Pam England recommends holding an ice cube in your hand for a minute. As you hold the ice cube, notice what happens in your brain and body instinctively. In the book, she shares many techniques to try while holding the ice cube to help your body learn to meet intensity—one of the best birth-prep exercises!

Another example: While pregnant with my first baby, I needed a cavity filled. I didn't want any numbing chemicals in case it was harmful to the baby, so I decided to use this to practice meeting sensations.

I remember sitting in the dentist's chair, holding James's hands hard, breathing through it. I felt the urge to push the dentist's hands away from my mouth and to dissociate, close down, or check out, but instead, I reminded myself to breathe and meet the sensation. I thought of my baby and let the love for her give me strength. And I did it without numbing! I was proud of that.

Other ways to practice meeting discomfort during birth could be holding squats against the wall as you breathe deeply (This can be longer or shorter than a minute, depending on your fitness). Or perhaps you stub your toe and use that moment as a chance to breathe deeply and meet sensation. Or maybe you have intense sciatica during pregnancy, and you use that to practice consciously welcoming sensation. Life is wickedly generous—it will give you many moments of discomfort to practice with.

You can also practice meeting sensations in a pleasurable way through sensuality. Sensuality grounds you into your five senses and into this moment, which is great birth prep.

There are many solo sensuality practices you can explore such as:

- Sway your hips to your favorite song.
- Learn belly dancing. (Rumor has it that belly dancing started as birth prep!)
- Massage your belly, hips, and feet with lotion.
- Give yourself a breast massage.
- Self-pleasure and feel the changes in your pussy.

- Cook your favorite food and take time to smell each ingredient.
- Lay in the sunshine. Even better if you can do so naked with the sun on your pussy.
- Take a swim in the ocean, lake, or river, letting the water ease any pregnancy discomfort.

All these practices are powerful ways to take you down from your head and into your body, which will greatly assist you in birthing. Once you access your own pleasure, you may feel more ready for sexuality.

Sex as Birth Prep

I'm going to make a controversial statement: **Sex is the best way to prepare for birth.**

Why? Because what makes for great sex also makes for great birth.

As Ina May says in her *Spiritual Midwifery* book, "What got the baby in is what will get the baby out."

There are five key skills you can practice during your lovemaking that will also serve your birth:

1. Follow your body's impulse.
2. Be aware of your breath.
3. Create limbic connection.
4. Experiment with sound.
5. Dance with pain vs. pleasure.

Let's look at each of these, step by step, and explore how you can practice these birth skills through your sexuality.

Moment-to-Moment Impulse

Think of the best sex of your life. Maybe it was recent, or maybe it was years prior. What made lovemaking so wonderful for you? Was it being fully in your body, and not in your head? Did you put down the to-do list and let yourself be absorbed by sensations and pleasure?

Note: If you haven't had this erotic experience yet, no worries! You can always discover this. My first book, Eros: The Journey Home, is a great resource for you here.

That is the same skill you will use at birth—letting go of the mental busyness and coming back to your body.

In moments of being fully present in your body, you can surrender to the moment—following your body and listening to an impulse for what happens next rather than having a plan.

You're following the natural, moment-to-moment erotic impulse. For example, maybe you two start making out, with your partner on top, and then naturally, you two roll over until you're on top, and later on, maybe you move into seated lovemaking. The dance is fluid, flowing, as you two follow the moment-to-moment impulse. No one is planning "First I'll do X, then Y, then finish with X"—no, it's a spontaneously arising movement. Have you ever experienced that?

This skill of moving fluidly, of listening to your body moment-to-moment, is also what is needed in birth. While giving birth, your body will need different positions, touch, movement, or locations. You'll want to listen for cues from your body like, "Do I want to walk? Or do I want to lay down? Do I want to sway or do I want to be still? What would most serve this birth?" The more you listen to your body and respond to the moment-to-moment impulse, the more fluid and flowing your birth will feel. Your body knows what to do.

You can practice this skill in your lovemaking by noticing any time you two fall into habits or a set plan of what to do next, and instead, get curious about where your bodies naturally want to take you.

> *The more you listen to your body and respond to the moment-to-moment impulse, the more fluid and flowing your birth will feel. Your body knows what to do.*

Breath

"Do you want to have a deeper and fuller encounter with life? Have a deeper and fuller encounter with oxygen." --Karen Maezen Miller, *Momma Zen*

We breathe all day long, but how often are we conscious of our breath? How often do we let ourselves surrender into a full-belly breath?

If you're like many of us, you spend most of your day breathing shallowly, up into your chest, which tenses your body and pulls your attention up into your mind. But this type of breathing keeps us in a state of fight-or-flight, vigilant and on guard. From this place, we are numb to the sensations of our body.

Birth requires safety and relaxation. We need to consciously move our nervous systems from hyperarousal, fight-or-flight, sympathetic activation into a place of softness, surrender, and opening (parasympathetic activation).

Breath is one of the most powerful tools you have in shifting your nervous system from sympathetic activation to parasympathetic relaxation. Breath can transform okay sex into extraordinary sex, or in birth, a painful contraction into an ecstatic moment of opening.

So, how do you use breath? There are a thousand different ways to play with the relationship to your breath, but here is a simple one:

To feel a melting experience and drop more fully into your body, soften your belly and take deep breaths into your belly and pussy. Try this now as you read this book. Consciously soften your chest and belly, and on the inhale, invite the breath down into the lowest parts of your body.

This is a strange but effective visual - imagine you have nostrils on your labia, and you can breathe air in through your pussy. Try it now. Can you feel that?

Then take a long exhale as you let all the tension in your body melt.

It may take a few breaths before your body is ready to soften and open.

Keep going.

Did you notice a difference?

You can try this "melting" breath during lovemaking to practice softening and relaxing every muscle in your body. Practice deep inhales down into your pussy, with long, gentle exhales.

When birth comes, this breath is so helpful in relaxing your nervous system during contractions, allowing your body to melt and surrender into the waves, releasing all tension and holding.

Occasionally, the moment calls for a different breath. If you breathe shorter, more quickly, with sharper inhales, you activate your sympathetic nervous system, which can sometimes ramp up the heat in the erotic experience. You'll notice that naturally, when people get aroused, their breath comes faster, with a more panting quality. You can enhance arousal by taking on this breath pattern if the moment needs more heat and fire.

The same is true for birth, especially in the pushing phase, which is a more fiery phase. Fast exhales or a ha-ha-ha sounding breath can help slow pushing so the baby doesn't emerge too quickly (which can increase the risk of tearing). Ask your midwife or doctor for breathing guidance if you want more information.

Either way, know that your breath is a powerful tool to directly impact your nervous system, muscular tension, and mental state. You can change your entire being simply by changing your breath. While you're pregnant, lovemaking is a great place to explore working with your breath.

Limbic Connection

In sex, two become one, and each person becomes more than they would be on their own. When you feel deeply connected in sex, you "merge" with each other, dancing and moving together in sync. In scientific terms, this state of merging is called "limbic resonance," where you two share deeply connected emotional, physical, hormonal, and nervous system states.

This limbic resonance can serve you deeply in birth. I remember one of the most profound moments in my first birth was eye-gazing with James, breathing together, imagining I was drinking in his strength. In the second birth, we rode every contraction together, breath-to-breath, sound-to-sound, and this gave me immense strength to rise up and meet the sensations.

Sex is a way to practice this soul-level merging so that when birth occurs and you need extra strength, you two know how to merge and access each other's capacities. Does it sound like a magic power? It is!

> *Sex is a way to practice this soul-level merging so that when birth occurs and you need extra strength, you two know how to merge and access each other's capacities. Does it sound like a magic power? It is!*

One of the easiest ways to tap into limbic resonance is by breathing together, matching your inhales and your exhales. Ask your partner to breathe in a deeper, more obvious way (e.g., expand their belly or make a sound on the exhale), and find your rhythm together. You may have to breathe faster or slower to find a middle place of resonance.

Once you two have found your rhythm, continue breathing together throughout the lovemaking or birth to feel a sense of being synced up.

Sounds

Most of us women have been trained to be quiet, little good girls, which is a real blocker in sex and in birth. When we tamp down our sounds, it also closes our vocal cords. Our vocal cords have a direct link to our cervix. This means that when our voice is open, our cervix and pussies open more easily.

You will feel more alive in your body during sex or birth as you unleash your voice and allow your body to make its innate noises. Release the restriction on your throat and notice how much more alive your pussy feels as you permit sound to naturally move through you.

Try it right now.

Take a deep breath in, and on the exhale, make a sound that represents how you feel right now. A sigh, a groan, a giggle, a growl... allow it to emerge.

What did you notice?

Next time you make love, let your partner know ahead of time (or surprise them!) that you will be experimenting with sound during your lovemaking, and then? Let it rip. Moan, groan, chortle, giggle, shriek, grunt, sing . . . Become curious about how your body and your vocal cords want to express.

Does this feel exciting or scary? Both?

After centuries of women's voices being muzzled, asking yourself to let it rip can feel like a tall order. Many of us have been conditioned to be quiet and this conditioning doesn't go away overnight.

Rather, allow this to be an ongoing exploration of 10 percent more sound. Just a little more noise than you might usually do. If you feel comfortable sighing, what about a gentle moan? If you feel at ease moaning, what about a groan? Let yourself experiment with sound in small, gentle ways that can build up to full expression over time.

Experimenting with sound in lovemaking will pay off big-time when birth comes, and you feel more free to let yourself make sounds. As you freely sound, your body will open more easily.

Pain vs. Pleasure

I remember a pivotal moment in my birth where it felt incredibly painful, and my midwife offered this sage advice:

> *"The only difference between pain and pleasure is how your brain interprets sensation. This could be pleasurable."*

In that moment, I made a decision to find the pleasure in the intensity, and guess what? I found it! Pushing out my first baby was a strange, delicious pleasure.

These moments are excellent teachers because they muddle the pleasure-pain divide in our brain. What if there is no "good" sensation or "bad" sensation, and it's all just sensations we can open to, welcome, and let tickle and touch us? Now that is a powerful spiritual practice!

Rumi, a famous poet, once wrote,

> *Out beyond ideas of wrongdoing and rightdoing,*
> *there is a field. I'll meet you there.*
> *When the soul lies down in that grass,*
> *the world is too full to talk about.*
> *Ideas, language, even the phrase "each other"*
> *doesn't make any sense.*

While Rumi was a man, I am sure he was talking about birth!

Just kidding, but I do think Rumi is pointing to a powerful spiritual place, where our thinking mind no longer sorts out "right" from "wrong," "good" from "bad," or "pain" from "pleasure." Instead, our mind lies down on the grass, welcoming the fullness of the moment, of our bodies' sensations. This potent place is lush and ripe for transformation.

We can consciously practice taking ourselves to this place every time we welcome sensation deeply without labeling it "pain" or "pleasure." Lovemaking is a great place to explore this.

> **Trigger Warning:** We're about to explore power dynamics and BDSM. If you find this triggering, feel free to skip this section.

BDSM as birth prep—we're going there.

When my midwife made the comment on pain/pleasure, it felt familiar to me as I had practiced that in BDSM. I had explored pain as part of a pleasurable (consensual) erotic experience.

My body remembered spanks that made me squeal with delight, or being scratched down my back in just the right way, or a fierce hair pulling that made my toes curl.

Have you ever tried "painful" erotic activities like spanking, scratching, dripping hot wax, or pulling your hair in the context of love and pleasure?

If not, would you like to?

I wonder, if you try these activities, could you find the pleasure even in the discomfort? Could you open deeply to the sensation without judging it? BDSM is a powerful way to practice meeting sensation and surrendering open to that spot where pleasure and pain meet.

This is a delicate practice, of course, that requires clear consent beforehand and during, plus after care. Before doing any type of pain play, share your boundaries and desires with your partner. Also, agree on a "safe" word that ends all play, something simple like "red."

Most of all, stay connected to your body throughout the experience, and if you sense a "no," stop the play. If you start to feel uncomfortable but aren't a total "no" yet, you can also say "yellow" as a way to ask your partner to slow down and check in with you.

I love the "Tantric BDSM" chapter in *Urban Tantra* by Barbara Carrellas. In this chapter, she says, "Both BDSM and Tantra produce intense erotic sensations that can create prolonged ecstatic states of arousal and altered states of consciousness."

Meeting intense sensations in an altered state of consciousness is the perfect way to prepare for birth. During labor, your body will remember how you opened to intensity in lovemaking and will respond similarly in birth.

A friend of mine experienced a "failure to progress" in her labor as the dilation of her cervix slowed down. She asked the nurses to give her fifteen minutes of privacy to see if she could hurry things along herself. She then whipped out her vibrator and proceeded to orgasm herself open through each contraction. Guess what?

Her cervix dilated quickly after that, and her baby came out easily. Pretty amazing, right?

For every woman, the journey of bringing pleasure into birth could look differently. While getting sexual during labor didn't feel right to me, I found that making out with my partner between contractions was supportive in keeping the love hormones (a.k.a. oxytocin) flowing.

Other ways to bring sensuality into labor could be kissing, massaging your breasts, receiving oral sex, or using a vibrator. All of these sensual activities help your brain reframe the sensation you're experiencing as pleasure.

In summary, every time you make love, you have an opportunity to prepare your body for birth. The skills of having magnificent sex easily translate into having an empowering birth. Exploring the link between sex and birth is a rich, fertile ground, ripe with potential for mind-blowing, soul-altering experiences—in the bedroom and in the birth room.

Go Do: Lovemaking as Birth Prep

You can explore birth preparation skills in your lovemaking, and in doing so, prepare your body to meet the intensity of labor. This will help you feel more confident and capable moving into your birth.

Instructions:

1. Reread through the five ways that lovemaking helps you prepare for birth:
   - moment-to-moment impulse

- breath
- limbic connection
- sounds
- pain vs. pleasure

2. Reflect on . . .
   - Which one of these five aspects would you most like to explore further in your lovemaking?
   - What would exploring this aspect look like, feel like?
   - How can you communicate this desire with your partner?

3. Share this section with your partner and invite them to explore one of the aspects with you in your lovemaking. This could be one of the themes for your love dates. Afterward, share what you each noticed.

RELATIONSHIP

Your birth is a pivotal moment in your relationship that you will remember for the rest of your lives. How you birthed together may ripple out into your parenting, your partnership, and your trust together.

I don't mean to add any more pressure than necessary, but it is helpful to think through how you want your partner to show up for you, and for this birth, before the main event begins.

For example, when you imagine giving birth, where is your partner? In the waiting room? Around to protect the space? Right next to you through every contraction, breath-to-breath? What would be most supportive for you? What kind of support would help you feel most loved, safe, and held?

There is no "right" way for your partner to support you during birth or labor—only *your* way.

I know some women who found it supportive to have their partner in another room, because their partner got queasy and scared during birth. These women loved knowing their partner was nearby but didn't have to worry about their experience while in labor.

During my first birth, I wanted James to help create the space—order food for the birth team, arrange the birth tub, put on the music, and lock the doors. His attention to the space helped create a place that felt safe and cozy for me, so I could focus more on my own experience than on the outer world.

For the second birth, I wanted him to drop all logistics and be near me, close, moving through every wave together. I hired a birth assistant to set up the birth tub, candles, and towels so that James could let go of the logistics and be fully present with me during every contraction. Different births, different desires.

When you imagine your partner during birth, where are they? What are they doing? How are they talking to you, touching you, interacting with you (if at all)?

Take time to really visualize the support you're craving and desiring.

Here are some examples of ways that partners can help during birth:

- Advocate for the birth plan with healthcare professionals.
- Order or prepare food.

- Ensure you are hydrated.
- Massage your back, feet, hands, and hips.
- Kiss you.
- Touch you in an erotic way.
- Touch you in a non-erotic way.
- Put on the music and playlist.
- Light the candles or beautify the space.
- Send birth updates to the extended family.
- Take care of other children or pets.
- Set up the birth pool.
- Speak encouraging words to you.
- Remind you to breathe deeply.
- Hold you close.

This is just a start! There are a million ways to support the birthing mama. Which items stand out as ways you'd like your partner to support you during birth?

Once you know your desires, be as clear and explicit as possible in your request. This is the moment to ask for 100 percent of what you want, unapologetically (while being open to hearing their yes or no, of course).

Know that while you can plan and ask for desires ahead of time, what you actually want in the moment may change. Perhaps you imagined wanting your partner to massage you during labor, but when the moment arrived, you couldn't stand to be touched. That's okay too!

This is your moment to *lead* the relationship through the birth portal, while listening to your body moment-to-moment.

He Surrenders to Her Power

The birth portal is a moment of true feminine leadership.

Normally, masculine energy leads—guiding and directing the moment—while feminine energy surrenders and receives. *Remember: we all have both energies, regardless of gender, but we may embody one energy more often.*

In birth, the energy is different. The feminine leads, while the masculine witnesses and meets her—but does not guide or direct.

This can be radical for many masculine-oriented partners, especially those born as men. Many men are used to directing, leading, and taking charge—it's what they have been culturally conditioned to do. Birth requires him to step back and move into a supportive role as he witnesses her power in bringing life to earth. He is not passive in birth, but he is also not leading. He is following her feminine leadership.

Ina May Gaskin says in her book *Spiritual Midwifery* (in her classic Southern accent) that "It does a man good to see his lady being brave while she has their baby . . . it inspires him."[3] She explains that this changes the way he sees her—forever. Many men report that they have never seen their wife as powerful and awe-inspiring as when they are birthing their baby.

This moment, as she is deep in her primal power, supported and witnessed by her partner, gives both people an embodied blueprint of the vastness and depth of the feminine. It is a transcendent moment that can change your relationship forever.

During my second labor, there was a moment when I was sounding deeply through a wave, rising up to meet the intense sensation as

---

[3] Ina May Gaskin, *Spiritual Midwifery*, 4th ed. (Summertown, TN: Book Publishing Company, 2002), page 193.

I rolled my hips, and James held me. He breathed with me and watched me, then told me I looked like this powerful earth witch, connected to ancient and primal wisdom. That moment has shaped the way he sees me, forever.

Open: Prepare for Birth Together

Since pregnancy and birth are both mysteries happening solely inside the birthing mama, it can be challenging to know how to create a partnered experience of this journey. Where does your partner lean in? How? What can you two do together during the pregnancy to prepare for birth?

That is what we will cover in this exercise.

Instructions:

There are many different ways you two can prepare for this birth. I recommend reading this list together, then choosing one or two ways that most appeal to you both and creating a plan on when you'll do them.

Here are a few ways to prepare together:

- **Practice meeting discomfort together.** Consciously welcome in intense sensation, together. Maybe you do an ice bath while he sits next to you, breathing with you (my personal favorite), or maybe you both hold ice cubes in your hand while eye-gazing to support each other. Maybe you hold wall squats together, encouraging each other. Or maybe you explore BDSM in your lovemaking. All of these are ways to see and be with each other while experiencing intense sensations, and through these, you'll learn what type of support works best for you.

- **Read birth stories together.** You can create a sweet ritual of listening to a birth story before bed. Then talk about your favorite moments from the stories, sharing what wisdom each story gave you.
- **Create your birth plan together.** How do you two imagine the birth going? Visualize together. Perhaps you two start with the birthing mama sharing her birth vision while the partner listens. Then the partner can add any ideas or insights, as well as figure out important logistics to support her vision (e.g., what to pack in the hospital bag, who will be on childcare for the other kids, etc.)
- **Make birth art together.** Find fun supplies (paints, pens, and crayons), and each draw out your ideal birth scenario. (No peeking!) It can be as abstract, silly, or realistic as you'd like. Then share it with each other and use these art pieces as a conversation starter for birth, and how you both imagine it might go.
- **Hands-on-body love.** This was game-changing for us— my midwife recommended fifteen or twenty minutes of nonsexual healing touch every night in the final trimester of pregnancy. My midwife explained that the mama is doing the hard work all day of carrying the baby, so the partner can offer twenty minutes of time at the end of the day to support this hard work.

  During this time, James massaged my aching back, rubbed my feet, or caressed me with oil, while I practiced relaxing fully with the help of his touch. This created a body imprint of relaxation from his touch, which helped immensely in labor. Just be sure to separate this time from your sexual foreplay so expectations are clear.

Which of these ideas intrigue you? Choose one idea to suggest to your partner. Do you have any other fun ways you'd like to involve your partner in preparing for birth?

Involving your partner in the birth prep can help you feel safe and loved, knowing that you are not facing this challenge alone. You are part of a team, with your partner there to protect you and take care of you.

Now let's look beyond your relationship to the broader ecosystem that holds your birth.

ECOSYSTEM

Remember how I described in chapter 1 what a plant needs to thrive? I talked about how each plant thrives best in a unique context. Some need more sun or less, more water or less, drier climates, hotter climates. There is no one "right place" for all plants to thrive.

The same is true of birth. Where you will most thrive during labor is unique, and it's important. If a plant is not thriving, we don't shame the plant for being broken. We look at the ecosystem that's around the plant and ensure it's best suited for the plant's thriving. Same with birth. If women consistently struggle to birth somewhere, or there are poor outcomes, perhaps it isn't women's fault, but rather, she was not in the most optimal context for her birth experience.

This can be a bit abstract, so let's break this up into three basic questions:

- Where will you give birth?
- Who will you give birth with?
- What other support might you need?

By answering each of these questions, you'll be well-equipped to create an ecosystem of support for your birth to thrive.

This is your baby, your birth, your initiation into motherhood. You are in charge here, and it's worth it to take time to set it up how you want. Birth is absolutely not the time to hand over your power to an authority outside of your own body, to defer to opinions that don't feel good, or to accept conditions that feel less than delicious to your soul.

> *When you are birthing, you deserve to be treated like a goddess at the height of your feminine power—because you are. Choose a setting and support that reflects that.*

When you are birthing, you deserve to be treated like a goddess at the height of your feminine power—because you are. Choose a setting and support that reflects that. This context will help your body produce the optimal hormones for a smooth birth (namely, yes to the feel-good, bonding hormone oxytocin, no to the stress hormone cortisol).

With the right context, you will discover a depth of power and capacity in yourself you never knew you had—and that will leave a lasting body imprint for your mothering.

Let's start with the location of the birth.

Where Will You Birth?

Imagine that you're going to have the best sex of your life. Where would you want this epic lovemaking to be? What type of environment would you want? You'd need to find somewhere safe and sacred, where you could fully let go of control and surrender into the experience.

For this epic lovemaking, you might want dim lighting, perhaps with candles or twinkle lights. Maybe you want music to set the mood. You probably want a clean, clutter-free space as well. You know intuitively that the space around you will have an impact on your ability to let go fully into the erotic experience.

As in sex, as in birth. Many women find creating a beautiful, safe place helpful to giving birth. Low lighting, music, cleanliness, and above all else, a sense of safety and privacy are key. You'll want to choose a place that feels most optimal for your surrender.

So where is that place for you?

Basically, you have three options of where to give birth: In a hospital, in a birthing center, or at home. Let's go in order.

The hospital might help you feel safe because you have immediate access to medical care if an emergency arises. You'll also be monitored continuously with doctors on call, and have access to pharmaceutical pain relief like an epidural. For some women, this may feel like the best, safest birthing place, especially if you have a high-risk pregnancy.

If you're in a hospital, you may still be able to create a cozy environment with candles, low lighting, music, and maybe a birth tub. Ask hospitals about their policies on this.

You could also give birth in a birthing center, which is a medical facility that specializes in childbirth. It's less restrictive and more homelike than a hospital. Birth centers may have cozier spaces for birth, such as a birth tub or bath, a private room, ambient lighting, and one-on-one support from a midwife. Your pharmaceutical options for pain are more limited, however, as most birth centers can't offer an epidural, and if a true emergency arises, you may need to transfer to a hospital.

Finally, you can give birth at home. I never imagined I would give birth at home. If you remember from my story above, I always assumed I'd give birth in a hospital like 98 percent of Americans. When I moved to Bali, I met women who had incredible home birth stories - and I began to believe that I, too, could have that type of experience.

But being the type A Capricorn I am, I first had to do some research.

First, I needed to know:

- What are the statistics around hospital birth versus home birth?
  - I was surprised to discover that home birth has significantly lower rates of maternal mortality, infant mortality, or serious complications[4] for low-risk pregnancies.
- What would I do in an emergency?
  - I found an experienced OB/GYN who would be on call once labor began, and we figured out what hospital I would transfer to in an emergency. I learned what would constitute an emergency, and warning signs for us to look out for.

---

[4] Patricia A. Janssen, Lee Saxell, Lesley A. Page, Michael C. Klein, Robert M. Liston, and Shoo K. Lee, "Outcomes of planned home birth with registered midwife versus planned hospital birth with midwife or physician," *CMAJ* 181, no. 6-7 (September 2009): 377-383, https://doi.org/10.1503/cmaj.081869.

- Who would guide this birth?
    - I found a midwife with twenty years of experience to help. I also did a lot of learning about the phases and stages of birth so I knew what to expect (as much as anyone can!) and could guide myself through most of the birth.
- What will I do for pain?
    - I learned many different pain-management techniques, such as those from *Birthing from Within* by Pam England and Rob Horowitz, and practiced these during pregnancy so I could be prepared to birth without medical pain relief.

In the end, I felt like giving birth at home was the right call for me and my family. I loved birthing at home -- I felt so empowered and safe here. I decorated my home with special art, candles, and music. I got to choose each person in my birth space and decide when they arrived. After the baby was born (in the birth tub), it was a four-foot walk to cozy up in my own bed with my new family. We didn't have to go anywhere or see anyone outside the birth team. Everything felt seamless, cozy, and natural.

If you're reading this and feeling curious about home birth, I invite you to go on a learning journey about it. Who do you know that has birthed at home? What information on homebirth would you need to feel safe?

After birthing both my babies at home, and witnessing many friends and clients give birth at home, I believe that home birth for low-risk pregnancies is most supportive of the physiology of birth. Like other mammals, giving birth in our "nest" is the most natural and easeful option.

That being said, where you give birth is a deeply personal choice. This is a moment for self-reflection and information gathering. Ask yourself, "Which of these three options for location feel best for me? Where will the "plant" of my birth most thrive?"

No matter which location you choose, you can have a beautiful, empowering experience by advocating for your desires during birth.

> Do you want extra privacy during labour? Ask for it!
>
> Do you want the baby to be on your chest during the "golden hour" after birth? Ask for it!
>
> Do you want delayed cord clamping? Ask for it!

All three locations can provide these options, and more, if you're willing to ask for it. Do your research on ideal practices post-birth and make a clear birth plan advocating for these desires.

No matter how you birth—unmedicated, medicated, Cesarean, vaginal, home, hospital, or otherwise—an empowering birth is possible for you. I'm in support of every woman choosing the birth place where she feels most safe, empowered, and relaxed.

Sometimes people may dismiss your birth plan with a well-meaning, "As long as baby and mama are healthy, the birth doesn't matter," but I want to say—your birth *does* matter. Enormously. This moment is one of the greatest challenges you'll ever face, and it has the opportunity to be deeply empowering for you, gentle for your baby, and sacred for your family.

Of course we want a healthy mama and baby. But that's not all—we also want a beautiful, empowering, and gentle experience for all involved.

Who Will Be At Your Birth?

Now that we've looked at the setting of your birth, let's explore who will be there.

When you give birth, your awareness and sensitivity is incredibly heightened. You can feel the energy of every person in the room viscerally, and each person's energy has an impact.

> Your husband's unprocessed birth fear? You'll feel it.
>
> That weird dynamic between you and your mother-in-law watching? You'll feel it.
>
> The random anxious intern that gets to attend your birth? You'll feel it.

With that in mind, less is more. Birth is like sex—it feels best with privacy. Birth is not a spectator sport, and every person in the room needs to be in full support of *you*, the birthing mama.

My midwife told me that in her experience, every extra person in the room adds an hour or so to the length of the birth (e.g., five people = five hours longer birth). Everyone in the room should actively support your birth experience, adding to your sense of comfort, relaxation, and love.

When you imagine giving birth, who do you picture in the room with you? Whose energy feels most relaxing, grounding, and supportive to you?

Both of my births had only my doula, my midwife, my partner, and myself. I found a midwife who supported my goal of deeply listening to my own body, where she would only intervene when I explicitly asked for help. As for my doula, during my first birth she was more hands-on (such as giving massages, aromatherapy, and helping me find positions), while in my second birth, she was practical support only (such as filling the bathtub, playing music, and arranging the lights) so that James could be more hands-on with me.

In both cases the doulas also took a couple of photos, as I opted not to have a separate birth photographer because I didn't want to be observed. Sometimes I feel sad that I don't have more photos or videos of this life-changing moment, but I also trust that I needed the privacy to have the primal birth experience I was craving.

What about you? Who do you want at your birth? Do you want your mom, your sister, a photographer? Is there anyone who it feels like you "should" invite to your birth, but you don't actually want them there? In that case, this is a moment to boldly claim what you want, and to courageously weather anyone's discomfort.

During my first pregnancy, I had many hard conversations with my family members about birth. My mother wanted to attend my birth, but I didn't feel comfortable with her in the room because she didn't have experience with home birth. She had two Cesareans, and one birth with me that had many interventions. In the room of my birth, I only wanted people who fully trusted that my body could do this without any intervention. While my mom and I are quite close, I worried that she may have unconscious fears or beliefs that would impede the birth, so I asked her to wait downstairs while I gave birth.

Similarly, my dad and stepmom wanted to be at the house as soon as the baby arrived to celebrate together, yet I knew I would need a few weeks to heal my body and adjust to motherhood before I could host family staying at my house. So I had difficult conversations with all my parents around what I needed. I cried, they cried. It was quite vulnerable. But I also was strong in my conviction of what this birth required and who was meant to be in that space.

Who do you want at your birth and immediately after? Remember that nobody is entitled to come to your birth, nor to meet the baby right away, no matter how close your relationship is. It's such an honor to witness a woman in labor, and your space is sacred. The only people who should be in the room are those who feel 100 percent supportive to you.

Here are a few roles to consider for your birth:

- **Who will manage the medical aspect of your birth?** Who will check the baby's heartbeat, watch birth progression, check cervical dilation (if you want it), and evaluate the baby's health on arrival?
- **Who will set up the physical space?** Who will put on music, dim the lights, or light a candle? *Remember: you can do this even if you're birthing in a hospital!*
- **Who will be hands-on support for you?** Who will massage your feet, press on your hips, give you aromatherapy, use a TENS machine, etc?
- **Who will be taking photos or documenting the journey, if anyone?** Who will send messages to the waiting family, or capture sweet moments on video?
- **Who will be there just after the baby arrives?** Is there anyone you want immediately there to bring you food, cuddles, or congratulations?

Remember, the same person can hold multiple roles (e.g.: photos + set up birth space), so you don't necessarily need a lot of people to be with you during birth. If you're birthing at a hospital or birth center, also check in with their regulations. Many places have a limit on how many people can attend the birth outside of staff.

If you're birthing at a hospital or birth center, also be sure to ask who else will be in the room to make sure it's only people you know and trust, like your doctor, rather than extra witnesses like medical students or interns (unless you don't mind extra observers).

Birth Opening and Closing Circle

A couple of weeks before each of my births, I held a **birth opening circle** with the birth team—my husband, doula, midwife, and myself. Over cookies and tea, we each shared about our dreams for the birth—how we imagined it might go and the role we would each play.

We also dove into fears we had and addressed each one together. I knew that any unaddressed fears that came into the birth room would impact how the birth went, so I wanted to face these fears head-on.

We closed the opening circle with a blessing for the birth. This circle was so powerful because it synced up the team, helped us create a common vision, and cleared the pathway for a beautiful birth.

Your situation may be different, and it may or may not be possible to do a birth opening circle depending on your team's availability. If they are willing, though, I highly recommend this ritual.

A few weeks post-birth we held a **birth closing circle**, where we reunited over tea and cookies again to share the birth story together. I recorded on my phone as we took turns sharing about what we saw and noticed at each phase of the birth. This helped me piece together the experience and create a cohesive narrative of the birth. It also gave me a chance to process any parts that were difficult or challenging and to harvest the lesson from each.

At the end of the circle, I shared a personal gratitude for each member of the birth team, thanking them for the way they generously supported me through this portal of transformation. It was such a touching, profound moment.

Again, a closing circle may or may not be possible for you, but I do recommend at least sitting down with your partner or a close friend to share your birth story as a way to digest and integrate the experience. More on that in the postpartum chapter.

What Other Support Do You Need?

While the biggest work of birth happens in the room with your birth team, you may also consider involving your wider tribe of support in the birth. It can be so beautiful to include the support of others who are not physically in the birth room, but who can hold you spiritually and energetically while you give birth.

During my second birth, I created a messaging thread called my "Birth Angel Team" with family members and friends who would say prayers and send warm wishes when I went into labor. When my water broke, we sent a message on the thread, and it was so lovely to hear all their excitement about the beginning of the birth. We sent a few more updates throughout birth and let everyone know when the baby arrived. Meanwhile, those on the thread lit candles, said prayers, made offerings, and sent warm wishes to our family.

It felt so good to know that my community was thinking of us and supporting us from afar, that this baby was held not just by me and by those in the room, but by the wider social ecosystem we're a part of.

I wonder how you'd like to call on your tribe and feel supported during your birth portal? What might help you feel the love of the wider web you're woven into?

These three aspects—location, who's attending, who is supporting—come together to create a powerful context for you to have the most beautiful birth possible. Of course, a birth plan is just that: a plan, so hold it softly, knowing that your body or baby may need something else in the moment.

Reflect: My Birth Ecosystem

Take the time to reflect on what type of ecosystem would most serve you and your birth.

Instructions:

1. Take out your journal and reflect on these questions:
    a. Location
        i. Where do I feel safest to give birth?
        ii. Am I curious to explore other options around location? If so, what other information do I need?
    b. People
        i. What roles do I want fulfilled at my birth?
        ii. Who do I want fulfilling those roles?
        iii. Is there anyone I feel like I "should" include but don't want to?
    c. Other support
        i. How might I include my community in the birth process?
        ii. What types of support could I ask for that would feel nourishing to me?

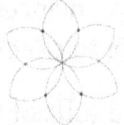

MY STORY

Below, I share my two birth stories. These were empowering experiences for me, and I hope that you find the stories helpful or inspiring. However, if you find these stories triggering or challenging, feel free to skip this section.

Lila's Birth

My first birth began at 2:30 a.m. on October 7th—my official due date! I woke up with contractions that felt more intense than the Braxton Hicks "practice" contractions I was used to from pregnancy.

I was in shock! I wasn't expecting the baby so soon, as I had heard most first pregnancies are "late" (on average, eight days late). In fact, I was so sure that labor wouldn't start yet that I had a big party planned that night with forty of our friends coming over to celebrate the end of pregnancy. Oops! Time to cancel the party.

I slipped out of bed, careful not to wake my husband, and went out on our deck. I watched the sun slowly rise over the horizon, feeling this deep sense of peace and joy as I realized this will be the day we meet our daughter.

When James woke up at 6:30 a.m., I excitedly told him labor was starting, and we breathed through the contractions together, imagining them as waves rising, cresting, and falling (I'll call contractions "waves" from now on as I find this term more helpful).

Our midwife and doula arrived shortly after, around 9:00 a.m. By this time, the waves were strong, requiring my entire attention to breathe through them. I was convinced that I must be almost fully dilated, so I asked my midwife to check my cervix.

Only four-centimeters dilated (out of ten)! I was so frustrated. I'd been giving this birth my all and couldn't believe I wasn't even halfway dilated. (Later, I realized *patience* was one of my big lessons from this birth!)

The midwife suggested we go for a walk in the garden, so off James and I went. It was lovely to be out in the sunshine, seeing the flowers and birds. I became less fixated and more relaxed about the whole experience. I took a dip in the pool, enjoying the feeling of weightlessness.

As I dried off from the pool, the waves got more and more intense. I bent over the counter, breathing deeply through each one. I threw up. I felt a primal urge to be in a dark, private space, so we moved upstairs.

I got on my hands and knees and roared through each wave like a lioness. I was angry! Angry at the intensity, angry it was taking so long, angry that it hurt. I was just spitting mad.

The midwife encouraged me to breathe the intensity down into my pelvis. I took a deep breath, imagining the uprising heat of my anger moving downward, melting my cervix open like fire on wax.

This made me very sleepy, and I lay down, falling asleep between contractions. My doula massaged my feet while James massaged my hips. The whole room got thick, deep, and dreamlike. It felt like time slowed down. We were deep in what midwives call "labor land," the ethereal, mindless space between worlds.

This full-belly breathing and conscious relaxation took immense focus. With every inhale, I said in my mind, "Soften." With every exhale, I said, "Open." For four hours! Then my midwife checked my cervix again (8 centimeters) and gave me the green light to go into the birth pool.

The hot water felt soooo amazing. I got on all fours and held James's hands as we eye-gazed. He looked so strong and so trusting of me that I drew on his strength and found new reserves of power.

It was an incredibly loving moment that brought tears to our eyes. He was in awe at the power and capacity of my body and the immense service I was doing, bringing our family to fruition.

Soon, the contractions changed sensation from a deep, aching opening feeling in my pelvis to a vibrating, pushing energy radiating from my pelvis to my whole body. My body began pushing for me with each wave.

I felt the baby move down into the birth canal and I panicked, fearing I'd be split into two.

I turned to the midwife. "I can't do this!" I cried.

She said, "I couldn't either . . . until I did." That line has stuck with me years after birth—a realization that I can do more than I ever thought possible.

I prayed to God between contractions. Eyes closed, I saw a visual of light coming through a round hole in a cave, and it felt like pulling my baby's spirit down. I talked to my baby, calling her to earth.

I reached inside my pussy to touch the baby's head. Feeling her, right there, gave me energy and courage. After a few good pushes, I felt her head pop out. What a relief! She felt so close to being born, I was ecstatic.

One more push, and her whole body slithered out. James caught her, the midwife unwrapped the cord from around her neck, and handed her to me.

I said over and over, "We have a *baby!*" in disbelief that this little perfectly-formed human creature came from my body. It was the most surreal experience.

She was so calm, not crying at all, just breathing and turning pink. We laid in the birth tub for a bit, then moved to the bed, where she crawled up my chest and latched on to breastfeed (called infant-led breastfeeding—it's amazing).

My mom, who had just arrived in Bali a few hours before, came up to see us. The room felt like a grand party full of love, tears, and cuddles.

The midwives checked me and gave me a couple of stitches. I was grateful there were no major tears. Meanwhile, we waited for my placenta to come, which took another four hours (and quite a bit of anxiety for me!).

We asked the baby if she wanted her cord cut. She started screaming, so we waited until the next morning to cut the umbilical cord when she felt more landed here on earth.

We named the baby Lila, a name we knew was hers even before we became pregnant. James, Lila, and I finally fell asleep peacefully, around midnight, resting joyfully as a new family of three.

Conscious Pause

Before reading the next birth story, pause to reflect for a moment:

- What parts of this story touch you? Scare you? Inspire you? Confuse you? Jot them down, as they can reveal aspects of your own birth belief system.
- How do you feel, having read this story?
- Are you curious about any aspect of the story, or about birth in general?

Birth stories are intense, vivid, and emotional, so it can be helpful to take a conscious pause after hearing or reading one to notice how the story impacted you.

Once you've paused to reflect, you can continue reading the second story below if you'd like.

Latham's Birth

Early Labor

My second birth started on a Thursday at 4:00 p.m. with my water breaking, just like in the movies! I was in awe at the amount of water my belly was carrying - it just kept gushing and gushing, like a waterfall. I felt joyful and calm.

Meanwhile, James was a bit flustered, which I found hilarious, as he is always the calm, cool, and collected one. He immediately called the midwife, anxious. He said that in all the movies, the water breaking is an emergency moment when the couple hails a taxi and heads straight to the hospital.

Our midwife reassured us that it was not an emergency and that the baby could be born tonight or tomorrow, but it could be a few days too.

Last birth I focused too hard too early and burned myself out, so this labor I decided I wouldn't pay much attention to birth until I had to. We had dinner and went on a walk around the neighborhood. The waves were mild. I felt calm, grounded, happy, content, and a bit dreamy, too, like my mind was turning into goo as I drifted toward "labor land."

Around 7:00 p.m., I took Lila downstairs to sleep with Oma (my mom) for the night. I felt relieved knowing she was in good hands so I could focus on the intense work at hand—birthing baby number two.

I knew birth could be a long way off (it was only 7:00 p.m.), so James and I made granola and slow-danced in the kitchen. I felt so in love, and we felt like giddy children, knowing our baby was coming soon. It felt like Christmas morning.

The waves picked up intensity, so we went to prepare the birth space. We lit candles and saged the room, turned on soft music, and pulled the curtains.

We invited our birth team to come spend the night in our guest room in case the baby made a quick delivery. Good thing we did, because the tempo picked up pace fast!

Active Labor

James and I tried laying down to cuddle through the waves, but quickly the waves became too big for me to lay down. My legs felt shaky with so much energy, as if I had quickly drunk ten Red Bulls. My body needed to get up and move that energy.

I walked around the room, swaying and circling my hips to primal drumming music. As each wave approached, I'd lean on James, forehead-to-forehead, and we breathed together as the wave moved through me.

After an hour, the waves were really big and I grew nauseous. I went to the bathroom and puked while leaking amniotic fluid all over the floor. So much for the cute little lacy black birth outfit I had picked out! (Birth is messy!)

My midwife and doula set up the space while I breathed through contractions. During a contraction, the whole team of four paused and breathed with me, like we were one big limbic system, all working together to ground the intensity of this birth.

When a big wave hit, I reminded myself that each wave lasts only four breaths (on average), and I could do this. As a wave approached, I smiled and said "Yes!" out loud.

When the waves ramped up, I felt this primal, guttural feeling unravel inside of me. I told James, "Fuck the good girl," and let out a roar as I pushed my hands into his shoulder. Inside, I felt a war between two parts of me—the "good girl" who wanted to birth "properly" the way I was taught, with long exhales and soft lips, and the wild one who wanted to unleash her wildness and roar the baby through.

The wild lioness won. I pushed hard into James, feeling my strength and my power. I scratched him, roaring through each wave as I pushed against his back and shoulders. Thank goodness he's as strong as he is!

Between waves, I joked with my team, talking about farts and poops and silly stuff. It felt so good to laugh, like being high and unfiltered.

The energy poured and poured through me, a fast-moving wave that couldn't be stopped. I surrendered to it. I moved into the birth tub, sitting in froggy pose, holding on to James tightly.

At this point, I knew I needed God's help. So, before every wave, I'd say, "God's got me. God's got our baby. Yes." Then I would ride the wave with everything I had.

Pushing Phase

Then the waves changed feeling, becoming more vibratory as my body began pushing on its own. I reached inside to feel the baby's soft, fuzzy head, which gave me strength.

I felt like we weren't progressing, so I asked my midwife to check me. My cervix wasn't fully open (I was at about 8.5 centimeters), so she invited me to consciously soften and open, as she used her fingers to help widen the opening. I imagined a wave of softness from my head down to my pussy, and in that instant, my cervix opened fully. She was amazed by how well my body responded to that visualization.

The very next wave kept going and going, as the baby moved quickly all the way out! I thought about trying to slow it down, but my body had other plans. I caught him instinctively, as both James and my midwife were stunned by how fast he came out—all in one single contraction!

He was triple-wrapped by the umbilical cord around his chest and arms. We later joked he was our little Shibari baby. I remembered that it's okay for a baby to be wrapped up like that—the still-pulsating umbilical cord is providing all the oxygen he needs, so we calmly unwrapped him.

He opened his eyes right away, looked up at James standing behind me, and down at me, and I felt this wave of love wash over me. Wow.

He took a few minutes to take his first big breath. Those few minutes waiting to hear him breathe felt like hours. I went into a deep, calm place, trusting that his soul would come to earth soon, as our midwife suctioned out his nose and mouth, listened to his lungs and heart, and rubbed his feet.

James and I talked to him, told him we loved him, and that we couldn't wait to welcome him to Earth and to our family. His heartbeat was good, but his breathing took a minute—I think he was in shock at his fast entrance into the world.

Then he took a big breath, and we all did too. Phew! Soon he was breathing and pink and happy, calmly looking around the room. He didn't cry for hours, just watched us all. He rooted around, making little snuffles like a baby piglet before latching on and breastfeeding.

After Birth

Meanwhile, I was waiting for my placenta to come. With Lila, this took four hours and was a whole journey of its own, so I was a bit anxious. My waves were small, nearly gone. My body felt so *done*. My baby was here, and I was so tired, I didn't want to push anymore.

My midwife was insistent and said, "Give it everything again." So, I did one last BIG push, as big as I had done to birth the baby, letting the wave tear my whole body open (or so it felt), and the placenta was born. A very big, healthy placenta.

Phew! We did it. The midwife checked me out and said I looked amazing down there! No tears, no grazes, and barely even swollen. I was amazed that I could have gone through such fast and intense pushing with no damage. (Except hemorrhoids. Holy hemorrhoids. That's for the postpartum chapter!)

We did it! I felt so empowered, so joyful, and so in love. I lay there, breastfeeding the new baby as the birth team emptied the tub and cleaned up the space.

I couldn't sleep afterward—I felt so high, so amazed, and so in tune with this little bubba that I just wanted to feel him breathing all night and give thanks to God. Wow.

Check-In

How are you feeling after reading these two birth stories? Do you feel inspired, nervous, scared, curious? Know there is no right way to feel, and all your emotions are welcome.

This would be a good time for you to open your journal and write down your reflections on the story.

CHAPTER 4 SUMMARY

1. Birth is a true Underworld Journey that invites you to face your fears head-on and meet intense sensations as you surrender your sense of control.
2. To prepare your mind, we looked at ways to mine your beliefs and unravel scary beliefs.
3. To prepare your body, we talked about how to meet sensations, particularly through lovemaking. Lovemaking helps you practice five key birth skills-- moment-to-moment impulse, breath, limbic connection, sounds, and pain vs. pleasure. These skills translate perfectly to birth.

We also explored your relationship in birth, getting clearer on how you want to be supported, and invited you to own your role as the feminine leader of the birth space.

Lastly, we looked at your ecosystem: where you give birth, with whom, and with what support systems you might want in place. The context of your birth is so important, as it will help you feel relaxed, safe, and supported as you undertake the transformational experience of your life.

Finally, I shared my two birth stories with you in the hopes that they inspire or help you.

Ways to GROW

In this chapter, I shared the following invitations for you:

- **Reflect: Mining Birth Beliefs**--This process helps us make unconscious birth beliefs more conscious, and it gives you the ability to influence what beliefs come with you into birth.
- **Reflect: Unraveling Birth Beliefs**--Three powerful ways to work with your fears or scary beliefs around birth.
- **Go Do: Lovemaking as Birth Prep**—Surprisingly potent ways to prepare for labor through your lovemaking. As they say, what got the baby in will get the baby out!
- **Open: Prepare for Birth Together**—Wonderful ways that you and your partner can connect through preparing for birth together and feel more synced up.
- **Reflect: My Birth Ecosystem**—An invitation to consciously design the setting, team, and support you want for a thriving birth experience.
- **Widen:** Here are the books I recommend to prepare for birth, in order of what I see as most important to least (but still so valuable!):
    - *Spiritual Midwifery* **by Ina May Gaskin:** One of the OGs of birth and full of inspiring, powerful stories. I highly recommend listening to the birth stories on audio.
    - *Birthing from Within* **by Pam England and Rob Horowitz:** Amazing guidance on how to trust your body throughout birth, including my favorite pain-management techniques.
    - *Ina May's Guide to Childbirth* **by Ina May Gaskin**—Another classic. This is a great place to start.
    - *Transformed by Birth* **by Britta Bushnell**—an incredible guide to the inner transformation that's possible through the birth portal.

- ***Give Birth Like a Feminist* by Milli Hill**—A deep dive into the history of birth and how to feel empowered and sovereign in your birthing choices.
- ***Orgasmic Birth* by Debra Pascali-Bonaro and Elizabeth Davis**—Ways to explore pleasure in your birth.
- ***Mindful Hypnobirthing* by Sophie Fletcher**—Full of techniques to manage pain and meet intensity with mindfulness.

Chapter 5

BEING REBORN
(THE FOURTH TRIMESTER)

Her pointed ear, like mine.
How is she so small?!

She nuzzles, nurses, and I feel
All the mama mammals with me.
Fierce, protective, soft.

I am an animal.
Bloody, swollen, so wildly hungry.
Always thirsty, sore.
A bundle of needs, holding my bundle of love.

Every nerve feels raw.
I'm reborn,
Holding my newborn.
We will figure out life together.

But first,
Let's just figure out how to eat.
Eat, sleep, cuddle, repeat.
Retreat, retreat, retreat.

BODY

Welcome to your fourth trimester! Congratulations, your baby is born! And if this baby is your first, you have just been born as a mother. You are a newborn mother to your newborn baby.

Now you have a tiny, helpless human who is fully dependent on you to meet every one of their needs. Plus you'll need to meet your own needs, not to mention you probably just did the hardest work of your life in giving birth and your body will take at least six weeks to recover.

All that to say—if you're feeling overwhelmed, that totally makes sense. It feels like a lot because it is a lot.

I'm going to keep things simple in this chapter, so here are the key messages I want you to receive for this phase:

- Go slow and gentle with yourself.
- Let yourself be tended to and taken care of.
- Embrace the duality of the death and rebirth you've undergone.
- Celebrate your body and come home to your sensuality.
- You and your partner are new to each other-- it may take time to rediscover each other.
- Discover how to tend to the earth while tending to your baby.

Ready to dive in?

Go Slow, Go Gentle

Right after your baby arrives, there is a golden window, an invitation to pause and slow down, to give yourself the grace of acclimating to this new reality. Your body is healing, you're learning to be a mama, and your new baby is still quite fragile (as are you!)

In the early days, just meeting everyone's basic needs for food, water, sleep, and pooping can feel like a massive undertaking. (Not to mention an occasional shower!) If you have older kids, even more so. I once heard this advice from a midwife: "Eat when the baby eats. Sleep when the baby sleeps." It's good advice. You'll likely be shocked by how hungry, thirsty, and tired you are during this time. Just like your little bubba!

For these reasons, many ancient cultures have a ritual of sacred pause after birth. For example, in Bali, where both my babies were born, new mamas and babies stay home for forty-two days. During this time, they receive help from the whole family—cooking, cleaning, and caring for the baby—so the mama can rest and recover from birth. What a beautiful tradition!

The book *The First 40 Days* by Heng Ou, Amely Greeven, and Marisa Belger taught me about the Chinese tradition of conscious ways to nourish the new mama with healing foods, rituals like Epsom salt baths, bodywork like massages, and cultivating beauty. The new mama is treated like a goddess during this window, pampered and tended to as she learns to tend to her new baby.

This is quite radical for many of us growing up in the Western world, where sacred traditions like these have been lost. There is a strong narrative to "bounce back," and we often celebrate people who recover quickly from childbirth. Instead of allowing this sacred pause, many women feel an urgency to get back to normal, to move on, to return to normal life quickly. Then she wonders what's wrong with her that she feels so exhausted, so overwhelmed, so depleted!

When my mother gave birth to me, my father took off a few days to help post-birth, but then he had to go back to work. She was alone with a newborn baby and a toddler (my big brother), trying to recover from birth while tending to herself, her babies, and the whole household. That's way too much for one woman! She had almost no family or friends around to support her. Unfortunately, that is many, many new mothers' experiences.

Of course a mother would be depleted in that narrative. It's absolutely not the season for her to be productive, to bounce back, to hurry. This is a time when the new mama needs slow nourishment, rest, and gentle care.

The need to be "mothered" ourselves is primal, urgent, and necessary.

Let Yourself Be Tended To

1. "I Need You, Mama!"

Two weeks after giving birth to my second baby, I became irritated.

My mom was visiting, helping us with the baby and our toddler, and for some reason, I felt so annoyed by her. She was annoyed by me too.

One day, I broke down crying while trying to have a conversation with my mom. I whined in this uncharacteristic baby voice, "I just want someone to take care of *meeee!*" More tears came. My mom quietly listened.

I continued, "I want someone to make me a cup of tea and run me a bath and hold me and tell me everything is going to be okay." I felt so fragile, so depleted, so raw.

My mom looked at me with tears in her eyes and said, "I'm upset too. I've been spending so much time with Lila (my firstborn) that I haven't been mothering you."

I cried more as I said, "I really miss your mothering. I need my mama."

It was such a raw, vulnerable cry for help, and I'm grateful my mama was up for it. After that pivotal conversation, we shifted a few things so she could nurture me more while I nurtured my babies.

One of our favorite rituals was every afternoon when my mom would make me a snack, a cup of tea, and run me a beautiful bath with candles, flowers, and herbs. She'd care for my little ones while I had thirty minutes all to myself. This act of nurturing and caretaking me meant the world to me. In the early postpartum, my attention flowed outward, tending to my babies, and I often felt depleted. When she poured attention into me, filling me up with beauty and nourishment, it felt life-giving.

Mamas need to be mothered too.

2. Get Ready to Receive

This is likely the most needy time of your life—and for a good reason! Having a baby is a rallying cry for your village, an invitation to pour love into your new or growing family. It's an honor to support a family post-birth.

I like to imagine, in our hunter-gatherer days, that people would naturally flock around the new mama and baby, providing food each day for them, protecting them from the elements or predators, and bringing them love and support. This community support is absolutely essential for the well-being and thriving of a new family.

Yet, in our modern times, many of us live quite isolated, residing with our nuclear families, in separate homes, in very separate lives.

Some of this isolation is financial necessity. Many of us have to return to work early: according to the advocacy group Paid Leave US (PL+US), **one in four women go back to work within two weeks of giving birth**! Your body takes at least six weeks to heal.

Or maybe we can stay home, but our partners need to go back to work, depriving us of critical support post birth. Even if both partners are lucky enough to be able to stay home, they are still often isolated from extended family or community.

This isolation is "normal" but it is not biologically natural nor healthy. It's no wonder many new mamas are not thriving in this context. We need more support!

> *This isolation is "normal" but it is not biologically natural nor healthy. It's no wonder many new mamas are not thriving in this context. We need more support!*

So what can you do?

Create your village and actively call on the support you need. You can do this regardless of your financial situation as support does not have to be paid.

Asking for support is a radical act of love. Many of us were conditioned from the time we were young girls to be independent, strong, and self-reliant. Our culture loves to celebrate the "self-made millionaire," forgetting that no one is "self-made." That is absurd. We're formed by the community and culture around us, held by friends and family, intricately woven into an ecosystem of reciprocity.

Now you're in the most needy time of your life, yet you may struggle to ask for help due to cultural conditioning.

What can you do?

1. Recognize that **asking for help is a gift to those you ask**. It is an invitation into deeper connection, away from the loneliness of staunch self-reliance and into the lush, nourishing realms of interdependence and mutuality.

   > **Asking for help is a gift to those you ask.** *It is an invitation into deeper connection, away from the loneliness of staunch self-reliance and into the lush, nourishing realms of interdependence and mutuality.*

   Yesterday, Lila and I had so much fun cooking energy balls for ourselves and for a new mama in our community. We decorated a card, made the balls, and sent it as a little care package. We enjoyed that action so much! It felt so good, so empowering to give to this new mama. That's the experience others can have when you ask for help.

2. Recognize that when you're nourished, your family thrives. When you receive help and support, especially around food and housework, you have more attention and presence to give to your new baby. Your baby gets a more attuned, attentive mama. What a gift!

3. Remember that, by realizing you deserve support, you are setting a standard for other women, helping all women around you remember that we are worthy of being cared for. By watching you receive support, your friends, your daughters, and even your mother gets the message that, yes, women are valuable and deserve nurturing. That is HUGE.

After my first baby, I spent a full forty days at home. I didn't leave my bed for two weeks, I didn't cook or clean, and I received nearly daily gifts from friends—meals and treats. It was so lovely.

During this time, my mother watched me receiving this level of support unapologetically, and she got teary-eyed about it, as her own postpartum time was lonely and isolated. Watching me receive so much support carved out a new pathway of how nourished mamas can be. So you're receiving not just for yourself, but for all the women around you.

So, ready to receive support? Let's do this.

3. What to Ask For

During the early days with your baby, you will likely feel consumed by tending to your baby and your own needs, much less the needs of your house. Just feeding you and your baby is a full-time job. Let me share some ways that others can help you:

1. **Bring home-cooked meals or deliver food to your house.** Not having to think about what's for dinner (much less cook dinner!) is such a gift. You can organize a meal train ahead of time, where people drop off meals on a schedule. I highly recommend this!

2. **Help out around the house.** The dream visitor brings you a meal, then does all the dishes afterward so you don't have to worry about it. Or pops in a load of laundry. Or tidies your living room while you breastfeed the baby. Don't be shy about asking visitors to help you around the house! *You should not be a host in this phase.* This is not the time to get your guests a glass of water or prepare snacks. There will be time for that later, but for now, you're in full-on receiving mode.

3. **Brings over groceries or snacks.** You probably never met hunger like postpartum hunger. Snacks may be your love language in the early days. (They were mine!) Bringing you healthy snacks (best yet if the snacks can be eaten one-handed!) is a great way someone can help you out.

4. **Mother the mother.** Pouring some maternal nurturing energy into you by running you a bath, rubbing your feet, and making you a cup of tea. Maybe they pet your hair and remind you everything will be okay. It's okay to need this type of maternal nurturing, too! Remember, you're a newborn mama, brand-new to this world of parenting.

5. **Take the older kids out.** If you have more than one child, your loved ones can take your older kids out on an adventure to the park, playground, or other fun spot. This can create some much-needed quiet time for you to connect with the new baby.

6. **Get your partner out of the house.** If you're co-parenting with your partner all day, your partner may start to feel a bit stir-crazy and restless in the postpartum cocoon. I remember James's friend took him to go play padel one afternoon early postpartum, and it rejuvenated him so much to take a break and have some fun with friends.

7. **Bring beauty.** Beauty and sensual delights are so nourishing in this stage (more on that in the sensuality chapter). Bringing over fresh flowers, potted plants, lovely skin care, body oils, and a candle are lovely ways that your guests can support your well-being.

8. **Emotional support:** Sometimes support is as simple as asking, "How are you, really?" and listening deeply. Early motherhood can be a lonely time, where you might be home a lot with just you and your baby. A quick visit, a text message, or a phone call can be just what you need to feel a little less alone and a little more connected.

If you can afford paid support, hiring someone to help cook or clean during your first 40 days can be a life-saver. Even if it's just a few hours a week, it can make a massive difference for your mental health. Postpartum doulas are specially trained on how to support a new mama through nurturing maternal energy and practical newborn help - another great investment.

Remember that it's an honor to support you and that, when you receive support, you become a better mama to your baby.

Go Do: Ask for Help

Having a baby is a tender, vulnerable time where you're meant to be held by the village. Unfortunately, for many of us, we've never seen this mythical "village" so we don't know how to support each other in this tender time. That means you'll need to be proactive about asking for the help you need and educating your loved ones about postpartum needs.

Ideally, you do this activity before the baby arrives, but if the baby is already here, now is also the perfect time to "go do" and ask for help. Let's walk through how.

Bonus: I have a beautiful PDF with the eight ways to support a new mama. You can simply download it and send it to loved ones as an easy way to ask for help. Find it at www.megandlambert.com/emresources.

Instructions:

1. Read through the list of ways people can help you. Choose one way that would be most supportive for you right now (or add your own if you'd like).
2. Reflect on who might be available to help you. A friend? A neighbor? A relative?

3. Call or text that person right now, and say "Hi (name), I hope you're well. I'm deep in the early baby days. It's beautiful and hard. I would love your support. Would you [item from the list]? Thank you so much."

4. Remember, whether they say yes or no is a reflection of their availability, not a reflection of their love for you or of the validity of your request.

5. Pat yourself on the back for doing something vulnerable and scary: admitting that you need help! It takes so much courage, and you are so brave. You are boldly carving a new path of motherhood—one that is supported, nourished, and held.

Welcoming the Duality

In becoming a mama, there's a duality—both the immense blessing and joy in caring for the next generation, and at the same time, the intensity, the stress, the overwhelmingness, the boredom, the feeling like you're missing out. All of that is true.

Just as you rode the waves of contractions during birth, this postpartum period invites you to ride the waves of your emotions. After birth, you will experience the biggest hormonal drop that humans experience at any point in their life. It's huge! So, if you feel weepy, rageful, or anxious, you're not going crazy. This is normal—it's at least partly hormonal, and you will move through it.

(Of course, if the feelings are persistent and long-lasting, please reach out to a mental health professional for support. You don't have to suffer through postpartum depression or anxiety alone. You deserve to receive all the emotional and physical support you need.)

During this time, I had many moments of awe, looking at his little arms getting chubbier day by day, and his perfect little ears. Some moments, I was in joyful tears at what a miracle it all was. Then there were other moments when I felt so bored, so lost, or so anxious at how fragile my tiny baby is.

> *For me, becoming a mother has never been all good or all bad. Instead, it's been an amplification of both the ups and the downs, the joy and the hardship. Becoming a mother made everything more vivid, more intense, more rich.*

For me, becoming a mother has never been all good or all bad. Instead, it's been an amplification of both the ups and the downs, the joy and the hardship. Becoming a mother made everything more vivid, more intense, more rich.

These emotions are not only normal, but they are also *useful*. These emotions give us great information on what we might need.

For example, if you're feeling anxious, that might be an invitation to cultivate a deeper relationship with Higher Power through prayer or meditation. Or your anxiety might be telling you that you need more grounding food and a nourishing touch. Anxiety often signals a need for experiences that drop you out of your mind and into your body, such as a warm, comforting stew or a gentle massage.

If you're feeling rageful, you might need more support or to set a boundary. Your rage may be an invitation to ask your partner directly for the help you need (rather than hope that they read your mind). Or maybe you need a boundary around the number of visitors coming by. Or maybe you need some space for yourself, to journal, to process this transition.

If you're feeling weepy or full of grief, is there a true loss you need to acknowledge and mourn? The loss of your freedom, perhaps, or

> *Your emotions are so wise. They are full of primal intelligence, guiding you on how to best care for you and for your baby.*

of your maiden days. This is a huge transition, and all transitions bring both joy and grief. Sadness often is an invitation to slow down, feel deeply, and rest more. Sometimes it also signals loneliness, or a need to be held and loved.

I wonder which of these resonate with you? Your emotions are so wise. They are full of primal intelligence, guiding you on how to best care for you and for your baby.

Many of these emotions arise because you're undergoing an enormous transformation from maiden to mother. It is a true death-and-rebirth experience.

The Identity Death of Postpartum

When a baby is born, the maiden dies.

If that sounds dramatic . . . it is.

For many women, the early days after having a baby (and early days can be weeks, months, or even years) are a time of true identity death. Who you thought you were falls away, clearing way to make space for who you might become.

> *The early days after having a baby (and early days can be weeks, months, or even years) are a time of true identity death. Who you thought you were falls away, clearing way to make space for who you might become.*

After my first baby, I was shocked at how suddenly I changed. My priorities, my values, my sense of meaning . . . All of it suddenly felt different. I felt like a newborn baby myself, raw and unsure how to move in this new world.

Who was I now? Everything felt murky, muddy, and unclear. It was so strange to do activities I used to do, like go to a friend's house or visit a café—with my baby. I felt like an entirely new person. Same context, new identity.

With my second baby, I didn't expect to have an identity death experience since I was already a mother. *Surely, I've done this death-and-rebirth dance, right?* But I was shocked once again by how dramatically my life changed by becoming a mama of two.

No longer could I carry on juggling work and homelife as I had before. My two babies kept my literal arms full, and my work went on the backburner. With one child, I could take turns with my partner, rely on a nanny, and continue working as before. With two children, finding time for work felt hard, if not impossible. In fact, I'm only writing this book now at 9:00 p.m. when my babies are asleep.

Dying away is the "boss babe" in me, who thrived on achievement, productivity, and external validation. Rising in me is the "homemaker," who loves making chicken soup for her family, and the nighttime dream-maker, who makes art while her little ones sleep.

Of course, if we listen carefully, we're always going through a death-and-rebirth experience. There is always a part of us dying and falling, and a part of us being born and rising. That is the nature of life—continuously, constantly changing, like waves in the ocean. It's just that, after birth, there is a particularly *big* wave of identity shifts.

After each birth, I spent months scrambling, trying to find footing on solid ground, trying to figure out: Who am I now? What am I meant to be doing?

During this time, I listened to the song "Phoenix Rising" by Fia, and one line stuck in my head everyday reminding me to go gentle, go slow, and taste life for the very first time. Great postpartum advice, right?

My client summarized this moment beautifully:

> "My rebirth after the third baby was not fun, and it didn't have anything to do with the baby. It was a death. And when I say "death" and "rebirth," it's not like a cute thing where you lay in your bed for a couple days and cry a little bit. It was a really intense experience, and I didn't think I was gonna make it out. Like, I was clawing my way out.
>
> I can see why it was such a death, because I wasn't capable of building what I'm building now with who I was before. Now I'm so happy and in such alignment, but it couldn't have happened without all the shedding, intensity, and death of who I was."

So, a question to you as you read this: What part of you is dying right now? What part of you is being reborn? Can you welcome this alchemical process?

Integrating Your Birth

Your birth was the climax of the birth-rebirth process—the ultimate moment of the old you "dying" and the new you being reborn. Birth is a pivotal moment of transformation, so it's worth taking the time to harvest the lessons.

Your birth may have been beautiful, empowering, and exactly as you hoped for. It may have been challenging, shocking, heartbreaking, or traumatizing. Perhaps your birth was a mixture of both of these.

Either way, there is gold here, with potent lessons to harvest and integrate.

Here is how I'd recommend integrating your birth:

First, resist the urge to look at any birth photos or videos. I want your first recollection of the birth experience to be from within your own body, rather than as a camera witness looking down at you. This keeps you in the driver's seat of the narrative rather than as part of the scene.

Next, take time to write or speak aloud your birth story to yourself. You can do this with pen and paper in your journal, as a note on your laptop, or as an audio note in your iPhone. However you do this, keep the story private to yourself for now so you can savor your own experience without interpretations from others. I wrote out my birth story while my baby napped during the first couple weeks and found it a beautiful solo practice.

Piecing together your birth story can feel like remembering a dream: emotionally vivid and intense at times, while other times may feel fuzzy or missing altogether. It's okay to not remember the exact specifics of what happened like the timing or the stage—focus more on the emotional tone and texture of the experiences.

Once you have completed your story, you may find it helpful to talk to others who were there about their experience. I mentioned a **birth closing circle** in the previous chapter, and this is a perfect time to do one.

A refresher on how a **birth closing circle** works:

- Invite those present at your birth to attend—your partner, doula, midwife, photographer, or doctor (if available).
- Ask your partner or friend to prepare some tea and cookies, and create a beautiful space where everyone can sit comfortably for an hour or so.
- You may want to record this session as a keepsake for yourself. If so, set up a way to record the session, perhaps

with a central microphone or a phone passed around while each person is speaking.

- Take turns sharing the birth story, hearing each person's perspective. Often they will notice things you didn't, or will help fill in the gaps in the narrative.
- At the end of the story, thank each person who supported your birth. I like to share an appreciation for each person on the birth team, perhaps a specific moment when they truly helped you, or a unique genius you saw in them during the birth.
- Close the circle with gratitude and cooing over the new baby!

This birth closing circle can help add a collective narrative to your personal narrative of the birth experience.

Finally, I'd take a few minutes to journal on the below prompts to help you fully digest the experience.

Reflect: Birth Wisdom

Your birth is a climatic moment of transformation and leaves a bodily imprint for years to come. By taking the time to digest the experience and gather the wisdom, you're setting yourself up for a more embodied, confident start to your motherhood journey.

Know that you can journal on these questions at any stage—whether your birth was recent or a while ago—and it helps to repeat these questions, as your responses may change over time.

Instructions:

1. Diving into your birth can be a tender, emotional process, so create a cozy little cocoon for this deep transformative exercise. Maybe make a cup of tea, get a blanket, and find a place where your body can relax fully.
2. Then, open your journal, notes, or audio recording.
3. Respond to the following questions:
    - What moments of my birth did I most feel my own power and capacity? When did I feel powerful, capable, confident? Anchor these moments in your body through writing about them.
    - What moments of my birth did I feel weak, vulnerable, scared, or lost? What resources—inner or outer—supported me to move through these moments? Keep this list of resources handy for future challenging moments!
    - When I look back at my birth, what am I proud of? Grateful for?
    - When I look back at my birth, what (if anything) am I upset about, heartbroken by, or traumatized by?

      If this question brings up strong feelings for you, it may be helpful to talk to a trusted friend, midwife, or counsel on these spots. Sometimes birth integration requires healing painful moments, and there are many trained professionals who can help with that.
    - How do I want to remember this birth? What will be the legacy of this experience?
4. Close your notebook—for now. Know that your experience of the birth will likely shift over time, as new layers reveal themselves. These are questions you can come back to again and again over the months (or years!) that follow.

Caring for Your Body

While your emotions and identity are moving through big waves of transformation during this postpartum time, so too is your physical body. In fact, your physical body is undergoing the most miraculous transformative recovery process of your life.

No matter how you give birth—vaginally or by Cesarean, unmedicated or medicated—your body has just done a heroic act of bringing new life to earth. It may have been the hardest thing you've ever done. (It was for me!)

Let's face it—postpartum can be a brutal time for your body. You may have hemorrhoids, stitches, bleeding for weeks, maybe a C-section cut, a swollen vagina, scar tissue, and more. Getting a baby out of your body, however it happened, is no small thing, and your body tells the tale. Which means that your body needs more love, care, and attention than ever before.

How can you support your body during this time? Here are a few ideas:

Shower Spa
One of my favorite postpartum rituals was what I call a "shower spa." I'd bring a speaker into the shower, put on my favorite songs ("Put Your Records On" by Corinne Bailey Rae was a favorite for me because it's about redefining yourself), and luxuriate in the shower.

I'd make a special scrub with coconut oil, salt, and essential oils, then give my body a good scrub down. I'd shave my legs and wash my hair, and basically feel all squeaky clean and fresh afterward. This shower spa only takes ten minutes or so, but it totally changed the way I felt about myself for the whole day.

Herb Bath
When I felt particularly exhausted, I loved drawing a bath with Epsom salts and healing herbs like lavender, calendula, and

rosemary. This bath supports not just your physical recovery, but can also help you decompress from the intensity of birth, sleep deprivation, and those chaotic early days. It's a balm for your body and your heart.

Coconut Oil Massage

After your bath—or at any time, really—taking five minutes to lovingly massage your skin with coconut oil can feel amazing. As you do, notice the new shapes and texture of your body (with as much self-compassion as possible). As you massage in the oil, imagine you're anointing yourself, honoring this vessel that has just grown life, given birth, and is now caring for new life. What a beautiful feat that is.

By noticing these changes and tending to your body with an oil massage, you're inviting a deeper relationship with your changing form. It's natural to be surprised by your belly pooch, or your stretch marks, or the new cellulite on your bum. If you notice self-critical voices or body shame come up, simply observe them. The harsh inner voices only have power if you fixate on them. Perhaps you tell yourself something like, "I'm not willing to shame my body anymore. I'm willing to love and honor my body." Would that feel nice to hear?

Nourishing Foods

One of the most important rituals during this time is feeding yourself well. Warm, nutrient-dense foods are best during this phase—think soups, stews, roasted veggies, and warm broths. Your body is trying to recover from birth, and is perhaps also making breast milk for your baby, so your need for quality nutrition has never been higher.

It can be so challenging, though, to feed yourself well while also tending to a new baby, so I highly recommend either a) cooking and freezing food ahead of time, or b) starting a meal train where friends and family drop off home-cooked meals for you throughout your first forty days. Just look up "postpartum meal train," and you'll find great sites to help you organize this support. (See section above on asking for help!)

Rest

Beyond food, your most crucial need is sleep and rest. Your new baby will eat every ninety minutes to two hours, day and night, so your days of uninterrupted sleep are behind you (for now).

You can expect to be sleep deprived and tired, but you should not be exhausted. If you are, it's a sign you need more support from your partner or your community.

Some practical strategies to get more sleep:

- Anytime the baby naps, you nap. If your mind is active and you can't sleep, listening to a yoga nidra or a sleep meditation can help (check out YouTube).
- Ask if your partner is willing to take the baby for an hour or two in the morning so you can sleep in. That solo sleep is precious, as you'll likely sleep deeper when you know your baby is in good hands. To do this, your partner may need to sleep in a separate room or the couch at night to get enough sleep themselves.
- Go to sleep for the night as soon as the baby does so your sleep schedules are synced up. Even if it's at 7:00 or 8:00 p.m., go to bed—it's worth it to feel rested!

Some parents found success with bottle-feeding the baby (with formula or pumped breastmilk), so they can take turns doing night feedings with their partner or a postpartum doula. That approach never felt right for me though, so I opted to exclusively breastfeed and bed-share. I just rolled over and fed the baby while side-lying, which meant I barely had to wake up. Even when the baby woke up four or five times per night, I still got decent sleep and felt rested. If you're curious about bedsharing, I recommend James McKenna's book *Safe Infant Sleep* on how to bed-share safely.

Now that your basic needs are (hopefully) covered—food, rest, nourishment—let's look at adding in elements of beauty, pleasure, and delight through your sensuality.

SENSUALITY

Rediscovering your sensuality

While sex may be far away, your sensuality is not. Birth heightens all our senses, which can make the window just after birth a beautiful opportunity for sensual pleasure. I remember, post-birth, being acutely aware of the smell of the room, the temperature, if the sheets felt soft or not. It was like my skin was raw and all nerve endings were tingling alive.

> *While sex may be far away, your sensuality is not. Birth heightens all our senses, which can make the window just after birth a beautiful opportunity for sensual pleasure.*

This sensitivity can be both pleasant and unpleasant. It means that anything ugly, harsh, or dirty may feel extra painful and dissonant to your sensitive system (like that ugly sock on the floor or the smell of a poopy diaper). But this sensitivity also means that, with care and tending, you can experience the deep satisfaction of beauty and sensual delight.

I highly recommend creating what I call a "sensual recovery cocoon," which is a space that feels wonderful to your body and senses, a place where you can truly relax and recover from birth while surrounded by soul-nourishing beauty.

How? Here are a few ideas:

- Put a special candle on your bedside table and light it as you get ready for bed. Allow the scent to waft over you.
- Create soft lighting. Purchase a lovely red salt lamp or throw a shawl over a lamp. (But check to make sure that the lamp doesn't get hot!)
- Put on relaxing music and sing to your baby. ("Goodnight Moon Child" by Beautiful Chorus is exquisite for this.)
- Ask someone to prepare a delicious snack for you and arrange it beautifully on the plate. Bonus points if they add a flower!
- Make a mug of your favorite warm drink (I love hot chocolate). Drink slowly as you look out the window.
- Bring a potted plant into your room and place it where you can see it from your bed (where you will likely spend a lot of time during these days).

However you create these sensual delights, the most important thing is your embodied pleasure of the moment. Let the beauty in, let it touch you, let it delight you. Breathe it in like a lover. Your sensuality starts with you, and it starts with being aware of your senses, right here and right now.

Your sensuality can be a haven of rejuvenation in these exhausting early days, a place where you go to fill up your own cup and rebalance your nervous system.

Coming Home to Myself

"Honey, can you please take the baby so I can have thirty minutes alone?" I asked James. I was four weeks post-birth with my second baby, trying to juggle nurturing a newborn and a (very emotional) toddler. I felt frazzled, exhausted, and wired.

James agreed, so I went into my bedroom and locked the door. I put on my favorite music and sat cross-legged, breathing, focusing on the inhales and exhales. Nothing extra. I allowed this simple focus on breath to slow my mind and bring me into the present.

(Perhaps you take a deep breath with me as you read this!).

Then I moved my chest slightly forward with the inhale and swayed backward with the exhales, letting my breath slowly move my upper body forward and backward. As my spine became a little less stuck, I began moving in circles, circling my rib cage and chest in rhythm with my breath.

At first, it was hard! I was stuck in my head, unable to drop into my body, but I continued moving and breathing. Every time I caught myself thinking about the to-do lists, or wondering if the kids were okay, I'd come back to the sensation in my body. Breathe. Move.

"This is my meditation practice," I'd tell myself to get curious again about the sensations in my body. Feeling soft carpet against my thighs. Feeling my back stretch as I lean forward. Feeling the muscles lengthen under my armpits as I reach my arms forward.

With each new sensation, I said "yes" out loud. "Yes, yes, yes." By saying "yes" out loud, I welcomed the sensation, which helped keep myself present to what I was feeling.

After a few songs, I started to feel my body more and it felt so good! *Wow, this is me. This is my body.* I experimented with different songs—some fast, intense, angry songs; some slow, soft, sensual songs; some upbeat, happy songs. I noticed which songs made me feel most alive.

After a half hour, I heard the baby crying and knew it was time to go back and take care of the kids. Before I left my room, I looked in the mirror, noticing the flush in my cheeks and the smile on my face. I felt connected to myself in a way I hadn't since birth.

By taking a moment to be with my breath, my body, and my sensations, I came home. The attention inward on my own experience nourished myself, after many days with my attention outward on the baby. After this practice, I felt full of pleasure and aliveness with a fuller cup to give to my baby and family.

Would you like to try this exercise? If so, return to the "Go Do: Sensual Movement Class" I shared in the Conception chapter for the instructions. May it nourish you the way that it nourished me.

Now that you've looked at reconnecting with your body's pleasure, let's explore reconnecting with your womb and pussy after birth.

Honoring your Womb and Pussy

Your whole body has gone through so much through pregnancy and birth, but the MVP of the "creating life" party is definitely your womb and your pussy.

Your womb expanded to the size of a watermelon, and now it's doing the massive job of shrinking back to smaller than a grapefruit. You may feel afterpains postpartum—a cramp-like sensation as your womb shrinks back to size—especially if this isn't your first child. This is your womb knitting back together after finishing the marathon of pregnancy and birth.

One way I honored my womb post-birth is with a simple one-minute ritual. *You can do it now with me.* I put my hands over my womb in a heart shape. Then I took three deep breaths as I sent love to my womb, thanking her for all that she has done during pregnancy, and wishing her well in the recovery. That moment of gratitude helped me connect with awe and appreciation for my body. How did it make you feel?

Next up: rediscovering my pussy! In my first book, *Eros: The Journey Home*, I shared the importance of getting to know this intimate part of ourselves. I invited the reader (you!) to take a mirror or phone camera to look at your pussy, while noticing the inner dialogue about this part of your body. It's a powerful, and often emotional, exercise for many women.

Now in this book on motherhood, we will do the advanced version and look at our pussies post-birth.

Honestly, I was scared to look at my pussy after my first birth because I didn't know what I would see. My first birth left me with a few stitches, and my vagina felt quite swollen. I was afraid that my pussy would look ugly, broken, deformed—but I was also committed to knowing myself intimately, so I got a mirror and looked.

At first I was a bit shocked. My pussy looked very different—swollen, tender, raw, red. I breathed and told myself, "This is my body. This is what's happening right now." I acknowledged all that my pussy had done during the birth, and realized it was an honor to see this season of my pussy.

Each week of my postpartum, I brought out the mirror and looked again at my pussy. Watching my stitches heal, the swelling decrease, and the redness go away was amazing—like seeing a miracle in real time. I became intimately acquainted with my own healing journey, which was such a beautiful experience.

Now, I wonder if you'd like to look at your pussy? This can be confronting, even if you've done this exercise before. This may be beautiful, triggering, or both. Either way, remind yourself that your body is resilient, that you can heal, and that seeing your pussy in this healing season is an honor.

For more instructions on pussy gazing and why it is important, I recommend reading my book *Eros: The Journey Home*.

Intimacy Post-Birth

The theme of this chapter is sensuality before sexuality, and that holds true in your intimate partnership as well.

While sex may be off the table in these early days, your intimacy should not be. Staying connected in a soul-to-soul, nonverbal way is invaluable as you two navigate your entrance into co-parenthood together. It's amazing what physical affection can do to curb nitpicking and fights.

I highly recommend that the early days postpartum are primarily about you receiving pleasure and touch. You're giving so much nourishment to your baby, so intimacy with your partner can be a refueling station for you, a place to get filled up. While it may be tempting to just "give" to him (perhaps to get it over with?), take a minute to really tune in to yourself and ask, "What would refuel me right now? How can I access some pleasure?"

Here are a few ideas . . .

It could look like pausing to really kiss each other for six seconds or more when you say hello and goodbye. (The Gottman Institute found that it takes six seconds for a kiss to cause your bodies to release the bonding hormone oxytocin[5].)

---

[5] Kari Rusnak. "The Six Second Kiss." *The Gottman Institute*. July 1, 2021. Accessed March 1, 2025. https://www.gottman.com/blog/the-six-second-kiss/.

Or perhaps a massage would be lovely. Your neck and shoulders will likely be sore after all the rounding over you'll be doing to feed and gaze at your baby. If your partner is open to it, a shoulder and neck massage could be lovely to loosen tight muscles. Or if you're breastfeeding, you could ask for a breast massage to honor all that your breasts are doing.

Even though you're deep in recovery mode, your partner's body likely still has their usual needs and desires. Here is one fun idea that worked well for us: If the baby was asleep and I felt rested enough, I would offer a few minutes of cock-sucking. We literally put on a five or ten minute timer, and I lavished his cock with attention until the timer went off. It was fun, playful, and helped me feel like an erotic being even while I wasn't ready for my own body to be touched yet.

The fact that this isn't reciprocal can make it extra fun. James still fondly remembers one night after the baby was asleep, maybe two weeks into postpartum, where I told him to lie back and receive ten minutes cock-sucking. Afterward, I tucked him in and told him to go to sleep. This is still one of his favorite postpartum memories!

We rebuilt our intimacy step by step after birth. We started by lingering kisses; then a few days or a week later, we made out; and then a couple weeks later, a breast massage; then later, he lay on me and we grinded together, still with clothes on. Then he went down on me, but with no penetration.

Each of these steps happened over the course of weeks. I felt like a virgin teenager, exploring my sexuality bit by bit, each tender step at a time. I paid extra attention to what I felt ready for, checking in with my body through each step, just like I did as a teenager.

Keeping your sensuality and intimacy alive in the early days truly helps. Even tiny ways, like a lingering kiss or a playful wink, helps keep the embers of your relationship warm.

Postpartum sexuality often feels like oil and water because women usually go from no sensuality at all, to expecting herself to be ready for intimacy as soon as she gets the six-week "all clear" from her doctor or midwife (or later, depending on her unique recovery).

By the "all clear" signal, she may feel like she "should" be ready for sex, especially if her partner is quite eager, yet the embers of her sensuality have gone stone cold. Or perhaps it's the other way around, where you feel ready for intimacy but your partner is not. Maybe your partner is struggling to integrate seeing you as "mother" and "lover," or maybe they are navigating their own intimacy challenges.

Either way, it can be a massive jump from nothing erotic to penetration. This can feel really jarring to the nervous system!

> *The embers of your intimacy may have cooled down too far to feel ready for sex, and that's okay! The only thing to do is to build your intimacy back, step by step, taking the pressure off to go "all the way," and instead focusing on creating tiny moments of pleasure for each other.*

The embers of your intimacy may have cooled down too far to feel ready for sex, and that's okay! The only thing to do is to build your intimacy back, step by step, taking the pressure off to go "all the way," and instead focusing on creating tiny moments of pleasure for each other.

After my first baby, we tried penetration a bit too soon, and it hurt. I stopped it, then we just cuddled and breathed together while holding each other. I was happy I listened to my body, as that builds self-trust—an essential element for good intimacy—and James was so understanding. A week or so later, we tried again, this time going very slowly and with lots of coconut oil. That felt good!

Your body knows what you're ready for. Listen to your body as you try different types of touch. Is there discomfort? That's a yellow light, telling you to slow down, go softer, or use more lubricant. Pain? That's a red light telling you to stop. (You can always try again in a few days or weeks.) Pleasure? Green light, go for it!

Beyond your physical body, you also have to check in with your emotional and social body. Is your heart ready? Is your relationship? Is there anything you need to say or share to feel more connected to your partner first? We will go deeper into these layers in the relationship section.

If you're feeling ready for sex and lovemaking, read on about ways to honor your first lovemaking post-birth.

Your First Postpartum Lovemaking

The first time you make love after birth is like losing your virginity. It can be so tender, so emotional, so much sensation.

> **Note:** Skip ahead if you don't like sexy stories! It's going to get juicy.

Here is the story of my first time being intimate after our second baby...

We gave the kids to our nanny and went upstairs. I didn't feel turned-on, or any desire yet, but I was willing. I wanted to connect with James this way.

I took a shower and put on pretty white lingerie. I chose the delicate laciness of the lingerie to match the soft sensitivity of my mood.

James and I lay down on the bed, moving so slowly. We breathed belly to belly, kissing softly. I felt my body warm up and soften, like butter melting on a sunny day.

Everything felt so intense and all my nerves were raw. When he moved inside me for the first time, he went so slowly, staying with my body's natural opening. I started crying. Tears pouring down my face, my heart felt so full, so tender.

He paused, not moving but totally present with me. My body was quivering, and he wrapped me up really tightly as if holding me together. We were forehead-to-forehead, just like in the birth, and I wrapped my hands around our faces, creating a dark little cocoon of love, safety, and pleasure.

We continued barely moving, breathing together, noticing the sensation of merging again for the first time. I felt so much love. I'll remember this moment forever, as it felt so sacred, virginal, and tender.

How do you feel reading this? Inspired, turned-on, judging my story, judging your story? May you bring some love and compassion to this tender moment of rediscovering sensuality.

The first time you make love post-birth is a *big* deal. It's like being a virgin again, and you may feel more intensity, emotionally and physically, than usual. You may be surprised what your body needs now—perhaps slower or more tender than you're used to.

You can honor your first lovemaking post-birth with extra attention, such as . . .

- Lighting a candle.
- Saying a prayer or mantra first.
- Putting on music.
- Eye-gazing before you begin.
- Journaling about the experience afterward.
- Sharing desires with each other before you begin.

All these actions, while tiny, can help create a more intentional, conscious space for your first lovemaking post-birth. When I talk about this, a common question arises:

What if I don't want to make love after having a baby?

The first and most foundational thing to say: you never have to. This is your body and your decision. That is a critical reminder in a patriarchal culture that has often treated women's bodies as property and reduced her sense of autonomy. Know that you never, ever need to make love if you don't want to. Please do not bypass your own bodily boundaries in order to please others.

Sometimes, **we may wish to avoid the erotic because (unconsciously) we want to avoid the uncomfortable, confronting aliveness the erotic brings.** Eros invites us to open our hearts and bodies back up—which can be a scary invitation at times!

> *Sometimes we may wish to avoid the erotic because (unconsciously) we want to avoid the uncomfortable, confronting aliveness the erotic brings.*

Maybe we have stuck emotions we've been numbing through busyness or social media, and we know if we create space for the erotic, these emotions will start flowing as well. Tears, grief, resentment, or anger may pop up if we let ourselves start feeling again. Maybe we feel tender, vulnerable, or raw—and fear being exposed through an erotic situation. Maybe we feel secretly angry at our partner, and so we withhold physical intimacy.

In short, **sometimes we put up walls to block the flow of Eros, of erotic energy, because it feels too confronting to be that alive, to welcome that much feeling.** We may be overwhelmed or unsure what to do with all those feelings or sensations. Or we may feel numb, stuck, and unable to access any sensation in our bodies. *Eros and turn-on is the warmth that would unfreeze the numb stuck-ness—if we let it.*

If you have a sneaky suspicion this might be behind your reasons not to be intimate, I invite you to ask yourself these questions:

- Is there a feeling or sensation I'm trying to avoid by avoiding the erotic?
- What is behind my resistance to being sensual?
- What do I need to feel safe here?

To create safety, I recommend you do *not* push yourself to be erotic if you don't want to. Instead, focus on bringing sensuality into your body through your five senses—slow down and notice tastes, smells, sights, touches, sounds. This gradually brings you back into your body and the present moment, which can help your nervous system feel safer to gradually open back up.

Sometimes you may not feel the desire yet, but you *want* to want to be intimate. You may see the benefits of intimacy for you and for your relationship and wish that you felt erotic desire. Have you had that experience?

If that is your situation, I'd recommend you go slowly, go gently, exploring small, "bite-sized" intimacy first, taking the goal of sex entirely off the table. Explore some of the other pleasure practices I've shared here, such as a breast massage or long, lingering kisses. As you do these activities, notice what feels good to you, where tiny pockets of pleasure may be. Then you can build from there, over days or weeks, of small and intimate moments.

Of course, all of this sensuality occurs in the wider context in your intimate relationship, so let's turn our attention to your emotional connection as well as the physical.

RELATIONSHIP

Your family has expanded from two to three (or more, if you have older children), and this is not just a practical shift. It's also a shift of your attention from looking at each other as a couple to looking at this third entity together—your child.

If you have older children or stepchildren, this shift in attention from being a couple to being co-parents may not be as dramatic—or it might be! With each child there is an invitation to expand your awareness to include the broader family nervous system, rather than just yourself or just your partner.

That shift of attention (and intention!) can create all kinds of thoughts and feelings, such as: "Does my partner even see me anymore?" You (or your partner) might feel invisible to the other, or miss the days when it was just the two of you.

All of that is so natural and so normal, especially in these early days as you ask the question, "What does it mean to be the three of us? How do we love in a new way, as a family rather than as a couple?"

It's no secret that as new parents you both will be *busy*. That's why tiny moments of connection are so important and life-giving.

Early postpartum probably isn't the season of Friday night date nights, two-hour afternoon lovemaking, or romantic weekends away with just the two of you.

Nope.

This is the season of "Finally, the kids are asleep. Hey you!" quickies during baby's naps and stolen kisses in the kitchen. When romance looks like someone else doing your laundry, bringing you water because you can't believe how thirsty you are while breastfeeding, or offering to hold the baby so you can shower.

Yeah, love looks different in this season.

It's normal and natural to grieve the days when you two had endless time and attention for each other. Just as you have undergone a massive identity transformation from maiden to mother, so, too, has your relationship transformed from couple to co-parents.

As with all transformation, the grieving and loss is real. You may not recognize your partner in the same way, or they may not see you in the same way either. They've never seen this mom-bun, milk-stained-shirt, belly-pooch you. You've never seen your partner so sleep deprived, so tenderly in love with the baby, so stretched in their capacity. You two are new to each other, freshly reborn as parents.

The early postpartum days are a time to be gentle with yourself and your partner, to be curious about who each of you are, and to get to know this new version of each other. Just as your sensuality may feel virginal and new after birth, so too may your relationship. This is a time for gentle curiosity and exploration.

A New Way to Love

I'd like to pose a question for you two:

- What does love look like for you right now?
- How would you like to give and receive love?

To help answer this question, let's explore *The Five Love Languages* by Gary Chapman. I recommend that you both take the quiz online and share your responses to it. Basically, there are five ways we like to give and receive love:

1. Physical touch
2. Gifts

3. Words of affirmation
4. Acts of service
5. Quality time

Which of these five ways is your primary way to give and receive love? Which is your partner's?

When put in the context of being new parents, here are a few ideas on how you can love your partner in the language they desire.

Physical touch:
- Hold hands while on a nature walk.
- Cuddle while watching a show after the baby goes to sleep.
- Linger on a six-second kiss when saying hello or goodbye.
- Give each other a big hug and breathe together.
- Stroke your hair until you fall asleep.

Gifts:
- Find a beautiful piece of jewelry to commemorate the birth.
- Buy a warm pair of socks or a sweater to make this postpartum cocoon extra cozy.
- Make your partner a scrapbook of the birth.
- Bring your partner home a bouquet of flowers or a potted plant.
- Book your partner a surprise massage.

Words of affirmation:
- Write a love note and leave it in their bag.
- Tell them three things you appreciate about them as a partner.
- Write a social media post bragging about what a great parent your partner is.

- Compliment her changing body, noticing what is beautiful about it.
- Express gratitude for birthing and tending to this baby, or for taking care of you well during the postpartum period.

Acts of service:
- Run your partner a bath with herbs and flowers.
- Offer them a foot massage.
- Do the laundry, fold, and put it away.
- Take on a chore your partner normally does (e.g., clean the kitchen or laundry).
- Make them a cup of tea or a snack.
- Set up a meal train with your friends so you don't have to think about what to eat.

Quality time:
- Take the baby so your partner can have an hour of alone time. (Yes, this is love too! It's quality time with themselves.)
- Spend thirty minutes talking about how you each feel in this phase of life after the baby goes to bed.
- Do a hobby together you both enjoy, like dancing, singing a song, making art, or playing a video game.
- Go on a drive together, hold hands, and talk. (I've found men that tend to open up a lot more when driving! It's a thing, try it.)
- Cozy up in bed and quietly read your books together.

These are just a few suggestions, a way to start the conversation about what love looks like to each of you now in this new phase of life. Since you two are likely quite busy with the baby, keep the acts of love small, simple, and intentional. It doesn't need to be a grand gesture to remind each other of your affection and commitment to your relationship.

Remember, you both have been reborn since birth. It's changed each of you on a cellular level. This period of time is a chance to see your partner anew, with fresh eyes.

Open: New Ways to Love Each Other

How do you want to be loved now, within the context of caring for a little one (or little ones)? This quick exercise will help you two feel closer and more connected.

Bonus: I have this list of ways to love each other as a downloadable PDF you can access free on my website: www.megandlambert.com/emresources.

Instructions:

1. Cuddle up with your partner and read this list together.
2. Each of you choose three ways of being loved that you'd most like to receive, then share it with each other.
3. Remember how your partner would like to be loved, and if a moment arises, offer them a gesture of love in that way (or a similar way).
4. If you'd like to go deeper into love languages, please explore Gary Chapman's work, including the online love languages test you can take.

But what if you don't *want* to be loving towards your partner? Well there may be resentment in the way. Let's explore . . .

"Maleness" vs. "Femaleness" in Postpartum

> **Note:** This section has gender generalizations based on heterosexual relationships. I've seen this dynamic often enough that it is worth stating, though it may not apply to your relationship.

It's 6:00 a.m., and we just woke up with our two-month-old baby for the seventh time that night. James jumps up to go pee, and I make a snarky comment about it: "Must be nice to just get up and think only of yourself . . ."

"You're mad at me for getting up to go pee?!" James demands angrily.

"Well, no, I'm not. It's not that I'm mad at you for getting up to go pee," I say defensively. "It's just that you don't even notice that you get to immediately get up and go pee when you first wake up. You can only think about yourself. Whereas, when I wake up, my first thought is, 'Does the baby need milk? Are they in a clean diaper?' And then only when my bladder is bursting do I realize I need to go pee."

James looks confused and angry. "I still don't get why you're mad that I go to the bathroom. Why don't you just wake up and go to the bathroom too?"

"It's not that easy for me! Can't you see?!" Now I feel misunderstood and slightly crazy. Yikes.

Of course I want him to tend to his own needs. Yet I feel rageful when I see him put himself first and take freedoms I feel like I don't have. What do we do here?

Have you had a fight like this yet?

If not, it's probably coming.

This is one of the most common fights that a heterosexual couple gets into after having a baby. It comes from two very different aspects of what it means to be a father versus what it means to be a mother.

I don't think men notice the freedom they have, and I don't think women can quite put their finger on why they get angry so often after having a baby. This can create a huge amount of misunderstanding and resentment in relationships.

See, mothers tend to be innately connected to their baby and family needs, aware of when the baby last ate, distinguishing his cries, tending to his needs, and noticing his nap schedule. In many ways, she's socially and biologically programmed to put the baby's needs before her own. Many mamas say it's hard for her to hear her own needs or desires while tending so deeply to her baby. Can you relate?

Whereas for the father, he will likely stay connected to his own needs quite easily, even while being a devoted and caring father or partner. He will usually notice his own needs first, then notice the needs of the family.

Why is that? Well, for one thing, his hormones haven't had the incredible shift toward nurturing a baby that hers have. And for another, women are culturally conditioned to be "givers" (a.k.a. focused on others) while men are conditioned to be "winners" (a.k.a. focused on their own success). This conditioning starts from babyhood for both genders, so it's invisible at first and hard to point to.

This difference can create resentments and misunderstandings. She might assume he's selfish, oblivious, or self-centered as he first tends to himself. He might assume she's being hysterical, silly for not just meeting her needs, or overly emotional about it all. Both are missing the deeper lessons.

There is an opportunity here to notice "maleness" and "femaleness," a.k.a. our inherent gifts in this spot, and our inherent blind spots or weaknesses.

"Maleness" is the privilege to stay connected to his own needs and enjoy being single-focused on the goal at hand—yet, he can learn to notice the sacrifices his partner is making on behalf of the family, and he can work on becoming more aware of the broader needs of the family.

When her mind seems full and bound up, he can assume it's because she's doing invisible emotional labor, tracking everyone's needs and pouring her diffuse awareness through the family.

What can he do? He can cultivate gratitude for this skill of hers, compassion for her tension, and awareness of places he can pick up some of the mental or emotional load. If he causes unintentional harm (like waking up the baby by noisily getting out of bed), he can take responsibility for the impact (ex: by putting the baby back to sleep), or at least acknowledge the impact this has on her.

Meanwhile, "femaleness" is the gift of intuitively sensing other people's feelings and needs, to track the family nervous system, and tend to others. She can learn from her partner by watching how he treats his own needs as immediate and important, and use that as inspiration to similarly value her own emotions and needs.

Many times, I've only taken solo time to nourish myself after seeing James take his solo time, and then I felt emboldened to take that time myself. I see him care for himself, and I remember to care for myself. He inspires me to remember my desires and claim them.

She can also acknowledge a simple, heartbreaking, beautiful, and complex fact—there is no one like the mother. As the mother, she has a unique role and burden that is only hers to carry. He will never fully understand, and no one can carry this burden for her. By accepting this weight, she can surrender to the fullness of motherhood and let it cultivate gravitas inside her.

This is a spot where men and women can learn from each other by valuing the gifts (and blind spots) that we each have.

Does that make sense? Does this dynamic apply to you and your partnership?

This is not necessarily a dynamic that needs to be fixed as much as it is an invitation to understand each other's worlds, to learn from each other's strengths, and to complement each other's blind spots.

The Resentment Wall

In these early days, I remember feeling shocked by how different life was for me compared to how different life was for James. He was so involved—changing diapers, burping, and bouncing, etc.—but it still wasn't equal. He wasn't breastfeeding around the clock, his body wasn't healing, and it wasn't his vagina that pushed the baby out. The work of baby care is not equal at all.

I don't know why that fact surprised me. Maybe because I had grown up in a feminist family who emphasized that women can do anything (especially professionally), and men should be involved with their families. With this conditioning, I don't think I quite realized how different becoming a parent would be for each of us.

James went back to work within a few weeks after the birth. I distinctly remember a Saturday when he led an all-day men's workshop, and was gone the whole day while I was home with the baby. I realized, "Wow, I feel like I'm in the 1950s." The gender roles became automatic. He easily took a day away from the baby, while I didn't feel comfortable doing so until over two years later. That is a *big* difference.

We chose these roles semi-consciously (but I'm sure there were also unconscious blueprints at play). I felt joyful in the sacrifice, and I truly wanted to spend that time with the baby, but I also felt uncomfortably stuck and tethered in a way that he didn't.

According to Pew Research Center, *Millennial fathers spend 3x as much time with their children as fathers in 1965. And yet, Millennial mothers feel more burned out and overworked than the previous generation*[6]. What is happening here? How can it be that men are far more involved than before, and yet the women feel even more burdened?

I believe a few factors are at play:

1. Mothers are *also* spending far more time on childcare — almost 50% more than in 1965. Why? The expectations of mothers have gone up. No longer is it enough that your children are fed, sheltered, and loved. Now a mama has to break "intergenerational trauma cycles," and "raise secure children," and "be present and attentive all the time," and ensure the children eat "nourishing, wholesome meals"— all while possibly working full-time as if she doesn't have children. Yikes! No wonder she's burned out.

---

[6] Pew Research Center, "Chapter 4: How Mothers and Fathers Spend Their Time," in *Modern Parenthood* (Washington, DC: Pew Research Center, March 14, 2013), , https://www.pewresearch.org/social-trends/2013/03/14/chapter-4-how-mothers-and-fathers-spend-their-time/.

2. Mothers are also working more than twice as many hours than in 1965 (25 hours a week on average, compared to 9 hours). So she's both working more and doing more childcare than her predecessors.
3. By men being involved, the work is (maybe) more equally divided, but so is the credit. No longer are women celebrated as the primary caregivers and life-providers. Her labor becomes even more invisible as his contributions are publicly celebrated and paraded ("Wow, what an involved dad you are!" he often hears).
4. He may be doing more physical contributions (e.g., changing diapers and burping), but she often still carries the emotional and mental load (e.g., knowing the baby's nap time and feeding schedules, monitoring for sickness, and tending to big feelings). This means that, while he is involved, the management and monitoring still tends to fall on her shoulders.

This inequity can lead to a wave of (often unexpected) resentment.

Around the same time, a few weeks after birth, my friend Florence, who is a mama of four, asked, "Have you hit the resentment wall yet?" I felt confused and asked what she meant.

She said, "That moment when you just look at your partner, and you feel resentment at how free his life is, and how not free yours is."

Ah, I understood. Yes, yes, I had hit the resentment wall.

Can you relate?

This is to not be a whiny victim, but rather to be real about the differences and challenges, particularly between men and women as you become parents.

This spot is ripe for resentment, which, left unchecked, can poison your marriage. Resentment is like a pesticide, slowly killing everything in its path. Yet resentment also has great wisdom for you—if you will listen to it.

If you have hit the "resentment wall," here are five steps to work with that spot:

1. **Speak to your world.** Acknowledge the differences without blame.

    For example, right now I'm writing this while breastfeeding my baby. I want to be doing this caretaking. But I also want to be *seen* in the caretaking, in the sacrifice. So, name these moments when you are deep in caretaking, when you see your partner have freedoms you don't necessarily have, as a way for your partner to understand your world.

    For example, "Honey, this is not to blame, and there is nothing to fix. I just want you to notice that I work while tending to the baby, while you work baby-free. Sometimes I feel sad or mad when I see how different our lives are right now."

2. **Empty the bucket.** My midwife gave us this powerful (and sometimes volatile) practice. At the end of the day, take turns sharing all the things you're annoyed about while the other person simply listens (do *not* respond).

    For example, "I'm annoyed that you forgot to buy diapers. I'm annoyed that you didn't refill my water bottle. I'm annoyed that I didn't get a nap today." The practice of speaking these out is so powerful in clearing the connection between you two, because many couples have a tendency to stuff all these annoyances under the rug, but then the annoyances become long-term resentments, which are much harder to heal.

By speaking about the annoyances each day, you clear the channels and also see what shifts might need to be made (see next point). The listening partner simply responds with "Thank you."

3. **Notice what needs to shift.** As you speak these annoyances out, you'll likely notice shifts that you need to make. Annoyances highlight places where you two can work together to create more flow and less friction.

   For example, with our first baby, I was often annoyed that James looked so rested after sleeping solo in his own room while I was up all night with the baby. As I shared these annoyances, I realized, "Oh, I actually need more sleep support." He saw it too, so after "emptying the bucket," we started brainstorming what to do. He began taking the baby in the morning at 5:00 a.m. so that I could sleep from 5:00 a.m. to 8:00 a.m. I remember the first time we did this, I starfished across the bed, relishing this space and time to rest. It felt so good! But we never would have come to that solution if I hadn't spoken up about my annoyances.

4. **Ask for what you need.** Our annoyances often highlight our deepest needs. So ask yourself: What does my irritation reveal about what I need right now? More sleep? More attention? More childcare support? More appreciation for all I do?

   It's natural that, as your life changes dramatically, so do your needs. And you may not recognize a new need until you feel annoyed. So notice the annoyance and dig underneath for what you really need or want here.

5. **Create a plan to meet needs.** Remember that, ultimately, you two are on a team and want each other to thrive. As you each share your needs, collaborate on how you can work together to meet those needs.

For example, does he need more appreciation? Maybe you can try to do at least one appreciation a day. Do you need more closeness? Perhaps you two can create a ritual of intimacy at the end of the day.

It may be a time to reallocate responsibilities or to become more explicit with who does what. For example, who wakes up to change the diaper? Who cleans the bottles if you're using them? Who takes time off work, and for how long? When do you take self-care time, like gym workouts or meditation?

These are important conversations to have. It's really important to be explicit about what you need and the expectations you have of each other—and both stick to the agreements—because this builds trust.

Having a baby requires more interdependence than you've ever experienced before, and that requires a lot of trust and clear communication about where you'll be, when, and what you can count on each other for.

6. **Give each other space.** Once a baby arrives, alone time has never been so precious. When irritations and annoyances build up between you two, sometimes the best thing to do is *not* talk about it, but instead, to give each other space to take care of yourselves. Take a nap, shower, go work out, eat something. It's amazing how the gift of self-care solves so many challenges.

Go Do: Take Down the Resentment Wall

Have you noticed anger or resentment in your relationship since having a baby? Walk through these five steps to take down this "resentment wall" between you two, brick by brick.

Instructions:

1. Notice a moment when feelings of anger, injustice, or resentment pop up. Acknowledge these feelings and welcome them as invitations for deeper connection.
2. Ask your partner for time to talk through what's coming up for you. A great time for this is when the baby goes to sleep at night or during a nap.
3. Speak to your experience with as much vulnerability as possible, highlighting differences between you two in a blame-free way.
4. Create space for each other to share annoyances or irritations while the other just listens.
5. Mine the irritations for unmet needs. What do each of you need right now? How can you support each other?
6. Make a plan for how to help each other get your needs met, reallocating responsibilities as necessary.
7. Last, give each other a moment of space and self-care.

These steps are acute remedies to fix an ailment in your relationship ("the resentment wall"), but of course, the best remedy is prevention. The following practice is one of the most powerful prevention exercises I know of to strengthen your relationship each and every day.

Daily GADs practice

On our couples' retreats, we teach a daily practice called GADs. It is one of the most celebrated and useful tools that couples learn and it's shockingly simple.

Think about GADs like your prenatal vitamin—just the right nutrients each day to prevent longer-term malnourishment or health challenges. In the same way, GADs is just the right dose of affection to create a deep sense of teamwork, to prevent bickering or growing apart.

How does this work?

It's simple. Each day you share:

- 3 Gratitudes
- 3 Appreciations
- 3 Desires

My favorite way to do GADs is to sit down together with a warm drink of choice and hold hands while we share these things. But life is busy, so sometimes we do GADs while we're driving, waiting in line somewhere, eating breakfast, or just before bed.

Once you're ready to start, take turns sharing three **gratitudes** each. What are you thankful for right now? What blessings in your life can you recognize? Maybe it's the healthy baby in your arms, or the meal your friend dropped off yesterday, or your cozy home. Look around. What can you give gratitude for right now?

Then take turns sharing three **appreciations** each. What did your partner do today, or recently, that touched you? Appreciation is most potent if it includes:

1. A specific moment (*ex: "When you figured out the birth certificate paperwork..."*)

2. How you felt *(". . . I felt relieved and loved . . .")*
3. The impact it had on you *(". . . because knowing you were handling the logistics of that freed me up to be more present with our baby.")*

Here are some more appreciation examples:

- When you brought me a snack while I was breastfeeding, I felt so loved, and it nourished me so that I could nourish the baby.
- When you came home and kissed me deeply, I felt turned-on and alive, which helped me remember that I'm a sensual woman, not just a mom.
- When you told your mother she can't visit the baby until next week, I felt protected and relieved that I don't have to host anyone right now. Thank you.

By highlighting these little moments and expressing the impact they had on you, you let yourself fully receive the love from that moment. You also help your partner feel important, valued, and useful, which is so easy to neglect in the chaos of early baby days. By sharing three appreciations daily, you create a virtuous cycle of appreciation and love.

Last, take turns sharing **three desires** each for that day. What do you really want to experience today?

Pause.

Ask your body.

What would delight me today? Do I want to go on a nature walk? Call a friend? Take fifteen minutes to dance? Take a bath? Taking time to pause and reflect on your desires is a discipline—one with immense rewards for you, your partner, and your family.

Remember that your aliveness is the light of the family. If you aren't doing something each day, just for yourself, it's easy for your light to get dim and dull and to feel like a martyr. You deserve joy too. What do you want?

Share your desire with your partner, and listen while your partner does the same.

Then it's both of your jobs to work together to make them happen. It's your job to make sure your partner gets their three desires, and it's their job to make sure you get your three desires.

In conclusion, this phase is an immense period of transformation for you two as a couple. The previous version of your relationship has died with the birth, and the early postpartum days are a rebirth opportunity to see each other with fresh new eyes.

Remember to stay curious about each other while discovering how each of you wants to be loved in this phase. Appreciate your inherent differences (the "maleness" vs. "femaleness" conundrum). Talk through annoyances before they harden into resentment, and make time each day to nourish your relationship with gratitude, appreciation, and desire. With these ingredients in mind, you two will be well on your way to a healthy, happy co-parenting partnership.

Now let's broaden the view beyond your relationship into the wider ecosystem that supports you and your budding family.

ECOSYSTEM

Finding Your Nature Haven

After birth, I felt ravenous for the feeling of earth under my feet, surrounding myself with natural beauty, and breathing fresh air. In the early days, I lay in bed with the curtains open, watching birds fly and the sky as it changed colors. As my body grew stronger, I took long walks with the baby in the carrier nestling up to me, noticing the big trees, beautiful flowers, and little butterflies around me. Nature felt like such medicine.

Looking back, it makes sense. Birth is such a primal, embodied experience—and afterward, of course, I'd crave a similar primal, embodied experience like being in nature. That is what we're designed for! We crave nature because it's natural to who we are.

> We crave nature because it's natural to who we are.

Have you felt a similar craving for nature through your journey of creating life? A yearning to be surrounded by life, while nurturing life?

If so, I wonder how you can access nature right now. Can you take the newborn for a walk outside? The gentle, steady movement often rocks little ones to sleep and soothes your frazzled soul. Seeing the plants sprout, bloom, and drop leaves reminds you that everything only lasts a season, even the hardest moments of new parenthood.

Or maybe you're still recovering in bed. If so, could someone bring you flowers so you have something beautiful to look at? Or maybe you could open your windows and let the fresh breeze tickle your skin?

If the weather is nice enough, you could take your baby outside and lay on a blanket together, watching the clouds roll by. Maybe you can tend to a few potted plants, delighting in little sprouts that emerge.

Go Do: Earthly Delights Walking Meditation

Taking time to enjoy the natural world nourishes our body and soul, reminding us that we're connected to all that is. This "walking meditation" can be done anywhere there are plants or animals.

Bonus: I have this meditation as an audio you can listen to for free on my website: www.megandlambert.com/emresources

Instructions:

1. Find a place where you can walk for 10–15 minutes with your baby. Somewhere that is safe and, ideally, surrounded by nature—trees, plants, flowers. If you live in a city, a park or even a street with a few trees will do.
2. Put your baby in a baby carrier, hold them in your arms, or put them in the stroller. Ensure you are both cozy and comfortably dressed for the season you're in.
3. Go for a walk! As you walk, take deep breaths down into your belly.
4. Listen to the sounds you hear. Can you hear any birds? Any insects? What else do you hear?

5. Find one beautiful thing to rest your eyes on. A flower? A leaf? A cloud? Spend a breath or two simply gazing at this beautiful, natural thing.

6. Take a big inhale and see if you can detect any smells. If there are flowers nearby, sniff a flower, or break off a leaf and smell it. What do you notice?

7. Are there trees nearby? Touch them. Feel the texture of the bark under your palms, notice the contours and design on the bark. Run your hands across the bark, noticing the way the texture tickles you.

8. Is there grass you can safely walk on barefoot? If so, take your shoes off. Feel the dirt and grass under your toes. Is it cold, warm, hot? What does it feel like?

9. Complete this nature exploration after a few minutes, and do a small bow to Mother Earth, thanking her for these earthly delights.

Receiving nature's goodness is such medicine postpartum. Now let's talk about how you can return the favor to Mama Earth by making eco-friendly choices.

Tending to the Earth and Your Baby

Having a baby is a notoriously resource-intensive activity. Between the thousands of diapers your baby will use, all the cute baby clothes your little one wears only once or twice, all the baby equipment that people say you "must have" . . . It adds up big-time for both your wallet and for the planet.

Your little baby needs a beautiful, healthy planet to inherit more than he or she needs yet another ruffle outfit or a baby swing. So how can you balance both providing a good life for your baby while caring for the earth?

Here are a few ideas:

Diapers: The average baby will use over seven thousand diapers in his or her lifetime, and each year in the US alone, thirty billion diapers go into the landfill. Most diapers contain plastic, which never breaks down and will continue to pollute our earth with microplastics forever. Bleak, right?

The most ecological option is to practice elimination communication, where you work together with your baby to use the toilet, even from birth. This is free to do, great for the earth, and great for the parent-child bond. We practiced this with both of our babies from birth, and found it to be so rewarding for us and empowering for the babies. The book *The Diaper-Free Baby* by Christine Gross-Loh is an amazing resource in learning about this option.

The second most sustainable option is to use reusable cloth diapers. I was skeptical of reusable diapers before having a baby, because I assumed they would require too much extra work, but I was pleasantly surprised by how easy they are. After the baby uses the diaper, you just put the diapers in a bucket of water with sodium percarbonate or baking soda until you can wash them in the washing machine. Done. And no, this doesn't make your washing machine smell or gross. Every so often, you can just put on a cleaning cycle, and it's good as new.

Reusable diapers are not only better for the earth, they are also far better for your baby, as they don't have toxic chemicals like disposable diapers do. They are also better for your wallet, with an estimated $1,200 savings over two years. Reusable diapers do require an upfront cost of a few hundred dollars, so this is a great thing to put on your baby shower wish list or ask people to contribute to a "diaper fund."

The third most sustainable option is to use eco-friendly disposable diapers, such as EcoBoom or Seventh Generation. These are expensive but they don't contain as many harmful chemicals as the mainstream brands, and they break down easier in landfills. We used these while traveling or at night. If you must use disposable diapers, it's worth it to get the eco-friendly option. You can ask for these diapers as a baby shower gift too.

Whatever you decide to do, I trust it is what's right for you and your family as you balance the competing needs of your family, your baby, and the earth. There is no perfect choice, just the one that feels most in alignment with your values and needs.

Clothes: Babies grow shockingly fast. Both of my babies had outfits that they simply outgrew before they had worn them more than once or twice.

While it's fun to buy all these cute little baby outfits, the eco impact adds up quickly. The fashion industry is the third-biggest contributor to climate change, and much of that is from children's clothing that is barely worn.

The best bet is to buy secondhand baby clothes. With our second baby, James and I each purchased one new baby outfit we loved, and we gathered the rest of the clothes secondhand from other families. This dramatically reduces our environmental impact, and we still could dress our baby in super cute, barely worn items for free or very cheaply. Ask around other families you know to see who might have baby clothes they no longer need.

If you do buy new items, seek out organic cotton, bamboo, or recycled polyester fabrics, which have a lower environmental impact than other fabrics. A great rule of thumb: Buy fewer but higher quality clothes that will last for generations.

Feeding: Breastfeeding is the most eco-friendly option, as it requires no additional equipment, parts, or formula. It's also well-known that breastfeeding is the healthiest option for a developing baby, providing all the essential nutrients, vitamins, antibodies, and probiotics the baby needs. It's as simple and natural as nature made us.

Of course, not every mama has the option to exclusively breastfeed. Perhaps her body can't produce milk, her baby has a challenge latching on, or simply, she needs more flexibility with her time (such as going back to work).

If you must collect and store breast milk, I love the Haaka, which collects milk from the other side while breastfeeding. It's simple, with no batteries or electricity required. If you're going for formula, seek out eco brands or low-toxicity options.

Other Items: As the saying goes, "Reduce, reuse, recycle." When it comes to baby stuff, this means thinking critically: Do I *really* need this item? What is the minimum amount of stuff I need? If I truly need this item, can I find it second-hand?

> *Babies need so little. They truly only need a happy, nourished mama who can take care of them. So focus more on your own self-care and nourishment than any more toys or items for a baby.*

Babies need so little. They truly only need a happy, nourished mama who can take care of them. So focus more on your own self-care and nourishment than any more toys or items for a baby.

Before having a baby, I assumed that I would need a whole list of things—strollers, bouncers, cribs, changing tables, toys, play pens, and stuffed animals. The truth is? I needed none of those things.

We baby-carried (no need for strollers or bouncers), we co-slept (no need for a crib), we changed the baby on a towel on the bed (no need for a changing table), we interacted with the baby, and we showed him the world (no need for toys or play pens).

Truth be told, I was shocked by how few things my new baby actually needed. Here is what I really needed for a newborn: diapers, washcloths, and a baby carrier. If I had lived in a colder climate, I'd also need blankets and clothes (but in Bali, my babies were often naked in the humid air). That's all.

So, forget the capitalist agenda that's pushing you to buy more, more, more by convincing you that your baby *needs* this. Companies try to push expecting parents to over-consume by convincing them they are taking better care of their baby if they buy X, Y, Z. **It's a straight up lie.** Your baby just needs you—your attention, your love, and your nourishment.

Remember, each item we buy has a carbon footprint in terms of manufacturing, shipping, and eventually, landfill. The best way to care for the earth is to quite simply buy less stuff. Go with the minimum amount of items, knowing you can always buy more later (ideally secondhand) if a true need arises.

By bringing awareness and attention to these everyday choices of diapers, clothes, feeding, and baby items, you're taking great care of Mama Earth, and in turn, the Earth is taking great care of you.

CHAPTER 5 SUMMARY

You are a newborn mama with a newborn baby. You need the same nurturing energy that your baby does as you devote yourself to caring for this little life. This is the time to ask for the support and help you need—to create the village that can hold you. Ask for help.

Becoming a mama is a true death-and-rebirth experience, full of mixed emotions and duality. In this new phase, it will take time to find yourself again. In the meantime, welcome all the feelings that arise as helpful information.

Birth is a climatic, pivotal moment of transformation. By taking the time to integrate this experience, you can gather valuable insight for your mama journey.

Your sensuality may feel far away right now, and that's okay! You can rediscover it, layer by layer, through bite-size intimacy and by engaging with your five senses before trying sexuality.

Your relationship has just had a baby bomb dropped into it, which can create both closeness and new feelings of resentment or anger. By openly sharing your experience and needs, you two can take down the resentment wall and find your way back to love. GADs is a powerful daily practice, a preventive "multivitamin" for your relationship.

Last, the Earth is a rejuvenating haven, just waiting to nourish you. I invite you to explore your five senses through a walking meditation. We also talked about ways you can help the Earth through your purchasing decisions and baby care options. Remember, less is more.

Ways to GROW

In this chapter, I shared the following invitations for you:

- **Go Do: Ask for Help**—A list of simple and practical ways for others to support you during this tender postpartum window. You don't need to do this alone!

- **Reflect: Birth Wisdom**--An invitation to mine your birth experience for deep wisdom and inner resources to support your motherhood journey.
- **Open: New Ways to Love Each Other**--An exercise to rediscover each other as co-parents, and find three new ways to love each other.
- **Go Do: Take Down the Resentment Wall**--Resentment reveals our unmet needs. This practice helps you two to explore your needs and how to meet those needs as a team.
- **Go Do: Earthly Delights Walking Meditation**--This simple practice will help you ground into your body and receive the nourishment of nature while with your baby.
- **Widen:** Here are books that you may find nourishing during these early days:
  - *The First 40 Days* **by Amely Greevan.** My copy of this book is dog-earned, covered in food, and deeply loved. I came back to this book hundreds of times in the early days postpartum and felt so nourished by the wisdom and recipes here.
  - *The Fourth Trimester* **by Kimberly Ann Johnson.** One of the best guides on how to tend to your body, nervous system, heart, and sense of self after having a baby. Highly recommend it!
  - *Body Full of Stars* **by Molly Caro May.** A beautiful narrative of a woman's journey to rediscover herself and her body post-birth. It brought me to tears!
  - *The Diaper-Free Baby* **by Christine Gross-Loh.** Practical information on elimination communication, which I found beautifully bonding for me and my baby and, not to mention, kinder to the earth.

Chapter 6

BABYHOOD & BEYOND (YOUR NEW LIFE)

You nuzzle up next to me,
Refusing to sleep even a foot away,
We're still so merged, aren't we?

I watch your impossibly sweet face sleep,
And say for the hundredth time today -
How is she so cute?

My heart is bursting.
Oops! So is my bladder.

You wake up and wanna go pee with me.
You hold out your little arms to be carried.
Please, please, can I just pee alone?
Nope. I snuggle in.

This is my season of . . .
so much closeness, so little freedom.
So much tenderness, so little certainty.
So much play, so little productivity.
So much love, so little time.

Here I am:
"Mama"

I know this is a season,
And like all seasons,
The only constant is change.
So for now, all I say is:
"Yes, baby, I'm here."

Moving Beyond the Baby Bubble

When my first 42 days ended, I cried. The Balinese tradition called for a home cocoon for these first 42 days, and then? The wide open world awaits.

I felt a mix of emotions—grief for how fast time was going and how big he was getting. Gratitude for such a beautiful pause. Confusion at why everything still feels so hard. Shouldn't it be easier by now? Fear and curiosity at how we will find our "new normal" as a family. What does life look like now?

As I slowly emerged from the baby bubble of the early days, I had a dawning realization that this is my new life. This is how it will be forever. Well, as "forever" as anything is with children, because if there is one thing I've learned while being a mama, it's that everything changes. Cliché, but true.

One minute, I will be in a glorious phase where my baby is smiling, my toddler is content and creative, my husband and I are connected, and everyone is healthy . . . It feels like an eternal summer. I can't believe how beautiful and blessed my life is.

The next moment? Baby is crying with gas pains, the toddler is having a tantrum for attention for the hundredth time that day, James and I are fighting, I'm exhausted and stressed out while running on a few hours sleep . . . those are the hard moments.

In the hard moments, I tell myself, "This too shall pass," and in the easy moments, I tell myself, "Not every moment will feel like this, but I sure will enjoy the ones that do." Because the truth is? Everything changes. Once I find a "new normal" or a set point—things change again.

When people would ask me how it feels to be a mother, I would feel at a loss for words. Miraculous? Heart-bursting open? Devastatingly tender? Overwhelming and stressful? Most beautiful thing of my life? All are true.

In many ways, motherhood *amplified* my life. The highs got higher, the lows got lower. It has invited me to expand my capacity over and over again, to stay present in an expanded range of sensations and emotions.

How has motherhood been for you?

How are you feeling, moving out of the early baby bubble and into your new life as a mama to a growing baby (or babies)?

In this section, we'll explore your changing body shape, your dynamic emotions, mom guilt, nourishing your relationship as co-parents, and how to raise children in a community and nature. There is so much to say about your "new normal," so let's dive in!

BODY

Let's start with the most obvious, tangible changes: Your body. Though the most intensive physical-recovery phase is behind you, your body will continue to change shape and require extra nourishment for months to come.

About three months after my second baby was born, I went to the shops, where the cashier told me, "Congrats on your pregnancy! That is so exciting!" looking down at my still-soft belly with the little bump. It was an awkward moment when I said, "Well, actually, I'm not pregnant. I'm postpartum."

At that moment, a part of me wondered, "When will I no longer feel (and look) pregnant or postpartum? When will I get 'myself' back—physically and emotionally?"

The truth is, there is no going back.

Physically, my body holds the imprint of my babies—the little stretch marks around my bikini line, my extra-big belly button; my soft, squishy belly; my breasts that swell or droop, depending on if the baby has fed yet. My body shows the story of growing and creating life.

Sometimes I mourn my maiden pre-pregnancy body, missing my flat stomach and perky breasts. And other times? I look at my body and feel such pride in what my body has created. Celebrating my body as a creator of life helps me have compassion for what's changed. These changes are not "pointless." They brought me the greatest gift I've ever had: my children.

I still remember being a little girl, tracing the silvery stretch marks across my mama's belly, the tracks that my brothers and I had left behind. I loved the way her stretch marks felt—so soft, so fascinating. She told me she didn't like them, and I felt confused. Why wouldn't she like them? They are cool!

All this to say, there is no right or wrong way to feel in your body in this phase. Maybe you're shocked at how great you feel and look postpartum, or maybe you're feeling insecure, shy, and ashamed of your new shape. Either way is okay.

My invitation in this phase is to get to know yourself deeply, to build a new relationship with your changing body. To explore and uncover: What's new? What's different? What parts of me are easy to love? What parts of me feel hard to love right now? Be honest and tender with yourself as you rediscover your body.

Let's explore ways to return to your body as a haven of rejuvenation and nourishment.

Coming Home to Your Body

Through the demands of motherhood and child rearing, your body can be a grounding place to resource yourself from.

I know, I know, a tall order as you're rushing around, changing diapers, tending to tears, and trying to figure out what is for dinner. "My body? What body?" you might ask. And it's true—there is often something so . . . heady, demanding, and depleting about motherhood.

Yet, when you take a moment to come back home to your body, you regulate your nervous system, unwind your tension, and become more present and alive for you and for your family. You can finally exhale and feel your center. Everyone wins when mama is grounded in her body.

Here are a few ways to come home to your body as a busy mama—all of which you can do in under a couple of minutes:

- **Conscious softness:** This is a great practice when you feel overwhelmed and overstimulated. Lay down on a soft, comfortable surface. Soften your belly, your chest, your pelvis, your throat. Take a few deep breaths, letting your breath open up tight places in your body. You can do this for as short as three breaths or as long as you'd like. The quality of your attention is far more important here than the quantity of time.

- **Dance it out:** When everything feels tense, nothing beats putting on a good song and moving your body. Dance silly, dance sexy, dance wild, dance free. You can get your kids in on this too, if they're willing. Music and movement is an amazing way to resource yourself and feel more present.
- **Find pleasure:** This is helpful when you feel dry and depleted by caretaking. Right now, find one place on your body that feels good. Your feet on the smooth ground? Your thighs on the chair? The breeze on your face? Bring all your awareness into that pleasurable sensation, letting it expand and nourish you. You can even make a game of this: Go find five pleasurable sensations right now. Try it now as you read this!
- **Enjoy food:** Preparing and eating food can be one of the most grounding, sensual experiences of your day. While cooking, can you smell the spices? Taste the soup? Watch the colors change? As you eat, can you slow down and deeply savor the food?

  The foods we eat, and the way we eat them, have a massive, primal impact on the female nervous system. What and how we eat signals to our body whether or not we're safe, cared for, or nourished. So it's well worth it to take the time to slow down; cook wholesome, nourishing meals; and let yourself savor and delight in the culinary experience.

Hopefully, one of these ideas appeals to you and gives you a way to connect with your body in just a few minutes amid the chaos and intensity of motherhood.

Your Changing Emotions

Motherhood is watching your heart move independently outside of your body—forever.

Have you heard this saying? It feels true to me! Motherhood is such a love-filled roller coaster. The joy in watching my babies grow up, seeing them roll over, sit up, and stand. Worrying if they will be okay, especially if sick or injured. I never felt such love or such anxiety before having children.

There is so much to feel here. Sometimes our culture highlights only one side or the other. You might hear people say, "You're so lucky!" or talk about how having young kids is the happiest time of their life. "Those were the good days," older people tell us nostalgically as they reminisce about raising their children.

Other times, you'll hear only the negative—the sleep deprivation, the overwhelmingness, the stress, the financial hardship. You'll see another mom friend exhausted, complaining about how hard this season is, how trapped she feels, how much she hates this. As always, the truth holds both.

Have you felt all these emotions? How do you welcome them all?

Imagine your emotions are like fish in the pond. There are many fishes, swimming around, gulping up at the surface, all different sizes, colors, textures. Yet you—you are not the fish. You are the pond. You are all of these emotions that you feel, and simultaneously, you're also the bigger self that witnesses and holds them.

Raising babies brings more fishes into this pond—bright, colorful fishes of joy and deep, dark fishes of grief, rage, and fear. Sometimes the pond can get quite crowded! You'll find relief and spaciousness by remembering you are the pond, not the fishes. When you are the pond, the witness, you can breathe with these feelings (these fishes) without having to "do" anything about them. They're just swimming around, and you're just breathing with them.

How do you do this? I like to close my eyes and imagine this pond of feelings. I name and spot the "fishes" as I sense them: "There is fear. Hello, fear. There is anxiety, swimming quickly. Welcome. Aw, look at love. Hello."

By naming the fishes and watching them move, I create a place to become the witness.

Mom Guilt

While we're on the topic of emotions . . . let's talk about mom guilt. Have you experienced it yet?

Mom guilt is the nagging, niggling feeling that there is always more you "should" be doing for your children. It's the self-criticism you inflict because you didn't live up to an expectation of yourself as a parent. It's painful, prevalent, and pervasive. (Triple P's!)

Mom guilt pops up like a weed in the gap between your idealized mama self and your real, actual mama self. It's everywhere your ideals diverge from your reality.

(PS Your guilt may not be around mothering. You may feel more "partner guilt" or "work guilt," or some other place in your life. The same method works for all of these types of guilt.)

For example, here are some moments when I've felt mom guilt:

I said while pregnant that I wouldn't let my children watch screens until they were older. Then the whole family gets sick, and you'll find us in bed, watching a *Frozen* movie, counting the hours until bedtime. Cue, mom guilt.

Or I sit down to play with my kids, hoping it's going to be this fun, connected experience, and I spend the time half-heartedly playing with stuffed animals while really thinking about my work to-dos. Oops! I lost my presence. Cue, mom guilt.

Or I see the still-empty baby books sitting on my shelf, remembering my intention while pregnant was to lovingly fill those out with each of my babies' firsts—first smile, first tooth, first steps—so they had a keepsake when they're older. And yet, the books are still empty. Cue, mom guilt.

Or my firstborn is crying because she wants to play with me, but I'm going to work. I think I "should" feel bad, but I'm actually just so excited and relieved to go to my office for some child-free time. Does that make me a bad mom? Cue, mom guilt.

Or I buy the adorable, brand-new plastic doll because my toddler really wants it, even though I'm trying not to buy plastic and I try to get most of our things secondhand. Cue, mom guilt.

You get the idea? Mom guilt can be everywhere.

I see two distinct ways of working with "mom guilt"—a feminine path and a masculine path. The feminine path asks us to drop the "shoulds," tune in to our desire, and trust our intuitive yearnings in each moment. The masculine path asks us to reflect on the "shoulds" to reveal our values and align our life more fully behind our values. The compass for the feminine is desire, while for the masculine, it's values. Both paths end with more self-compassion and clarity.

I wonder which path resonates more with you? Remember, we all have both energies inside us, and at different times in our life, different energies will appeal to us more. I'll outline both approaches below.

The Masculine Path

The "shoulds" we tell ourselves; the moments of guilt or regret; the itchy, uncomfortable feeling that we could be a better mom

. . . this is part of the inherent tension of growth that happens in motherhood. Mom guilt is creative tension, pulling us toward the best version of ourselves.

When I first felt the painful sting of mom guilt, my instinct was to find a way to get rid of it. I just wanted to stop feeling bad about my actions as a mother. Can you relate? Yet if we try to "get rid" of mom guilt without first listening to it and understanding it, we miss a valuable lesson on who we are and who we want to be.

How do you work with mom guilt?

1. **Look at your "shoulds."** Write out all the things you think you "should" be doing or feeling as a mama (or partner, or employee). For example, here are some of mine:
    - I should be present and attuned to my kids.
    - I should love spending time with them.
    - I should only buy secondhand items with minimal chemicals.
    - I should be recording all their firsts in the baby book.
    - I should be ready to play when Lila gets home from school.
    - I should only work when the kids are sleeping.
    - I should make nourishing, home-cooked meals for them.
2. **Find your values embedded in your "shoulds."** Each "should" reflects your idealized version of yourself as a mama, and in a very real way, it's revealing your values. What is important to you? What qualities do you want to embody as a mama? Here is my list again, with the values highlighted.
    - I should be present and attuned to my kids (presence).

- I should love spending time with them (delighting in them).
- I should only buy secondhand items with minimal chemicals (eco-awareness).
- I should be recording all their firsts in the baby book (presence).
- I should be ready to play when Lila gets home from school (presence).
- I should only work when the kids are sleeping (quality time with the kids).
- I should make nourishing, home-cooked meals for them (wellness).

3. **Make a list of your values.** Take out any that are redundant and simplify your list. Now you have a beautiful list of what you value as a mother.
   - Presence
   - Quality time together
   - Delighting in my children
   - Eco-awareness
   - Wellness

4. **Reframe mom guilt.** Now you can see the beautiful values hidden inside the insidious voices of mom guilt. There is gold here, you just have to clear through the muck. Here is what to do when you feel a moment of mom guilt:

   a. Notice the values you hold that aren't being lived in that moment (e.g., presence, attunement.)

   b. Have compassion for yourself when you're not living 100 percent up to those values. None of us will be.

   c. Find specific ways to move closer to your values.

The masculine part of us asks us to look at this moment as a chance to reveal our values and to make choices that are more in alignment with them.

For example, if you value presence but are always on your phone in front of your kids, that's a chance to realign behind your values and make a change. Perhaps you decide to put your phone in a drawer while you're playing with your kids so you're not tempted by technology. This is how we create integrity in our mothering and clarity on how we want to show up. The masculine gift here is clarity, integrity, and honor.

The Feminine Path

Meanwhile, the feminine part of us scoffs at our mom guilt, because the feminine part of us intuits that these voices are conditioning, cultural doctrines that have nothing to do with our inherent truth.

When you're feeling guilty for going to work and leaving your children at home . . . Whose voice is that anyway? Where did you learn to feel bad about that choice?

Mom guilt is born from mind-based "shoulds," an unrealistic ideal likely passed down to us through our cultural conditioning, while our innate truth resides in our body's moment-to-moment intuition and desire.

The feminine asks, "What feels good to me right now? Where is my desire calling me?" Then she trusts that above all else, especially when it "makes no sense."

For example, maybe you grew up with a working mom and you always thought you'd be a boss babe too, creating your empire while raising your family. But when your baby is born, all you want to do is spend all day with him, cuddling him, cooking, and tending to the home. When you think about going back to work, you feel itchy and unhappy.

So you choose to quit work and focus on your family. Maybe you feel immense guilt for not earning money for the family, or guilt that "all" you do is stay home. Yet at the same time, you feel such relief and joy in getting to be with your kids. Your heart feels so full, so nourished by it.

That is working the feminine path of desire.

Or maybe your story is the opposite! Maybe you waited your whole life to be a mother and imagined that you'd want to be home with the little ones because you always hear that "it goes by so fast," yet when the time comes? You crave the freedom and creative joy of being back at work.

You might feel guilty leaving your little ones, but once you're in your office, diving into your service to the world, you feel such joy and enthusiasm for what you're doing. It just feels right.

That's also the feminine path.

> *From a feminine perspective, mom guilt and shoulds are not a good compass for your life. They are mental confusion, mind pollution, that blocks you from the crystal-clear knowledge of your desire, of the wisdom of your body.*

All this to say, from a feminine perspective, mom guilt and shoulds are not a good compass for your life. They are mental confusion, mind pollution, that blocks you from the crystal-clear knowledge of your desire, of the wisdom of your body.

Hearing the deepest desire in the moment is not always easy. **Convenience sometimes masks itself as desire**. For example, you may think, "I want to buy that, so I will," when your deeper desire is to save money for a house. Or you may think, "I want to watch a movie, so I will" when your deeper desire is to be outside more with your kids. Sometimes you won't know if it's a convenience desire or a true, deep desire until afterward.

The way you can tell the difference is how you feel after you move towards the desire. Expansion, joy, or enthusiasm? You're on the right path. Shame, restless, or numb? Time to redirect your actions.

So part of the feminine path of desire is to notice a desire, follow it, and then feel the results. For example, while watching the movie, do you feel joyfully relaxed and in alignment? Or do you feel itchy, restless, like this is not quite it? Trust the way a desire makes you feel and keep moving toward what feels good and true to the deepest part of you.

Remember the analogy of your friend whispering something truly important in your ear at a rock concert? Your deepest desires are the whispers, yet the "mom guilt," or the pull toward convenience, is the noise of the concert—blaring, noisy, and persistent. So the trick is to get quiet enough, and still enough, to hear the subtle whispers of your body's yearning. Then, to trust that yearning above all else.

Both of these ways to handle "mom guilt" (or any "should" voice) are valid. The masculine side of us demands integrity, calling us to live up to our highest values, while the feminine side of us whispers that the deepest, truest version of ourselves is not found in any "shoulds," but in our deepest desires.

Which path resonates more with you right now?

Which path feels familiar versus foreign? Sometimes the more foreign, or unfamiliar, path is actually the one to take, because it offers fresh and novel wisdom.

Both paths will help you find clarity and power under the mom guilt. However you travel, may you find the wisdom that lies just behind the feelings of "mom guilt," and may you stumble into a lush place of delicious self-love and self-awareness.

Meeting Your "Mother" Self

As your baby is born, you are also born as a mother. Right now, you are likely a new, tender mother just learning to "walk" in this role. But someday you will be an experienced, wise, and confident mother who can handle all the ups and downs of raising children. The good news? You can tap into that older part of you right now.

How?

By imaging yourself ten years into the future. The following meditation was inspired by the book *Playing Big* by Tara Mohr, and I adapted it to be specifically for mothers. I personally found this process incredibly profound, and I hope it benefits you as well.

Are you ready?

Go Do: Meet Your Mother Self

This meditation will give you a glimpse of the wisest, most mature part of you, and then she can become a guiding light for you in challenging moments of motherhood.

> **Bonus:** For best results, I highly recommend listening to the audio version of this meditation, which you can find at www.megandlambert.com/emresources.

Instructions:

1. Find a place where you can be uninterrupted for twenty minutes. Lay or sit down somewhere comfortable where you can relax—but won't fall asleep.

2. Close your eyes and take deep, long breaths. Feel the sensations in your feet.
3. Then bring your awareness up your calves, thighs, and hips, noticing sensations and inviting these parts of your body to relax. Continue to your pelvis, lower back, chest, and upper back. Finally, relax your face and neck.
4. Once you're fully relaxed, imagine leaving your current body, watching it float away, as you dive into a magical time portal that can transport you ten years into the future. Imagine this portal as a rainbow beam of light, carrying you into the future.
5. When you land, you're facing yourself ten years from now. See your family in front of you. How old are your children now? How many children are there? Who else is present in the room?
6. Notice the energy of yourself ten years from now. How does she feel? What is her energy like?
7. Get even more specific. What is she wearing? What room is she in? What is she doing?
8. Notice now the way that she parents the children. What is her energy toward the children? How does she respond to them? What is she doing with them?
9. Imagine that the children are having a hard day and being difficult. How does she respond? What does she do?
10. Last, go up to her and ask any mothering question you have right now. Perhaps you ask how she handles when the children are sick, or how she handles when they cry, or how she takes care of both herself and the children. Whatever challenge is arising for you right now, bring it to her. She will have wisdom for you. Listen.

> 11. When you're ready, slowly come out of meditation. Then open your journal and take notes on what you noticed.
>
> The version of you that you found in this meditation is *you*. It's the wisest, deepest part of you, the part of you that knows how to handle the ups and downs of motherhood. You can call on her anytime you feel confronted or challenged by motherhood.
>
> I recommend coming back to this meditation again and again as motherhood brings you fresh, new challenges.

SENSUALITY

"Quick! The baby is asleep, let's go," I whisper to James. We had planned to make love during the baby's naptime, but she took forever to fall asleep.

We begin kissing. My body feels stiff and tense, not yet flowing and sensual, but we continue. I breathe deeply into my belly, soften my chest, and find pleasurable sensations. I'm not turned-on, but I'm willing.

We move together, breathing together. James takes off my clothes and strokes my body in long caresses. I feel my center heat up. "Ah, there is my turn-on!" It feels delicious, and I wonder why we went so long without this.

Things get hotter, and we're just about to make love when we hear her rustling awake in the bed nearby. "Damn," he says, looking over to check on her. Yup. She's waking up. "Go back to sleep!" I hiss, like that will do anything. I try to settle her, but to no avail.

I feel frustrated and bummed but also grateful that we got a few minutes of feeling sensual together. Even a few minutes feels precious during those intense early days. I know that someday we will once again have hours with just the two of us for lovemaking, and that thought comforts me as I return to the season of hurried naptime quickies.

How do you feel reading that story? Can you relate to any parts of it?

Finding time to be sensual (much less the energy and willingness) is notoriously difficult with small children. Yet it can be so nourishing, so important for you and your partnership.

On the individual level, neglecting your sensuality will leave you feeling dry and depleted. Life without Eros feels less juicy and vivid, more monotone and dull. It's like all the color and sensation has been sucked out. Have you felt that?

On the relationship level, when a couple stops being intimate physically, it also dries up the lifeblood of the partnership. They fight more often, they feel like roommates, they check out on each other. Sensuality is the fire that keeps the relationship warm, a haven for intimacy—both emotional and physical. It draws you two close, reminds you that you are a team, and brings out the best in each of you.

James and I have seen this time and again with the couples we coach: When they prioritize their sensuality and lovemaking, everything flows better. As one couple put it, "Making love is like putting oil in the car—all the gears work better. Without oil, we're headed toward disaster."

You have every excuse in the world *not* to be intimate in this phase. Sleep deprivation, overwhelmingness, stress. When?! Fights with partners, feeling touched-out, and more. It's totally valid for your erotic life to take a back seat to your budding family.

And yet? If you're reading this, you're clearly someone who values Eros—your erotic aliveness, your passion, your vitality. So let's talk about practicality. Let's talk about *how* to nurture your sensuality in this phase of your mama journey.

Schedule Love Dates

The first thing is to **schedule love dates**. Am I a broken record yet? Great! Love dates are essential with little ones. So open your calendar and put them in. You may need a bit of flexibility, depending on how much childcare you have from a nanny, daycare, or loved one.

I don't recommend planning to make love after the children are asleep, because chances are you'll both be exhausted by then and aren't at your sexiest. Instead, I'd make use of nap times, committing to a window of time when you two will be intimate, depending on when your little one falls asleep (which, obviously, you can't 100 percent control).

If you have childcare, it's even better so you don't need to keep one ear out for your baby or children while they nap. This can help both of you to surrender into the experience more fully, knowing that your little one is in good hands.

Nourish Your Sensuality

The second step is to **nourish your sensuality solo**. For some reason, this was a big lesson I had to learn postpartum. I'd show up to our love dates dutifully and willingly, but with zero personal time beforehand to get into a sexy state of mind. Part of me expected my partner to turn me on and get me juicy, but that's a tall order! It's like pushing a stalled car up a hill.

The truth is, reclaiming my erotic aliveness is an inside job—my job. When I first take the time to remember my pleasure and activate my erotic energy, everything flows.

It helped me to take fifteen minutes before our love date to shower, brush my teeth, and do a short five- or ten-minute solo pleasure practice. The list before in the body section, "Coming Home to Your Body," is a great place to start. All of these practices will give you a chance to let go of the mental chatter and come home to the sensations in your body.

As you come home to your body, you naturally start to feel more sensual and alive. From there, you can explore the erotic, either in a solo practice or in a partnered love date.

Show Up Goalless

The third step is to **show up goalless**. So, you've scheduled your love date or self-pleasure session, you've nourished your own sensuality, and now you're standing in front of your partner, ready to feel Eros together.

The problem? Erotic pleasure is a shy creature; it hides under pressure. So if you're standing there, expecting yourself to be turned-on, rushing yourself to get aroused already, thinking about how long this will take, feeling bad that you haven't had sex or self-pleasured in days . . . That is not a conducive environment for turn-on to arise.

Instead, try to drop the goal and experiment instead. Imagine there is no "end destination" to get to—sex is

Erotic pleasure is a shy creature; it hides under pressure.

not the goal, your partner going over is not the goal, even feeling aroused is not the goal. The "goal" is simply to be with yourself and your partner, willing and open to connect, to see where the erotic wants to take you today.

That can feel radical for many people, so if you're doing this with a partner, I recommend talking about this idea together beforehand.

Even better, if intimacy is a tough spot for you two, *get support*. There is nothing like a coach or mentor who can help you two share desires, hear each other, and move together as a team toward a sexier future. Becoming co-parents is HUGE for your relationship. Now, trying to be lovers *and* co-parents? This is a delicate spot that often benefits from coaching and support.

Explore Desire

The fourth step is to **explore desire**. The story below highlights this practice.

We put on the timer for twenty minutes, with a bell at ten minutes. We turn and face each other, bowing our heads to each other and to our higher power. This is the ritual we've created together to begin our love dates, to separate this sacred space from the rest of our daily life.

Then I begin. I close my eyes and ask my body, "What would feel good right now?" At first, I felt stumped. A breast massage? No. Making out? No. Finally, I found a desire.

"I want to dance with you," I said. He puts on a song, and we sway together. Mmm, that's nice. Being close to him, feeling his body, I notice my breath deepening and softening. After a few minutes, I sense it's time for a new desire.

"I want you to kiss my neck," I say. He kisses my neck slowly, suggestively. I feel a bit of heat building and share a soft "mmm yes". I tell him that I want him to bite my neck, and he does. More heat.

Every minute or so, I tune in to my body, listen for a new desire, and ask for it. When the bell goes off after ten minutes, we switch roles.

He asks me to make sounds on my exhale. Move my spine. Touch his cock. I move toward his desire, seeking to bring us both pleasure as we explore what our bodies are wanting.

After twenty minutes, we move into erotic freeplay, letting our bodies talk without words.

_____

Are you intrigued by this practice? Give it a try!

Open: The Desire Game

This little twenty-minute game is a great way to jump-start your sensuality, especially if it feels a bit stalled at the moment.

This practice helps you stay active as an erotic participant, listening to your body and communicating your wants, or offering pleasure and sensuality to your partner. This way you are 100 percent responsible for creating the sensuality you're craving.

Instructions:

1. During your next love date, talk to your partner about starting the date with a twenty-minute Desire Game. If they're willing to try it, share these instructions with them.
2. Decide who is person A and who is person B.

3. Set your timer for ten minutes. During these ten minutes, person A will ask for their desires, one at a time.
   - Challenge yourself to ask for novel desires that you haven't tried before.
   - If you can't think of a desire, just guess! You can always course correct as you get started.
4. When person A asks for a desire, person B can say yes or no.
   - If they are unwilling to do the desire person A asked for, they ask for a redirect by saying, "Thank you for the desire. I'm not up for that right now. Can you give me another desire?" This way you express gratitude for your partner's willingness to vulnerably share a desire and respect your body's "no" at the same time. It's not a rejection, it's a redirection.
   - If they're willing to do the desire, continue playing the game.
5. When person B does the desire and it feels good, person A says "yes" and shows the pleasure through their body. They can ask for as many different desires as they want during their ten minutes. Try for a minimum of five desires and no maximum!
6. After ten minutes, switch roles.
7. Once the twenty minutes is up, you can either end the love date or continue with erotic freeplay.

Every couple I know who has small children go through dry spells where sensuality and sex feels more challenging. That is normal! The question is not whether you two will experience challenges reconnecting as lovers (at some point, you will!), but rather what you will do when that happens.

These four steps—scheduling intimacy, nourishing your solo sensuality, showing up goalless, and exploring desire—are a time-tested and proven way to reignite the spark and heat your relationship back up.

The question is not whether you two will experience challenges reconnecting as lovers (at some point, you will!), but rather what you will do when that happens.

For more support, reach out to us for couples' coaching. Our specialty is helping couples keep the spark alive, especially after having a baby. See www.megandlambert.com for more information.

Now, let's explore some of the broader relationship trends and themes you'll notice as you move into the babyhood years and beyond.

RELATIONSHIP

Welcome to your co-parent era! This era of your partnership looks infinitely different from any that have come before.

There are moments when I look at James, holding our sleeping baby and toddler as they nap in his arms, and my heart bursts. How can I love a man this much?

Or when I see him playing with Lila, watching how much she adores him, and I feel so grateful that I chose this man to be my children's father.

Or when we're holding hands, on a nature walk with our little ones, and life feels more perfect, more *right* than it ever has.

Those are the easy moments of our relationship, when love and togetherness feels effortless.

Then there are the difficult moments.

When we get to the end of the day, both totally depleted, yet still somehow need to wrangle a toddler into PJs and bed while caring for a fussy baby.

When we're up all night with a feverish child, scared and beyond exhausted, bickering about what to do for her.

When we pass each other in the kitchen, having a quick conversation about logistics, passing the baby like a baton, hurrying to our next thing, and I realize I miss "us"---that slow, deep, loving version of us.

Having children together is the ultimate capacity expander, the ultimate selflessness, the ultimate call for greater teamwork.

For the first time, it isn't about either of you, or your coupledom. It's also not just about the kids. It's about you two as the foundation for the family. Your relationship is the bedrock of your children's sense of security and safety.

(That's not to say that if you're divorced, remarried, separated, or single that your kids can't have security or safety. They absolutely can.)

The well-being of your partnership ripples out and touches your children, creating a sense of calm, safety, and okay-ness that your little ones feel. When your children see you and your partner being affectionate with each other, talking kindly and laughing together, they are reassured that everything is okay. So taking time to tend to your relationship is always worth it.

I often see couples turn 100 percent of their focus to the new baby, giving the little one all their love and attention, while neglecting to also turn toward each other. This is so understandable. Biological, even. And yet? It causes immense harm in the long-term. The relationship needs tending to just as much as the baby does.

The relationship needs tending to just as much as the baby does.

From my client Jess, Mama of Two:

> "My husband and I always felt we had the most epic relationship (and we do). Our friends have always come to us for relationship advice, and we have also had the willingness to work through any bumps in the road.
>
> After about one year into parenthood, we felt overwhelmed by the challenges we were facing as a couple. All this old stuff (that we thought we had dealt with!) resurfaced. We experienced increased resentment toward each other.
>
> After investing in a beautiful coaching intensive with Megan and James, our relationship transformed. We took away so many incredibly simple and effective tools to support us in the sore spots, and probably even more profoundly, support us to actively put attention on what we wanted to grow and create for our relationship.
>
> Key tools have been GADs (from the previous chapter)—especially the appreciations. To hear and receive all the ways in which your partner sees what you're doing is *huge*, and then to be able to offer that back is a gift. Life-changing."

Like Jess's story shares, the first year (or more!) after having a baby can be rough on the relationship. Even strong couples will have some bumps in the road and new terrain to navigate together. The question is, how can you resource yourself now so you two are strong when the tough times come? What can you do to actively strengthen and fortify your relationship, starting today?

When my first baby was little, my friend, a father of two, shared this life-changing tip with me. *"One of you should be president of the kids, while the other person is president of your partnership."* This means one person is more fully responsible for tending to the little ones, while the other person helps keep the spark alive, reignite the romance, and tend to the health of the relationship. This helped us a lot, as it gave each of us a "focus" and ensured that our own relationship was not forgotten in the process.

What can the "president of the partnership" do? What does tending to your partnership look like, while balancing children? Here is a 1:1:1 rule I love.

The 1:1:1 Rule for New Parents

Bonus: I have this 1:1:1 rule as a downloadable PDF on my website that you can save and send to your partner: www.megandlambert.com/emresources

Once a day: Carve out time to check in with each other and share your emotions. This can be as simple as, once the kids are asleep, taking ten minutes to really be present. A great opening question for this is: "What's been on your mind today?" or "How did you feel today?"

Once a week: Each of you takes responsibility for initiating intimacy once a week. It may not "work"—your partner may be too exhausted or busy at that moment—but the simple act of each person initiating weekly ensures that you both feel wanted and desired, and that the relationship's erotic aliveness is resting solely on one person. Better yet, schedule at least one love date each week and both commit fully to it.

Once a month: Have a date night! If you can do more often, great, but as a new parent, this was about as often as I could manage it. Your date night could even be an at-home date once the kids are asleep. Perhaps you order takeout, throw a blanket on the floor, and have a picnic. Or you ask your parents to watch the baby while you two get ice cream together. Or you pull out a board game and invite your partner to play. Whatever you do, prioritize fun and simplicity in these early days.

To summarize:

- Once per day: Check in with each other emotionally
- Once per week: Initiate intimacy
- Once per month: Have a date night

If you can keep this up, your relationship will have a more solid foundation as you navigate the turbulent waters of new parenthood. This 1:1:1 rule prevents you two from the all-too-common tendency to drift apart once children arrive.

Weekly Planning Ritual

Having children requires more independence, teamwork, and collaboration than you've ever had before. Suddenly, you need to know where your partner is nearly at all times, what you can count on them for, and who is doing what. It's big! This level of collaboration requires new tools and practices.

A simple ritual that has helped James and I is our weekly planning ritual. On Sunday nights, once the baby is asleep, we sit down with a big piece of paper and colored pens (and we often give our toddler a video to watch. I know, I know, screens, but it's worth it for the focused time to plan together).

We start with reflecting on and sharing our intentions for the week. How do we each want to show up this week? We each choose one to three intentions. For example, wanting to have clearly separated work versus children time, or wanting to create special memories with the children, or wanting to feel relaxed even in the busyness. These intentions are more about ways of *being* than things we're *doing*. We write down our intentions on the paper.

Then we each choose a word for the week that will help us anchor into our intentions, such as creativity, joy, clarity, presence, or calm. That one word becomes a mantra for the week.

Last, we go through the week, day by day, sharing about our plans and requesting any support we will need from each other. We clarify who is taking care of which child and when, as well as making sure we both have fun, nourishing things during the week (e.g., Pilates, a friend date, or morning meditations).

We usually write out the schedule using different colors for me, him, or us together. Then we hang up the paper on the fridge so we can refer to it throughout the week. .

This simple ritual helps us avoid so many fights (e.g., "You never told me you had boys' night tonight!") and feel like we're on the same page.

I'll be honest, sometimes this weekly planning ritual turns into a fight over time management. Who gets to have their "fun" time, and who takes the children? Time feels more precious—and more scarce—than ever once you have children. Can you relate?

The best way I've found to navigate conflict around time is to be on each other's team to get both of your desires met. For example, if

James wants to go to the gym three times per week, it's my job to help him find time for that. If I want to see a friend, it's his job to help me find time for that. That changes the energy from me-versus-you fighting over time, to being on each other's teams and trying to find a way to bring joy to the other. Fight *for* each other rather than *against* each other.

Fight for each other rather than against each other.

It also helps to zoom out from individual needs and desires (what *I* want vs. what *you* want) to look at the family system as a whole. What does our family system need this week? How is our collective nervous system? What does our family dynamic need more or less of? This broader perspective helps us realign behind our family and feel more like a team.

Getting Support

External support is important at any stage in the relationship, but possibly, the transition into becoming co-parents is the most important time to get support. This can look like having a couples therapist or coach, going on a couples retreat, or having a mentor.

If resources are tight right now, this does not have to be paid support. You can consult with a wise friend or family member who can give advice and see things you two can't see alone. Having an outside perspective is invaluable in getting out of sticky spots together.

When Lila was nine months old, I found a couples retreat I wanted to attend with James. He was skeptical, citing how busy we are and how hard it would be to leave our baby with a nanny while we attended the workshops. He said the clincher line, "This just isn't a good time."

Yet, I argued, this is the best time, when everything feels full and complex, when we navigate this transition together. We went back and forth for maybe a month on this. I was careful not to pressure him, but at the same time, I didn't let go of the desire to be on this retreat together. I held the vision of it, and the certainty that we needed this external support.

James eventually decided it would be good for us, and we went. We had the best time! We stayed on-site with our baby, and our nanny helped us during the workshop times. It was so beautiful to have the space to reconnect with each other as lovers while our nanny lovingly tended to our baby. After just a few days, I felt so rejuvenated and in love. It was profound for us and for our family.

Going away on a retreat together is a privilege that may feel far away right now. If that's the case, what kind of support feels manageable? Who could you reach out to for perspective? A spiritual leader from your church? Your mom? Who could help you remember your highest, wisest self in the midst of co-parenting turmoil? Ask for help, get support. We are not meant to do this alone.

Lastly, Don't Forget Fun

Ironically, fun was the first thing to go when we became parents. Suddenly, life felt full of important responsibilities. We spent less time dancing and more time discussing baby strollers. Less time laughing and more serious and logistic conversations.

After a while, I realized—I miss laughing together. I miss just having spontaneous, frivolous *fun*. What do we do that is goalless, that has no point beyond the pure joy of it?

In my opinion, the two most bonding activities for a couple are sex and laughter. There is something so powerful about making love and laughing—both occur in the moment, in your body, in the pure joy of the experience, for no other reason than it feels good.

So if you're feeling like your relationship could be better, consider: What makes you laugh? How do you two have fun together? Here are some ideas:

- Dance together.
- Play board games.
- Wrestle with each other.
- Be silly with funny accents.
- Laugh about something funny the kids did.
- Do a competitive game like padel.
- Play little pranks on each other.
- Make a scavenger hunt.

The way you laugh is not important. It's only important that you two do something together for fun and keep the laughter alive. It's amazing what *fun* and *laughter* can do for a relationship!

Reflect: Relationship Tune-Up

The first year(s) after having children can take its toll on your partnership, but it can also be a beautiful time of expansive and family togetherness. Take time now to reflect on what nutrients your relationship might need right now.

Instructions:

1. Read through the tools and practices I listed in this chapter:
   - The 1:1:1 Rule for Parents
   - Weekly Planning Ritual

- Getting external support
- Having fun

2. You may also want to refer to relationship tools from the previous chapters, such as:
   - Practicing daily GADs (gratitude, appreciation, and desire).
   - Taking down the resentment wall by mining annoyances for deeper needs.
   - Planning love dates.
   - Learning each other's love languages.
   - "See into My World" process to more deeply understand each other.

3. Now imagine yourself as a relationship mechanic, with all these powerful tools in your toolbelt, ready to bring your relationship to the next level through a Relationship Tune-Up.

4. Ask yourself:
   - How are we doing right now as a couple?
   - What do we need more or less of?
   - What tools would most serve our partnership right now?

5. Then commit to bringing that tool into your relationship. Perhaps you schedule time into your calendar now, carve out time to talk to your partner, or simply make an internal commitment to bring that element in.

6. **Remember:** If you notice something is missing in your relationship, it's yours to bring. You have the power to create the love that you want.
   - Don't wait for them to initiate what you're wanting, nor do you need to talk about the issues endlessly. Just bring in the energy or tool that you notice is missing.

ECOSYSTEM

I'm sitting at a long wooden table, playing board games with two friends, while my other friend holds our baby, cooing over his little smiles. Nearby, I hear the laughter of two toddlers, Lila and her friend River, as they run through the garden with another friend of mine.

Looking around at my babies, loved and cared for by my friends, is like balm to my heart. It fills me with the most unexpected joy, this feeling of community raising our babies together. There is something so natural, so primal about this moment. Everything just feels *right*.

It reminds me that this is our nature, the way humans have lived for millennia—together, in a tribe, raising babies collectively. My soul is at peace.

Yet this is not the norm for many of us, for most of the day. Most of us live isolated, in nuclear families, only seeing other families for a lunch or two here and there. This is lonely and unnatural, both for us as adults and for our children. It can feel empty in a way that's hard to put your finger on, yet that emptiness points to a need for connection, for community.

Our babies are meant to bond deeply with many adults, to feel the freedom that they can run from adult to adult, always finding a smiling face ready to give them hugs, snacks, or a gentle boundary.

Our babies are meant to bond deeply with many adults, to feel the freedom that they can run from adult to adult, always finding a smiling face ready to give them hugs, snacks, or a gentle boundary.

In the previous chapters, we talked about the need for interdependence, to gather your village. In this era, while raising your little ones ... this is where the village shines. This is where it all comes together.

Perhaps you read this with a sense of longing that you want this but aren't experiencing it yet. If that is you, I am sending you so much love. It is so natural to crave a community to raise your babies in, and *it's never too late to create that community*.

How do you create a community for your little ones? Here are a few ideas ...

- Spend time at the playground near your home, watch the kids your little ones gravitate toward, and strike up conversation with other parents.
- Seek out a local community center and see if they hold a mother and baby group, or a family play date time.
- If you have a library nearby, check out if they have a children's reading circle. This can be a great place to meet other families.
- Invite your friends to spend the night at your house, or go away together for a weekend if you can. This time spent living in community, even if just for one night, is like turbo fuel for relationships.
- If you live in an apartment or housing complex, host a swim party to meet other families who live nearby.
- Drop off baked goods at your neighbor's house and introduce yourself. I know, so old-fashioned and quaint, right? It works!
- Bring out some toys like chalk, a ball, or a frisbee, and start playing on your front lawn or on your street. If neighborhood children pass by, invite them.

- Ask your friends to introduce you to other families they know who you might get along with.
- If your children attend school, get to know the other parents in their class. Perhaps arrange a monthly coffee date for the parents at a café nearby.

Building a community can feel like dating. You're seeking out families who have a natural resonance with your family, or in other words, "You vibe together."

From there, you take little steps toward deepening intimacy with the family, getting to know the adults and their children, and allowing them to get to know yours. It's tender and intimate but so immensely gratifying.

Parenting Philosophies

Being around other parents can help you discover your own parenting philosophies as you notice what you like or don't like about how others parent. Aligning around others with similar parenting philosophies is also a great way to build community. Both elements go together.

There are so many different parenting philosophies—classical attachment parenting, Aware Parenting, Montessori parenting, permissive parenting, or authoritative parenting, to name a few.

I wonder which philosophies align the most with you? This is a deeply personal question as you reflect on the parent you are today and the parent you want to be.

A few questions to consider:

- What is important to you in raising your babies?
- What type of children do you want to raise?
- What values do you hold as a family?

> If you'd like a structured approach to this conversation, I recommend checking out my Parenting Manifesto resource that helps you two craft your own parenting philosophies. You can find it at https://www.megandlambert.com/resources/parenting-manifesto.

For James and I, our core values in raising children are gentleness, attunement, and trusting our children's innate wisdom (and in doing so, supporting our children to trust themselves). We want to raise children who are connected to their inner voice, who know their yes and their no, who are sensitive and heart-led, and who are connected to the people and ecosystem around them. We trust that children are inherently wise and gentle when treated with gentleness and respect.

We've naturally gravitated toward a Montessori-style, which fosters children's growing competence and encourages children's self-directed learning. We also have been deeply touched by Aware Parenting, which supports a strong attachment between parent and child, nonpunitive discipline, and listening to our children's feelings.

We studied with Marion Rose, author of the books *The Emotional Life of Babies* and *I'm Here and I'm Listening*. Her work, particularly on listening to children's feelings, has been life-changing for us.

Lila, my firstborn, slept terribly, waking up every sixty to ninety minutes for her first two years. We were very attentive parents, always trying to respond to her cries right away. Yet, looking back, I also saw it as my responsibility to "soothe" (a.k.a. stop) all of her tears. I believed that if I were truly responding to all her needs, she shouldn't need to cry.

It's funny, because I've taught adult women for almost a decade to reclaim the power of their grief and their rage, to let it all out—and yet, when it came to my baby? I didn't want to hear her cry. Oops!

After we discovered Aware Parenting, we stayed present with her and listened to her feelings, tears, and tantrums. And guess what? She slept better! I now believe so much of her sleep challenges were from repressed feelings that she never had a chance to express and heal from.

With our second baby, we listened to his feelings right from birth, and he hasn't had nearly the sleep challenges that Lila did. He is also a very calm and happy baby.

All this to say, Aware Parenting has changed our life. But the most important thing is to learn what philosophies resonate with *you*. What are your values? What is important to you? How can you align the way you show up as a parent behind your values? What resources might you seek out to better understand different parenting philosophies? A few of my favorites are in the resource section.

The Earth Your Kids Inherit

I distinctly remember looking at my newborn baby while sitting in our garden, and realizing—my goodness, I care so much more about future generations now. Suddenly, my heart felt tied to the future of the planet in a way I never anticipated.

Sometimes I flash-forward to my children as teenagers, when the earth has disintegrated more than it already has, and my children ask me, "Mom, what did you do? You knew what was happening . . . what did you do to stop it?" I don't want to have to say "Nothing." I don't want to admit that I stood idly by when the earth burned around me. No. That will not be my legacy.

This is heavy, I know. You may want to skip the section, and I don't blame you. But the good news is, we're also role models for a future generation. We have agency and power, we stand as guardians of our future and of our earth.

It is not hopeless.

I love the quote by Greta Thunberg, a young eco-activist, who said, "We've already solved climate change. The solutions are already here. We just need to wake up and change our behaviors."

> I believe that mothers will lead the eco-revolution, precisely because we can feel how intricately linked our children's well-being and the earth's well-being is.

Young people like Thunberg bring tears to my eyes and hope for the future. I believe that mothers will lead the eco-revolution, precisely because we can feel how intricately linked our children's well-being and the earth's well-being is. Mother Earth tends to us all, and we're being invited to tend to her.

What does that eco-awareness look like in your mothering journey?

It will look different in every family, as each of our contexts and capacities are unique.

Eco-awareness develops through three interconnected steps: heart, head, and hands. Our **hearts** first get called to care, to grieve over what's happened, to feel anger by the actions of past generations, to be moved by it. Our hearts wake us up.

Then our **heads** get busy learning. What can we do? What can be done? I love the Instagram accounts @commonsearth and @imagine5_official for great information on this. We learn, we study, we understand what's happening, we get to the root cause of the situation.

Then our **hands** make new choices. We use our deep care and our information to guide new choices. We give up disposable diapers, we stop buying new baby clothes, we turn down the heater, we fly less, and we vote for the presidential candidate who cares about the earth. We make tangible life decisions, guided by our hearts and our heads, investing in the future we want to see.

Being around a like-minded community that also cares deeply about the earth is essential. It helps us feel powerful, connected, and motivated to keep going.

Hearts, heads, hands. These three interconnected elements guide us on how to live in a more sustainable, earth-regenerating way.

One of the greatest gifts you can give your children is a healthy, beautiful environment to grow up in—and help them foster a love of nature so they, too, learn to protect the earth.

At the start of this book, we looked at you, the Eros Mama, as the seed growing into the thriving tree of motherhood. We understand that if the seedling isn't thriving, you first look at the context it's in—does it have enough water? Food? Space? Sunlight?—then adjust the context accordingly.

The same is true for yourself as a mother, and it's true for your babies. They need good nourishment, water, sunlight, space to grow, and a healthy ecosystem surrounding them. So, by tending to the earth, you tend to their well-being too.

CHAPTER 6 SUMMARY

It is quite likely that everything has changed since becoming a mother: your body, your emotions, your priorities, your sense of self. In this chapter, we explored how to be with these changes, move with them, and trust the process.

I shared two ways to work with "mom guilt," which pops up in the gap between your idealized-mother self and your real-life capacities and desires. I also offered an invitation to connect with your future mother self—the wisest and deepest part of you—to help guide you in your current decisions.

Moving from a couple to co-parents is a major shift in your relationship, and it requires new tools to adapt. In this chapter, I share the 1:1:1 rule for new parents, as well as our weekly planning ritual. I encourage you to reach out for external support and remember to have fun together.

Expanding beyond your home into the broader ecosystem, we looked at the profound and ancient beauty of raising children in a community, and how to create that village for your children. We explored different parenting philosophies (more resources on this in the "Widen" section). Last, we looked at the Earth our children will inherit and what we can do now to tend to Mother Nature by engaging with our hearts, heads, and hands.

————————

Ways to GROW

In this chapter, I shared the following invitations for you:

- **Go Do: Meet Your Mother Self**—A profound meditation practice to connect with the wisest, deepest part of you and bring her into your motherhood experience.
- **Open: The Desire Game**—A simple and playful way to invite erotic exploration back into your partnership, especially if you two have hit a dry spell.
- **Reflect: Relationship Tune-Up**—An invitation to reflect on all the relationship tools throughout the book and identify the ones that your partnership needs right now.
- **Widen:** Here are books that you may find helpful in your motherhood journey:
    - On your inner world
        - *Love Your Kids Without Losing Yourself* by Dr. Morgan Cutlip
        - *Mothering from Your Center* by Tami Lynn Kent
    - On your relationship
        - *To Have and to Hold* by Molly Millwood
        - *Baby Bomb* by Kara Hoppe and Stan Tatkin
    - On your parenting
        - *Hunt, Gather, Parent* by Michaeleen Doucleff
        - *The Emotional Life of Babies* by Marion Rose
        - *I'm Here and I'm Listening* by Marion Rose
        - *No Bad Kids* by Janet Julian
        - *The Montessori Baby* by Simone Davies and Junnifa Uzodike
        - *Safe Infant Sleep* by James J. McKenna
        - *The Happiest Baby on the Block* by Harvey Karp

CONCLUSION

Today, I'm at an ecstatic dance, which is a delightful sober Bali rave that has become a weekly ritual for us. I'm swirling and moving my body to the music on this wood floor that is so familiar, worn by years of dancing. I first met James on this dance floor, the incredible man who became the father of my children.

I've danced here hundreds of times, but every time, I relish this moment to come home to my body. My days with a toddler and a baby are full, to say the least, and this weekly dance ritual is my favorite form of self-care.

When I first met James here six years ago, I felt excited, nervous, and a bit self-conscious. I wondered how I looked, if he liked me, how I was meant to dance. Now I notice how much freer, more relaxed, and more easeful I feel today than I did six years ago. So much of my own self-consciousness has fallen away, as my priorities, hopes, and concerns have deepened through motherhood.

Speaking of motherhood, I feel curious how the little ones are faring, so I peek over the banister to see our three-year-old and eight-month-old playing in the courtyard. The eldest is singing and munching on fruit, while her baby brother crawls around her feet and our devoted nanny watches them. I smile, feeling their joy as my own.

James comes up behind me and holds me. In silence, we look down at our little ones, at this family we've created together, and it all feels so special that my eyes get teary. Some moments it just hits me like that—how sacred this is.

Between the diapers and the chaos of tending to two, it's easy to forget. But today, as I am perched above, on the dance floor, watching my babies, I'm struck with gratitude. Wow. How did I get here, to this beautiful life?

I kiss James on the cheek, a friendly kiss full of love and familiarity, this life partner of mine, before heading inside to dance again.

A while later, I met his eyes across the dance floor. *Hello, you.* I move toward him, and we dance together. I flirt with him, giving him a cheeky smile over my shoulder, as I twirl. Even though we've been together for over six years, I love flirting with him, dancing with him as if he were still a stranger to me.

He spins me around, pinning my arms behind me. I feel the heat of his body, and my own body heats up in response. Mmm . . . yum. I smell his sweat, so manly and earthy, familiar yet erotic. A primal "yes" floods through me. After years of deep lovemaking, my body instinctively knows his body, and remembers the pleasures we've shared.

Not every moment feels this passionate with two kids (Truthfully, most moments don't!), but when we create a moment of body-to-body intimacy, like now, our chemistry is right there, just an inch away. It's delicious, enlivening, exhilarating.

The song changes and becomes a playful, upbeat number. We laugh and dance together, doing silly dance moves. I realize how much more at ease in my body I've become over the years, how much easier I can let myself go into the music. I have more wrinkles now, and a soft, stretch-marked belly, but far less mental hangups.

After a bit, we turned toward each other. "Ready to see the kids?" he asks. I nod. We descend the stairs together, hands interwoven, to go greet our little ones.

Our oldest runs into our arms, full of squeals, and our youngest crawls after her, desperate to keep up. I smile. Yes. This.

I scoop them both up into my arms, and James wraps his arms around me. My arms are full, my heart is full. I'm about to jump back into the chaos of diapers, messy snacks, and endless demands of my attention, but first, I send a silent prayer up to God for the beauty of this moment, for the grace of becoming a mama.

This journey has taken me into my depths, into an underworld of letting go of all that I've clung to, only to be reborn anew as a mother. A woman who knows herself more fully, who feels her power deeply, and who loves more fiercely and broadly. An Eros Mama.

As I hold my family today, reflecting on my journey from maiden to mother, I also wonder about the future. As my children and I grow up together, who will I become? What more will I learn about this journey of motherhood? Of womanhood?

Someday, if I'm blessed enough to live that long, I hope to discover what it means to be in my crone years. I dream of becoming a grandmother, of seeing my children's children, and seeing the future of our Earth. The thought feels so sweet, so tender, so full of possibility. I wonder what wisdom the decades will give me, what insights I will gather and share in my crone years? I hope I am privileged enough to age into that phase of life.

But for now, all I can do is hold my family close, honor the journey so far, and look wide-eyed at what is unfolding right here, right now.

YOUR INSIGHTS

What about you, Eros Mama? How has the journey into motherhood changed you? How has this book impacted you?

Take a moment to reflect. How has this book changed you? Perhaps . . .

- You feel more connected to your body or your emotions.
- Your intuition speaks louder to you—and you listen.
- You feel more confident owning and speaking your truths.
- You know how to awaken your pleasure and sensuality.
- You have new tools and practices for your relationship.
- You and your partner have weathered storms together—and emerged stronger.
- You've created a beautiful, cozy home for your family.
- You've gained insight about your ecosystem, or a deeper connection to nature.
- You've created a stronger community and are building your village.

Is any of this true for you? Which of these speak the most to you?

Remember that shifts can be slow and gentle. Perhaps you feel only 10 percent more connected to your body, or you've tried just one tool from the book, or you feel a little more aware of your body's messages. That is more than enough!

This journey is not all-or-nothing. It's a series of tiny steps toward becoming the woman and mama you were born to be. Celebrate your progress and keep your eyes on where you want to go.

Every woman reading this will have such a different path into motherhood. Your journey is uniquely your own, with challenges and joys as distinctive as your fingerprint. Maybe some parts of this book resonated with you, while other parts didn't. That's great! As always, take what you like and leave the rest. *You know your story best.*

My final invitation: Take a minute to reflect on what you want to take away from this book. **Which practices, tools, or insights are you leaving here with?**

Here is a little summary to jog your memory:

EROS: Eco-aware, radiant, open, and sensual—motherhood is available to you at any time. It requires four pieces:

> **Body:** Your body holds immense wisdom—if you're willing to listen. By noticing your sensations, emotions, and gut truths, you will have the wisdom you need to move toward the path of your soul.
>
> **Sensuality:** Your sensuality is a pleasure-filled pathway home to your body. It creates a haven for rejuvenation and remembering your inherent power. Sensuality includes your sexuality and expands beyond it.
>
> **Relationship:** Your love created this little human, and with patience, compassion, and the right tools, your partnership can be a steady foundation of your family. Your emotional and physical intimacy can nourish you both and bring warmth to your family.

Ecosystem: Like a plant, you need a healthy ecosystem of community and nature to thrive. By sensing your interconnectedness to all living things, and tending to the web around you, you can create an environment where your family flourishes.

These four aspects—body, sensuality, relationship, and ecosystem—come together to help you live a life that is rooted in your body and the earth while being alive with pleasure and connection. You become a mama who is lush, radiant, and unapologetically feminine.

JOURNAL

Now open your journal and write. Consider these questions:

1. What were three insights you gained from reading this book?
2. What was your favorite practice or tool?
3. What practices would you like to incorporate into your life?
4. How has reading this book or doing these practices shaped your motherhood journey?
5. Name three shifts you've experienced, no matter how subtle. (Remember: 10 percent is enough!)

I hope this book has served your motherhood journey, and helped you remember your power and capacity as a woman in a deeper, richer way.

And as you embark on your own journey, may I leave you with one final poem:

The Mama Call

Mama, you did it.
You bravely called new life in.
You grew a precious little soul in your womb.
You opened wide, surrendered deep to bring this life to earth.
And now, you're caring for the next generation.

This is big work, deep work, profound work.
The start of a lifelong relationship,
Between you and your baby,
Between you and your mother self,
Between you and the divine.

A cycle of seasons, of firsts and lasts.

First steps, last crawls.
First foods, last breastfeeds.
First night away, last time living at home.

While your baby's growth is obvious, celebrated, documented,
Your growth is just as deep and profound,
Though far less visible.

Every day, you're evolving into a richer,
more nuanced version of yourself,
Both fiercer and softer,
Both stronger and more tender,
Both more confident and more humble than ever,

You're growing into a woman who can hold these paradoxes,
Holding her own heart as she holds her little one's hands,

This journey of motherhood,
That is aching vulnerable, so rich and true.

While deep in the caretaking of little ones,
May you remember that you too need tending.

While consumed by the monotony of motherhood,
May you continue to be awed by the sacredness of it.

While challenged and confronted by the intensity of it,
May you find strength you didn't know you had.

While your heart is stretched—or ripped—open wide,
May you feel the grace and expansion of loving so deeply.

You've transformed from a maiden into a mother,
And yet the transformation isn't done with you.

It's an every day, all day, kind of work.
It's a never-not-going-to-be-surprised kind of work.
It's losing yourself, and rediscovering yourself, daily,
in the act of mothering.

Next time you're knee-deep in diapers, tears,
and sleepless nights
Remember, your work may feel mundane,
But it's the most sacred work there is.

The greatest calling of a lifetime,
To become a woman who can
Raise the next generation.
Regenerate our future.
Rebuild community.
Together.

You've got this, mama.

SHARE YOUR EXPERIENCE

I wrote this book with the hope of supporting this new way of mothers—women who are connected to earth, body, and Eros, and who lead the way for us all to find a way to thrive.

You are part of a movement! If something in this book touched you, I love when you share quotes or favorite parts on Instagram and tag me @megandlambert or tag #ErosMama. If you have any reflections from this book that you'd like to share privately with me, you can send me a message on Instagram at @megandlambert.

I'd also love it if you left a review of this book wherever you purchased it, or shared this book with a loved one. This helps spread the word of a new type of motherhood journey! Thank you so much; I am eternally grateful for YOU.

GO DEEPER

If you loved *Eros Mama*, here are 3 ways you can go deeper with my work:

1. **Read my first book *Eros: The Journey Home***

   Eros: The Journey Home invites you to come home to your body and deepest desires. It's full of exercises, meditations, and practices to feel more lush, juicy, and alive, as well as intimate stories from myself and clients to bring this transformation to life.

2. **Listen to my podcast "Eros Mama with Megan Lambert"**

   Over the last 5 years, this podcast has been an evolving platform sharing my personal journey, transformative client coaching sessions, and insightful interviews with industry experts. Each episode is unique, ranging from relationship, to intimacy, to eco-awareness.

3. **Apply for private mentorship**

   Each year, I support a limited number of private clients through my 1:1 or 2:2 (couples') mentorship. This is the deepest and most transformative way to work with me, and the spaces go quickly. It's my greatest honor to walk beside a woman through her motherhood and relationship journey. Check my website for current availability, as well as client testimonials.

ACKNOWLEDGEMENTS

First off, shout out to my amazing husband, James Mattingley, who is right now putting our babies to bed while I finish yet another round of editing deadlines. He is the rock of our family, my steady anchor in life's storms, and the one great love of my life. Thank you for everything you do to care for me and our little ones. It is no exaggeration that *none of this would be possible without you*.

Second, big hugs to my babies - Lila and Latham. Getting to be your mama has been the biggest blessing of my life and I give thanks every day for you two. It's such a joy and miracle watching you grow up. Maybe someday you'll even read this! How fun.

Third, thank you to my amazing Eros Mama beta readers! Your encouragement, wisdom, and insights have made this book far deeper and richer than it would be otherwise. So much gratitude to Adriana, Alex, Alie, Anne, Bindi, Catharina, Carla Ann, Carly, Carolina, Ellie, Eri, Jess, Joy, Juna, Kori, Lisa-Maria, Madiha, Mahika, Pia, and Sandra. You rock!

Fourth, thank you to my editor Tara C. Allred for your incredible guidance during the refinement process, and helping me make this manuscript into a far more potent reader experience. The readers and I thank you! You are truly in your calling doing this work.

Additional thanks to proofreader Caitlyn Nichols for your final set of editorial eyes—you helped bring this book to its finished state.

Finally, big thanks to my parents for giving me a secure start to life and laying the blueprint for how to be a parent. I am the mama I am today because of the work you did to break generational patterns and love me and my brothers so fiercely. *Your endless support is the wind beneath my wings.*

ABOUT THE AUTHOR

Megan D. Lambert is a mama, coach, and community builder who facilitates transformational experiences for deeper connection to the earth, body, and the feminine.

In her twenties, she was a Fortune 100 senior leadership consultant specializing in helping companies and teams create a deeper sense of purpose and interpersonal leadership. She traveled all over the world designing and facilitating award-winning learning experiences.

After that, she went deep into the world of mindfulness, sexuality, and feminine embodiment, eventually leaving the corporate world to move to Bali and start her own business as a master-certified intimacy and relationship coach.

While in Bali, she met her now-husband James Mattingley, and the two of them began coaching couples and leading retreats together.

Over the years, she has run many sold-out international couples' retreats and women's retreats, coached hundreds of couples and women, written a best-selling book *Eros: The Journey Home*, and taught thousands more about the transformative power of the feminine.

Then, motherhood came—along with another massive wave of transformation.

When her two babies were born, her focus moved to earth regeneration and motherhood as a transformational journey. She became the domestic goddess she never knew she could be, suddenly making homemade cashew milk and non-toxic cleaning spray. Who knew?!

While raising her babies, she and her husband also built their dream co-living community space for families to connect with nature in Bali. This special place is called IBU (meaning "mother" in Indonesian). IBU will open in June 2025 for families from all over the world to experience the deep rejuvenation and reconnection available in lush mama Bali.

Currently, she lives between Bali and California. You'll find her making chocolate cookies with her little ones, having a dance party in the kitchen, working with her clients, having epic love dates, or hosting friends over for swim parties. Connection, creativity, and community are her key values.

www.ingramcontent.com/pod-product-compliance
Lightning Source LLC
Chambersburg PA
CBHW011947090526
44580CB00011B/138/J